MOTORCYCLING ALABAMA

Published in cooperation with the
BARBER VINTAGE MOTORSPORTS MUSEUM, Birmingham, Alabama

MOTORCYCLING
ALABAMA

50 RIDE LOOPS THROUGH THE HEART OF DIXIE

DAVID HAYNES

THE UNIVERSITY OF ALABAMA PRESS • TUSCALOOSA

Copyright © 2011
The University of Alabama Press
Tuscaloosa, Alabama 35487-0380
All rights reserved
Manufactured in China
Published in cooperation with the Barber Vintage
Motorsports Museum, Birmingham, Alabama

Typeface: Arno Pro and Corbel
Book design by Michele Myatt Quinn
All photos courtesy of the author unless otherwise noted

∞

The paper on which this book is printed meets the minimum
requirements of American National Standard for Information
Sciences—Permanence of Paper for Printed Library Materials,
ANSI Z39.48-1984.

Library of Congress Cataloging-in-Publication Data
Haynes, David (Roy David), 1954–
Motorcycling Alabama : fifty ride loops through the heart of
Dixie / David Haynes.
   p. cm.
Includes index.
ISBN 978-0-8173-5528-9 (pbk. : alk. paper)—ISBN
978-0-8173-8157-8 (electronic)
1. Motorcycle touring—Alabama—Guidebooks.
2. Alabama—Guidebooks. I. Title.
GV1059.522.A2H39 2011
796.709761—dc22   2010030811

CONTENTS

Foreword   ix

About This Book   xi

PART I **Planning Your Trip**

1 Mapping Your Trip   3

2 Motorcycle Safety   5

3 Motorcycle Camping   16

4 On the Road   27

PART II **Rides in Northeast Alabama: Ride Loops 1–10**

Ride Loop 1: Paint Rock River and Monte Sano State Park Ride   36

Ride Loop 2: Springville, Gallant, Oneonta, Remlap Ride   40

Ride Loop 3: Brompton and St. Clair County Ride   46

Ride Loop 4: Lake Guntersville State Park, Sand Mountain,
Langston Ride   51

Ride Loop 5: Little River Canyon, Mentone, DeSoto State
Park Ride   56

Ride Loop 6: Hammondville, Scottsboro, Stevenson Ride   66

Ride Loop 7: Falkville, Eva, Florette Ride   71

Ride Loop 8: Heflin, Piedmont, Talladega National Forest
Dual-Sport Ride   77

Ride Loop 9: Blount County Covered Bridges Ride   83

Ride Loop 10: Blount County Covered Bridges Dual-Sport Ride   90

PART III Rides in Northwest Alabama: Ride Loops 11–20

Ride Loop 11: Bankhead National Forest Dual-Sport Ride   99

Ride Loop 12: Lewis Smith Lake and Bankhead National

    Forest Ride   106

Ride Loop 13: Hamilton, Natchez Trace, Florence Ride   111

Ride Loop 14: Joe Wheeler State Park, Lexington, Cairo Ride   119

Ride Loop 15: Lake Lurleen State Park Ride   124

Ride Loop 16: Eutaw, Aliceville, Gainesville Ride   128

Ride Loop 17: Brilliant, Haleyville, Bear Creek,

    Hackleburg Ride   132

Ride Loop 18: Warrior, Arkadelphia, Maytown Ride   136

Ride Loop 19: Brookwood, Windham Springs, Tuscaloosa Ride   141

Ride Loop 20: Lacon, Hartselle, Addison, Clarkson Ride   146

PART IV Rides in East-Central Alabama: Ride Loops 21–30

Ride Loop 21: Alabama-Georgia State Line Ride   153

Ride Loop 22: Wetumpka, Weogufka, Clanton, Pine Level Ride   157

Ride Loop 23: Wind Creek State Park, Lake Martin Ride   162

Ride Loop 24: Lanett, Wadley, Horseshoe Bend Ride   168

Ride Loop 25: Cook Springs, Logan Martin Dam,

    Highway 25 Ride   172

Ride Loop 26: Cheaha State Park Dual-Sport Ride   177

Ride Loop 27: Cheaha State Park, Talladega National Forest

    Road Ride   184

Ride Loop 28: Mount Cheaha Ridges Dual-Sport Ride   191

Ride Loop 29: Oak Mountain, Highway 25, Montevallo Ride   197

Ride Loop 30: Chilton, Talladega, Coosa Counties Ride   203

PART V Rides in Southwest Alabama: Ride Loops 31–40

Ride Loop 31: Boligee, Demopolis, Cuba Ride   211

Ride Loop 32: Bladon Springs, St. Stephens Ride   218

Ride Loop 33: Roland Cooper State Park, Davis Ferry Ride   225

Ride Loop 34: Paul M. Grist State Park, Selma, Camden Ride   233

Ride Loop 35: Calera, Montevallo, Centreville, Sprott,
    Maplesville Ride   239

Ride Loop 36: Clanton, Selma, Billingsley Ride   244

Ride Loop 37: Mobile Bay Ferry Ride   251

Ride Loop 38: Greenville, Fort Deposit, Burnt Corn Ride   261

Ride Loop 39: Hope Hull, Lowndesboro, Fort Deposit Ride   269

Ride Loop 40: Mobile Bay, Bayou La Batre, Grand Bay Ride   274

PART VI Rides in Southeast Alabama: Ride Loops 41–50

Ride Loop 41: Chattahoochee State Park, State Line Ride   283

Ride Loop 42: Eufaula, Abbeville, Clayton Ride   287

Ride Loop 43: Blue Springs, Smuteye, Ozark Ride   291

Ride Loop 44: Hope Hull, Ansley, Lapine Ride   297

Ride Loop 45: Opelika, Tuskegee Ride   302

Ride Loop 46: Florala, Geneva, Opp Ride   306

Ride Loop 47: Evergreen, Andalusia, Brewton Ride   310

Ride Loop 48: Frank Jackson State Park, Stanley, Red
    Level Ride   315

Ride Loop 49: Baldwin County Ride   320

Ride Loop 50: Fort Deposit, Luverne, Brantley Ride   324

Index   329

FOR ME, NOTHING CAN MATCH the sensation of leaning my motorcycle through the twists and turns of a country lane in the springtime.

When everything is just right, bike and rider can become one, leaning into the turn, rolling on the throttle, feeling the *whish* of the wind, smelling the honeysuckle, and gliding through a blur of oxide greens and blooming wildflowers. And all the while I know that my mount is able and willing to take me wherever I choose to go.

My reason for writing this book is to help others find these sensations for themselves, here in Alabama. To my knowledge this is the first motorcycle guidebook dedicated to the roads in Alabama.

In the almost two years and more than fifty thousand miles I logged seeking out the routes for the ride loops in this book, I found that Alabama has a wealth of great motorcycling roads and locations.

I won't pretend that all are equal. They are not. In general, the areas with more hills and mountains make for better motorcycling. In Alabama most of this terrain is north of Montgomery. After all, the curves we all crave to carve are usually there when a mountain is being crossed.

But to my surprise I also found wonderful motorcycle riding in the southern parts of the state, and after much searching I believe some of the roads mapped out in these rides can be just as satisfying in their own way as the mountain roads up north.

The overriding thing I learned about my state in all those miles is just how much of it is still rural. Except for the immediate areas around the major metropolitan cities of Birmingham, Huntsville, Mobile, and Montgomery, most regions still offer the escape of hours and hours of riding through a rural landscape with little traffic.

In this book I intentionally left out any rides through metro areas and sought out back roads wherever possible. Except for the start and end points for rides, the routes never touch interstate highways. And four-lane roads are only traveled when absolutely necessary. Who needs a guidebook to find interstates anyway?

Some of the rides are tailored for dual-sport motorcycles, which can handle paved streets, gravel roads, and some easy trails.

It is my hope that Alabamians reading this book will take advantage of rides close to home as well as ones on the other side or other end of the state. And I hope that readers from outside the state will come away with a new appreciation for what Alabama has to offer the motorcycle enthusiast.

Riding Alabama 49 on a lovely day in May

ABOUT THIS BOOK

IN PLANNING FOR THIS BOOK, I divided the state of Alabama into five regions and mapped out ten ride loops for each region. Fortunately, the locations of interstate highways in the state made ideal division lines for the regions, which I have defined and named as follows:

Northeast Alabama—
Areas east of I-65 and north of I-20 (Rides 1–10)
Northwest Alabama—
Areas west of I-65 and north of I-20/59 (Rides 11–20)
East-Central Alabama—
Areas east of I-65, south of I-20, and north of I-85 (Rides 21–30)
Southwest Alabama—
Areas west of I-65 and south of I-20/59 (Rides 31–40)
Southeast Alabama—
Areas east of I-65 and south of I-85 (Rides 41–50)

Each of the rides makes a closed loop, beginning at and returning to the same point, and each loop is between 75 and 150 miles in length. All together, the fifty rides total more than 4,800 miles.

To ensure that the start and end points can be easily located, each one is either at an interstate highway exit or at the entrance to one of Alabama's state parks. Additionally, GPS coordinates for the start/ end points of each ride are included at the beginning of the section for that ride.

The routes for each ride loop intentionally steer clear of interstates altogether and four-lane highways where possible, except for

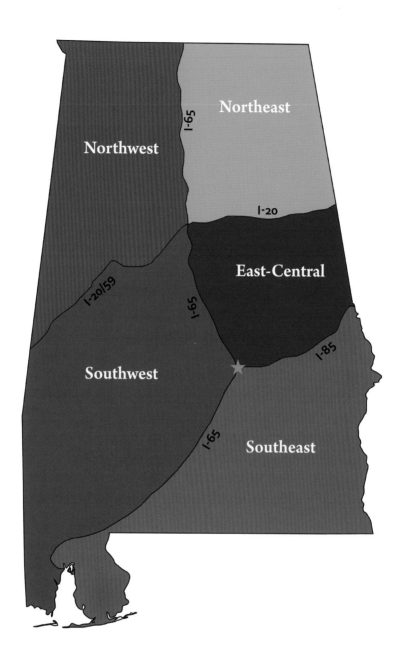

Northeast

I-65

Northwest

I-20

East-Central

I-20/59

I-65

I-85

Southwest

I-65

Southeast

the start and end points. The rides are almost all through the back roads of our still mostly rural state.

The names of roads and their decriptions were accurate at the time of riding, but please remember that counties may change the names of roads. Also, some routes take forest roads, which may be redirected or closed by the Forest Service. When riding any of the dual-sport loops, riders should pay careful attention to the distances between turns because often these gravel roads are completely unmarked. Also, I highly recommend that riders obtain detailed topographical maps of the area to have along for reference.

The ride descriptions include information on lodging and points of interest along the way, but the focus of each ride is the experience of the ride itself. In other words, the routes were selected with preference given to the most enjoyable roads for motorcycling rather than the attractions you might pass along the way.

A project like this book is never the work of a single person, and this book is no exception. I'd like to thank my good friends David DeBandi, David Elder, Joe Copeland, Bart Jones, Ken Ivey, and Don

Author David Haynes on his motorcycle (Photo by Ken Ivey)

Harbor, all of whom at one time or another got up early on a frosty morning or suffered through sweltering heat to ride along and help me when researching the routes; Craig Remington and the Cartographic Lab at The University of Alabama, who created the maps; Randy Mecredy, Greg Hester, Rusty Smith, Aceynith Alexander, and Jim McLean, who test-rode the routes; many members of the ADVrider.com online motorcycle community (whose real names I do not even know), who assisted with advice and suggestions; and Elizabeth Motherwell, whose encouragement and guidance were invaluable. And finally, I'd like to thank my wonderful wife and partner in life, Beverly, for making it possible for me to follow my dreams.

Please visit motorcyclingalabama.info, the interactive companion website for this book, which includes downloadable GPS coordinates for all of the rides as well as extra features, including updates for various rides.

MOTORCYCLING ALABAMA

PART I

PLANNING YOUR TRIP

1 MAPPING YOUR TRIP

THIS GUIDE INCLUDES A MAP with turn-by-turn directions and a brief description of each ride. However, road names frequently change, and particularly with the dual-sport rides, rural and forest gravel roads may change.

When planning a ride, I recommend obtaining the DeLorme *Alabama Atlas and Gazetteer,* a book that divides the state into sixty-four map pages measuring 11 by 15½ inches with much more detail than any single foldout state road map. If space is available on the motorcycle, this is great to carry along on any ride.

Another excellent resource for planning a trip is Google Earth and Google Maps online. These offer zoom-able views of road maps, terrain, and satellite imagery as well as street-level photos of some areas.

Each of these resources will help give the rider a sense of the character of the area through which a ride loop passes.

I also recommend having a Global Positioning System (GPS). These days most everyone knows about GPS, and more and more navigation features are being added to everything from dedicated GPS devices to cell phones.

For me, a GPS unit is one of the first accessories I'll put on any motorcycle I own. It just opens up so many possibilities.

Even if not using the GPS unit to follow a route, it's very nice to be able to see what kind of road is coming up (and how sharp its curves). And if I'm navigating a route and I want to go down a different path to check out something, the GPS will automatically recalculate a new route as soon as it senses I'm off the original one.

GPS display at Davis Ferry

For those who have GPS units, this book offers plenty of options for taking advantage of GPS features in conjunction with these ride loops.

Each of the fifty routes in the book is saved as a ".gpx" file that purchasers of this book can download from the book's website at motorcyclingalabama.info. After downloading the .gpx file, the route can be simply transferred to a GPS unit and then accessed and activated from the route list in the unit. Once activated at the start/end point, the GPS unit will give turn-by-turn prompts along the way for the route path.

2 MOTORCYCLE SAFETY

"I'd rather sweat than bleed."

MOTORCYCLE SAFETY GEAR

A FEW YEARS AGO, SOME buddies and I were stopped at a gas station on a midsummer ride when some other motorcycle riders pulled in.

One of the other riders—dressed in shorts, a sleeveless T-shirt, and sneakers—asked how we could stand to wear all our protective riding gear in the 95-degree Alabama heat.

"I'd rather sweat than bleed," my buddy told him. And I think that one statement sums up the philosophy known as A.T.G.A.T.T.: All the Gear, All the Time. This means making it a habit to wear all the gear—helmet, boots, gloves, riding jacket/pants, etc.—on every ride, even short ones.

By its very nature, motorcycle riding has some built-in hazards, the most obvious of which is that even if not moving the motorcycle will fall over if not on its kickstand. And if the motorcycle hits something, the motorcycle rider will not be protected by the enclosure, seat belts, air bags, and such of a car or truck.

To make these situations as painless as possible for the operator of a motorcycle, a dizzying variety of safety gear is available. This chapter will examine the typical kinds of gear on the market—at the time of this writing—and briefly discuss some pros and cons of each.

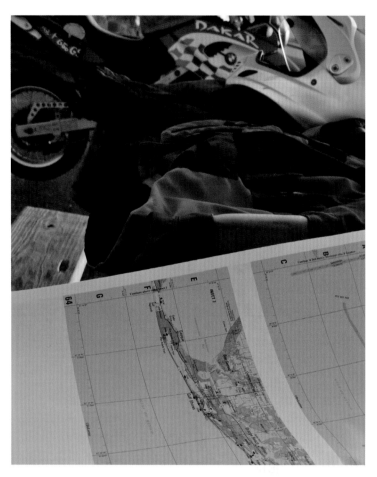

Mapping a route at Gulf State Park campground

Helmets

Helmets are the most basic form of safety gear for motorcyclists, and, in fact, the State of Alabama's laws require that a motorcycle operator and any passengers wear a helmet approved by the Department of Transportation (DOT) when riding on any public road.

Some states do not have helmet laws, and I understand that some riders believe it is their right to not wear a helmet if they so choose. But the fact is that Alabama does have the law, and to ride legally here requires a DOT-approved helmet, regardless of the philosophical arguments for and against it.

Many kinds of helmets carrying the DOT sticker are available, ranging from the ones shaped like a basketball cut in half that offer protection only to the head from the ears up to full-coverage helmets that surround the head from chin and neck up.

My personal choice is a full-coverage helmet because of the protection it offers. Mine has a face shield/visor that hinges up or down and also prevents bugs or other debris from hitting me in the face or eyes.

The first year I had this helmet, I experienced a very minor get-off at less than 30 miles per hour on a gravel road. That one incident convinced me I made the right choice. Had I not been wearing a full-coverage helmet, the left side of my face and jaw would have likely required stitches at a minimum, and very possibly surgery to repair broken bones. But thanks to the extra coverage on this style of helmet, I didn't receive a scratch, although the scrape marks on the helmet are a daily reminder of what could have happened.

The way I see it, the only reason I'm wearing a helmet is to protect my head. Why would I want to protect only a part of my head when other designs offer protection for the entire head?

Another interesting fact about helmets is that professional motorcycle racers always use helmets with maximum protection. Hmmm. . .

Several designs are available that offer protection levels from the full-face to the salad-bowl designs.

The second-highest level of protection is available from a helmet in which the hard shell extends down over the ears but leaves the face exposed.

So-called modular helmets feature a hinged chin bar that can be raised for putting on or taking off the helmet and lowered and locked into place for riding. These are popular with riders who wear eyeglasses because a rider can don or remove it while still wearing glasses.

Whatever style is used, it should fit well. If the helmet is too loose, the safety features of the design can be compromised. If it is too tight, the helmet will become a torture chamber on a long ride. With full-faced helmets, the ventilation system becomes an important comfort feature as well.

When it comes to helmets, the old axiom "you get what you pay for" is usually true. I personally recommend always trying on a helmet before buying because sizing among manufacturers is not standardized. Also, riders with oval-shaped heads will find that certain brands of helmets tend to fit them better, while people with rounder heads will prefer other brands.

Gloves and Boots

Gloves and boots protect the hands and feet and can make a huge difference in comfort on a ride. Because the controls of a motorcycle are operated by the rider's hands and feet, gloves and boots should strike a balance of flexibility, comfort, and safety to make riding a pleasure during a range of conditions.

Generally speaking, motorcycle gloves fit into two categories: summer and winter. When the weather is warm, the main function of the glove is to provide protection and comfort, usually through ventilation. Many summer gloves have leather palms and knuckle protection with a mesh material in between to allow airflow. Some riders like gloves with cutout fingers for summer that offer a minimum of protection but a maximum airflow. However, the fact is that in a mishap the rider's hands are likely going to make contact with the ground or road surface at speed. For that reason, I always wear vented summer gloves with full fingers in warm weather.

Winter gloves in general will offer more abrasion protection because they will be made of thicker material. These are available with a wide variety of features, and typically the higher-priced gloves will be warmer and more comfortable.

My preferred winter gloves are a hybrid of leather and textile outer shell, lined with synthetic material and a Gore-Tex layer that makes them both waterproof and windproof. Mine also have a long gauntlet that extends well past my jacket sleeve and can be cinched tight with a shock cord using one hand. My hands stay warm and toasty even when temps dip into the teens.

I use summer gloves until the temperature drops below about 50 degrees, then switch to the winter gloves. The biggest downside to warm winter gloves is that they are usually bulkier and allow less "touch" with the operating controls.

Some motorcycles have heated handlebar grips that can help keep digits toasty on a cool day. Riders with these "hot grips" can use summer-type gloves in lower temperatures.

Motorcycle-specific boots are another item that I consider essential. In general, boots are categorized into street boots or off-road boots. The off-road boots are usually much stiffer and offer better protection for the ankles. The street-oriented ones tend to be more waterproof and flexible, but offer somewhat less protection.

I prefer a boot that falls in the middle of this range—waterproof and insulated for warmth and flexible like a street boot, but with a steel shank through the length of the bottom and ankle and shin protection. Some riders I know wear hiking or Army-surplus combat lace-up boots and are very happy with these as well.

My first boots were at the bottom end of the price scale for motorcycle-specific boots—about $95—and did not have a steel-reinforced sole area. On a slow-speed gravel road fall, my foot got bent around the left-side foot peg between the bike and the road for about twenty feet. Because I wore motorcycle boots, no bones in my foot were broken and I wasn't even scratched up. But because they did not have the reinforced bottom, my foot was severely bruised and required several weeks of recovery. Had I been wearing the boots I now have—which I purchased within a week after this mishap—I would likely not have been hurt at all. We live and learn.

Riding Jacket/Riding Pants/Riding Suit

These items complete a rider's A.T.G.A.T.T. gear. They are usually made from either leather or some kind of abrasion-resistant textile, or a combination of the two. The better garments will also have body armor inserts at the shoulders, elbows, knees, and back.

The idea here is that, if the motorcycle goes down at speed, the rider's skin is protected for at least a time before making contact with the pavement or ground. Of course, in some accidents no amount of armor would help. But this protective layer can often mean the difference between simply sacrificing the gear and having medical procedures such as skin grafts.

Leather gear is typically recognized as having the best abrasion resistance, but some textiles now incorporate Kevlar—the same material used in bulletproof vests—which offers substantial protection. In general the leather will be difficult to wear in hot weather because it's not as breathable. Other gear has high-impact, tightly stitched, and abrasion-resistant nylon with strategically positioned armor and zippered vents that can be opened in summer and closed in colder weather.

Pants can either be dedicated riding pants or the over-pant style designed for the motorcyclist to don for riding and then remove at the destination.

For additional safety, many jacket/pants combos zip together to avoid separation in the event of an accident.

Another popular style is the waterproof and armored coverall-style suit with zippered vents. This can usually be donned over street clothes or removed in less than a minute. Armored mesh jackets that offer cooler riding in hot weather with some protection are another option for summer riding.

Designs and gear are constantly being improved as new techniques and materials evolve, so whatever is the best today likely will be improved next year or the year after.

Rain Gear

There are three main types of rain protection:

1) A rain suit—either a jacket and pants or waterproof coverall—that is worn over the riding gear
2) Jacket and pants or coverall suit made of waterproof materials
3) Jacket and pants liners made of waterproof materials

Each of these works well if quality gear is selected, so it comes down to the personal preference of the rider as to the best approach.

Riders in Basic Rider Course at the University of Montevallo

Rain gear designed for use only in the rain—the type that goes over the outside of the regular riding pants/jacket—allows the everyday jacket/pants to be designed with better ventilation for summer riding. To use this kind of gear, the rider has to stop, retrieve the rain gear from its storage place, and put it on, then remove it once the rain ends.

Riding gear made using waterproof materials is seldom truly waterproof, because zippers and other closures often allow some water to make its way inside. But it is convenient because there's no stopping to put on or remove gear. However, in the heat of summer this gear is seldom ventilated well enough to be truly comfortable.

The gear with removable liners under the jacket and pants is great for winter when the liners can be left in all the time, and this gear can be truly waterproof, even in heavy downpours. However, in summer the liners make the gear too hot above about 75 or 80 degrees. I wear this type of riding gear, and I use the liners during cool weather and ride without liners in summer, carrying a one-piece coverall-type rain suit in case of rain.

As noted at the beginning of this chapter, the only safety gear required by law in Alabama is a DOT-approved helmet. But this does not mean that a helmet is the only protection you should use. My reason for harping on this is that in my years as a newspaper photographer I have been unlucky enough to see firsthand the results of motorcyclists not wearing safety gear. I have seen crashes in which injuries or even fatalities could have been completely avoided had the rider used some of the safety gear discussed above. I have also seen many cases in which riders wearing protective gear walked away without a scratch because of their gear.

Riding a motorcycle is one of the most enjoyable experiences in my life, and using safety gear is a habit that in no way diminishes the experience for me.

Motorcycle Safety Training

In a car or other four-wheeled vehicle in which the passengers are surrounded by a curtain of steel, safety is important. But the issue of operator safety becomes a much more urgent concern for the motorcycle rider.

The very unrestrained freedom motorcycles offer by putting the rider "out there" makes the experience of two-wheeled travel more potentially hazardous, for obvious reasons.

This fact alone should be reason enough for any new rider to want to develop and hone his or her riding skills to become as proficient and safe at motorcycling as possible.

Fortunately in Alabama there is an excellent place to learn these skills. Based at the University of Montevallo, the Motorcycle Safety Program of the Alabama Traffic Safety Center offers intensive training in both motorcycle riding skills and motorcycle safety. The courses are offered year-round at the Montevallo headquarters as well as at other sites throughout the state.

In fact, for the beginning class, the Basic Rider Course, they even provide the motorcycle—a lightweight 200–250cc bike. This three-day course typically begins with Friday evening classroom work, followed by all-day riding training on a closed course on Saturday and Sunday. Students begin by learning the basics of using the clutch and shifting gears and by the end of the weekend are proficient in advanced braking, swerving, and cornering techniques.

The other two courses in the Experienced Rider Course–Skills Plus are designed to help experienced riders polish riding and safety skills. For these courses the rider uses his or her own motorcycle, and each course lasts a single day. One course is for a single rider, and the other focuses on the skills required for a rider to safely carry a passenger on a motorcycle.

For additional information on these classes, you can call the Motorcycle Safety Program's offices at 205-665-6740 or visit the program's Web site at www.montevallo.edu/ATSC/Motorcycle.

3 MOTORCYCLE CAMPING

"Wherever you go, you're there."

I'M CONVINCED THAT CAMPING from a motorcycle offers the best of all camping experiences. As an avid camper over the past forty years, I've sampled a variety of ways to camp, including car camping, backpacking, canoe and kayak camping, and even a bit of bicycle camping. For me, motorcycle camping has them all beat hands down.

Camping from a car limits the roads I can explore (most cars can't get down a muddy dirt road). Backpacking lets me go anywhere, but range is limited to how much I can walk in a day. Camping from a canoe or kayak limits the range to the particular river or lake I'm on, and bicycle camping puts severe restrictions on what comforts I can bring along.

But I can load up food, tent, sleeping bag, and more on my motorcycle and ride until I'm ready to stop. And wherever that happens to be, I'm there.

It could be a developed campground in a state or national park. It could be along a free-flowing creek or river in a national forest. It could be just on the side of a road. My destination is wherever I want it to be. And that's the point!

Those of us who ride motorcycles are already used to being out in the elements, so camping is not as big of a jump as it might be for people who are always separated from the real world by the steel and glass enclosures of a car or truck.

Of course, many riders prefer to find a room at the end of the

Winter camping at Blue Springs State Park

day's adventure, and that's fine, too; but if you like to camp, you'll love motorcycle camping. There's just something about pulling up to a beautiful, secluded spot, setting up camp, and being lulled to sleep by a mountain stream gurgling or the wind whispering through the pines. I also love to sit around a campfire—with no one but me and my camp mates within miles—and recount the day's riding adventures.

I believe strongly that camping should be as enjoyable an experience as possible, and so I bring along what I consider my essential comforts. If it's a cool or cold night and I don't have a sleeping bag appropriate for the weather, I'm not going to enjoy the experience and will be less likely to do it again. Thus my policy has always been to buy the best gear I can afford. I like to follow that old saying attributed to the Chinese: "Buy the best and only cry once." Over the years this practice has served me well.

What follows are a few lessons I've learned firsthand about motorcycle camping and some tips for making the experience more pleasant. I don't claim to know everything about the subject, but these are things that have worked well for me.

PACKED SIZE IS KEY

One of the most important features to look for when selecting motorcycle camping gear is its packed size. This is true for the tent, sleeping bag, sleeping pad, cookware, and so on.

For backpacking, usually the most important feature is weight. For motorcycle camping, however, bulk actually trumps weight. While my motorcycle can carry much more weight than I'd want to put in a pack on my back, it can quickly begin to bristle with bulk if I'm not careful. And a motorcycle must be packed in a way to be as safe as possible en route to the campsite.

Much of the gear used by backpackers is good for motorcycle camping—goose-down sleeping bags, inflatable sleeping pads, two- and three-person tents, compact cookstoves; all pack reasonably small. Backpacking gear is also lighter weight than gear intended for car camping.

Sleeping bags are a good example of variance packing size. A synthetic-fill sleeping bag will often be twice the packed size of a down bag for the same temperature range. The same holds true for tents: a six-person tent might seem like a good idea in the store, but tying a tent that measures three feet by one foot on the motorcycle leaves a lot of excess.

CARRYING CAMPING GEAR ON A MOTORCYCLE

There are lots of ways to secure camping gear to a motorcycle. For

Exploring Alabama

safety reasons, it's important to keep the weight distributed as evenly left to right as possible and to keep the heaviest items as low as possible. At all costs, avoid putting heavy items up high because the handling characteristics of the motorcycle could be compromised.

The two most popular ways for carrying camping gear on a motorcycle are hard cases made of aluminum, steel, reinforced leather, or plastic, and soft luggage which is usually made of leather, nylon, or vulcanized rubber.

Whatever is used should be waterproof. Just trust me on this. Because it's not unusual to encounter rain on a trip, keeping things like sleeping gear dry can mean the difference between a great camping experience and a miserable one. A goose-down bag doesn't keep its occupant warm when wet. And putting up an already soaked tent in a rainstorm is not any fun either.

What has worked well for me are aluminum panniers on either

Camping in Coosa County

side at the rear of the bike to carry the heaviest items such as a tent, water bottles, and food. Mine have locking waterproof lids with wire racks on top where lighter items can be tied or strapped on if need be.

I also have various tail bags—which are waterproof or have rain covers—that mount behind the seat and carry sundry lighter items or gear I might want to access while on the road.

For longer trips, I also have a dry bag made of vulcanized rubber that is watertight and can be tied on between the seat and tail bag.

Some riders like to carry often-needed items such as sunglasses, cell phones, and wallets in a tank bag. Just remember that, in a heavy rain, any case or bag not waterproof or protected by a rain cover will result in wet gear.

WHAT I CARRY FOR CAMPING

The following is a list of the items I typically carry when camping and where they are situated on the bike:

Compression bags—For me these are indispensable for motorcycle camping and allow me to pack large items into a small space. The ones I like best are made of very thin silicone-impregnated ripstop nylon and have a lid connected to the main bag by four webbed nylon compression straps that tighten one way and lock when pulled.

Using these bags to carry items that tend to billow out, like tents, sleeping bags, or clothing, I can usually condense to about one-quarter to one-half of their "loose" size. These bags make a huge difference in how much gear I can pack into the limited space available on my motorcycle. In some cases I can pack twice the gear or more into the same space that would be required without compressing the gear. This usually makes the difference in my being able to carry my "luxuries" or not.

Tent—I take a three-person backpacking tent with separate rain fly and large vestibule (to keep riding gear out of weather). My tent/fly is separated from the stakes and tent poles, stuffed into a compression bag, and packs down to about eight by fourteen inches in size. It goes in one of the side panniers. Tent poles, stakes, and ground cloth are in individual small bags and are wedged into the panniers where space is available.

Hammock—For humid summer camping in Alabama, I often substitute a hammock for the tent. Mine has a rain fly and mosquito netting built in and packs to about the size of a five-pound bag of sugar. If using the hammock, because of its lightweight and small size it goes in the dry bag behind the seat. Because I need less of everything in summer, I can often use only a tail bag and dry bag for a summertime trip and leave the aluminum panniers at home. If temperatures are going to be much below freezing at night, however, I go with the traditional tent because keeping warm in a hammock that's hanging off the ground requires about as much extra gear as just carrying the tent.

Sleeping bag—Mine is a goose-down bag that's rated down to 0 degrees Fahrenheit. I put it into a compression bag that packs slightly larger than a five-pound bag of sugar, and it rides in the same pannier as the tent.

Sleeping pad—Technology is changing all the time, and I recently discovered an air mattress in which the tubes are also filled with goose down. This provides amazing comfort and warmth com-

Enjoying the sunset while hammock camping on the Alabama River

pared to one of the self-inflating mini-cell foam sleeping pads often used by backpackers—which are also quite good. Again, the big advantage of this air mattress is packed size, which is about two-thirds the size of a bag of sugar. Compared to the foam pad I used previously, this one measures about one-fourth the packed size. It rides between the tent and sleeping bag.

Hatchet—This is handy for driving in tent stakes or splitting firewood. Because of its weight, it rides at the bottom of the pannier with the tent, bag, and pad.

Folding saw—If you're going to have a fire, this is an important item. Mine weighs less than a pound, folds to one inch by eighteen inches, and will cut through a six-inch-diameter log in thirty seconds. The saw rides next to the tent poles in one of the panniers.

Camp cooking

Stove/Cookset—You will find lots of choices here, but think backpacking stoves that will be small in packed size. Mine is a compact stove that nests within a large coffee cup and uses propane canisters. I also have a companion two-quart cook pot in which I store additional fuel canisters and a dishcloth. This often doubles as a bowl to eat from as well. Knife, fork, and spoon (plastic or titanium) also nest inside the pot. All this goes in the other pannier, along with a box for food (think compact dry food packages of rice or pasta that you would take backpacking).

Chair—Taking along a comfortable chair is one of the luxuries I insist on. A two-week kayak trip through the Grand Canyon taught me to appreciate a good chair at the end of the day. Mine packs down by rolling up into a sleeve that can then fit sideways in the pannier opposite the tent.

Water—There are several options here. If I anticipate having a good water source at the campsite, I'll bring a water bladder or bag. If I'm unsure, I typically fill two to four plastic water bottles and pack them—because of weight—at the bottom of the pannier with the chair.

Clothes—I usually put clothing into large zip-top bags that can be squeezed to remove excess air, then wedge the bags around the chair, water bottles, and cooking equipment in that pannier.

Shoes—I always carry either sandals (in summer) or sneakers to wear around camp. These are usually bungee-tied to the top rack of one of the panniers or kept behind the seat with a bungee net.

I always bring along various other small items on a camping trip: camera, first aid kit, shaving/bath kit, cooler, and so on. These usually go either in the tail bag or are stored beneath a bungee net between the tail bag and the back of my seat.

One very important item to always carry (even when not expecting to camp) is a flashlight of some kind. I'm partial to the relatively new LED "headlights" that mount on an elastic headband. They seem to give just enough light right where it's needed, and the batteries seem to last forever. Mine is usually kept in one of the tail bag pockets for easy access.

AT CAMP

When you're making camp, consider some of these lessons I've learned (sometimes the hard way) about general camping habits.

Often campsites require you to park your motorcycle on grass or in soft dirt or even mud. Be especially wary of these conditions, and select a place with good support for the kickstand foot. I've seen people park a bike on soft ground at a campsite, and slowly the bike leans farther and farther over until reaching a tipping point during the night. If the ground is mushy, find a rock or limb to put between the kickstand and the ground. Some folks carry a piece of plastic similar to a drink coaster to place under the kickstand.

When selecting a tent site, do not pitch the tent downwind of the fire location. Also, it's a good idea to make sure all motorcycles are upwind and a safe distance from the fire.

As mentioned above, my tent has a huge vestibule—the covered area between the rain fly door and the sleeping area of the tent. Mine is actually as large as the sleeping area. This allows me to put all my gear—panniers, tail bag, boots, riding pants and jacket, helmet, and so forth—out of the weather but not where I'm actually sleeping. If it's raining or there's a heavy dew in the morning, you'll appreciate having your gear under cover.

If possible, allow the tent to dry before packing up. But due to scheduling and weather, sometimes you'll have to pack a wet tent. When this happens, pitch the tent in the sunshine when you return home or as soon as possible to prevent mildew. Mildew can turn an expensive tent into a leaky sieve within a few days. It's also smart to always store all camping gear in oversized, breathable bags in a warm, dry area of the house. I store my gear in the top shelf of a closet.

4 ON THE ROAD

LITTLE THINGS CAN MAKE THE RIDE BETTER

As EXPLAINED AT THE BEGINNING of this book, all the rides covered here are between 75 and 150 miles in length, and all can be accessed and then followed either at the start or end point or at a point along the way.

The reality is that for many riders the overall distance from their home starting point to the loop and back will be double the loop itself or more. So it's important to plan ahead and bring along some tools that will be helpful on a long ride.

Before taking off on a lengthy trip, I've found it prudent to pack some items that can add to the enjoyment of the ride, whether or not any problems arise. But there are other items I always carry with potential problems in mind, so that I can get home a little more easily should I have a flat tire or other roadside malfunction along the way. Motorcycles made in the last two decades are much more reliable than those of years past, but it's still not uncommon to have to make roadside repairs—most commonly fixing a flat tire.

TIRE PROBLEMS

I highly recommend that each rider learn what is required to fix a flat tire on their bike, practice the procedure *before* heading out, and have the necessary tools for the job on the motorcycle in case of a tire problem.

All of today's motorcycles will fall into one of two categories when it comes to tires and tire repair: tubeless tires and tires with

Rainbow after a shower

inner tubes. You need to be familiar with the repair procedure according to which type of tires are on your bike.

Repairing Tubeless Tires

Of the two types of tires, tubeless tires make roadside repairs much easier. With a tubeless tire, you can perform a temporary repair on the road in just a few minutes using a tire plug that works exactly like that used to plug a tubeless car or truck tire.

To do this kind of repair, you need only an inexpensive tire plugging kit and a way to put air back into the tire once the hole is plugged. This can be accomplished with a small air compressor that runs off of the motorcycle's battery, a manual tire pump, or a CO_2 cartridge equipped with an adapter allowing it to connect to the valve stem. These devices are all available at motorcycle dealerships and online.

I must emphasize here that tire plugs will not work on some holes that are either too large or on the tire's sidewall, and that in all cases plugs should be viewed as a temporary measure. In fact, I've found that many motorcycle dealers will not repair a damaged tire at all because of liability issues. Therefore, if you have to plug a damaged tire, be mindful of how far you ride on it afterward. Riders I've met have different opinions on riding with a plugged tire. I know some who ride a plugged tire for thousands of miles. Others discard the tire and replace it as soon as they return home. In my opinion, the safety of the tire should be a deciding factor in these situations, since having a flat tire on a bike at high speed could result in catastrophic consequences.

Repairing Tires with Inner Tubes

If your bike has tires with inner tubes, the repair will take longer, because in most cases the wheel has to be removed before making the repair. This is why it's important to practice removing and replacing the wheels in the comfort of your own garage or driveway *before* having to do it on a roadside in less than ideal conditions.

In my experience, most flats seem to happen on the rear tire, perhaps because more of the motorcycle's weight is riding there. For a bike with a chain, removing and reinstalling a tire will mean also dealing with the chain and rear sprocket. Again, it's much better to have practiced this previously!

Once the wheel is off, one side of the tire bead must be pried off (using tire irons) so the inner tube can be removed. In this situation, having the right tools can make a huge difference. Technically, a screwdriver or other tool handle could be used to remove and replace the tire bead on the rim, but this often results in other holes being poked in the tube during the reinstallation.

When the tube is out, it must be either patched (again, using readily available kits and following the directions) or replaced with a new tube if you have one ready.

Again, a source of compressed air—hand pump, compressor, or CO_2 cartridge system—will be needed to reinflate the tire. I always—and I urge you to follow my advice on this—air up the repaired tire and wait a few minutes before reinstalling the wheel, to prevent having to remove it a second time should there be any leakage due to a pinched or damaged inner tube.

This procedure may sound daunting, but once I did it a couple of times, I found it was really no big deal. The main thing is to make certain you know how to do it and that you have the proper tools on the bike. One tool you may want to have on hand is a center stand, which will make the repair job much more pleasant.

Tire Goo

Another option for both tubed and tubeless tires that I've seen used with varying degrees of success are the aerosol cans or plastic bottles of gluelike goo that are sprayed through the valve stem into the tire or tube. The idea here is that the air pressure exiting the hole will expel the goo and simultaneously dry it out to form a plug and stop the air leak.

In my experience, tire goo works best on smaller punctures near the center of the tire. And it makes the next tire change a nightmare because the excess goo residue has to be cleaned up.

If you opt for an aerosol can of tire goo, make sure to get the kind with a pigtail to connect to the valve stem. With the other type of aerosol—designed for car tires—the can must press straight down on the valve stem to release the pressurized goo. The centered placement of most motorcycle wheels' valve stems will not have the clearance for this to work.

Valve Core Removal Tool
This tool is essential to remove the valve core on a tube or tubeless tire. The most convenient type to have combines a valve stem cap with the core removal tool on the opposite end. These tools are very inexpensive, so I suggest that you keep one on both wheels, so they are there when and where they are needed.

WHAT I CARRY ON EVERY RIDE
The following is a list of the must-have items I carry on any trip to help me deal with roadside issues and add to my personal comfort.

Tool kit—Because my bike uses inner tube tires, I carry the bike manufacturer's tool kit that has the necessary tools to remove and replace both wheels. A note here: luckily the bike I ride came with a fairly good tool kit. In a recent trend, motorcycle companies have pared down the tools in the supplied kit to the point that they are sometimes useless. Make sure you know what the supplied tools can and cannot do *before* heading out. My kit includes the wrenches to remove both wheels, a spark plug wrench, pliers, a couple of screwdrivers, and hex (hexagonal) or torx wrenches to remove anything I'd need to get to on the road.

To this basic kit I have added the following useful items:
1. About twenty **plastic wire ties** of varying lengths. These are very handy to tie things up or make quick repairs. They take up a negligible amount of space and weigh practically nothing.

2. Tape pencil—My father taught me this trick: I pull off about six feet each of plastic electrical tape and silver duct tape from their rolls and then wrap each length around a pencil that's just long enough to hold the combined widths next to each other. With that I have twelve feet of tape in a compact package that's about four inches long and just over an inch in diameter.

3. Epoxy putty stick—This comes in a one-by-four-inch tube, and when sliced off and kneaded together makes a stick-to-almost-anything epoxy putty to make temporary repairs.

4. Leatherman-type knife/pliers multitool—This tool takes up little space and comes in handy for lots of small jobs.

5. Miniature air compressor—The one I have packs into its own six-by-six-by-two-inch case and is wired to connect into the accessory outlet on the bike. It will pump up a tire in less than five minutes.

6. Tire gauge—The reasons for this tool are obvious.

7. Tire irons—I carry three nine-inch-long steel irons that have one flat end and a slight hook that makes getting under the tire bead easier when removing the tire. It's important to have three because, when you are working the tire off the rim, two are holding the progress you've made and the third is used to get the next "bite." Trust me on this. I stack the irons together and tape them to prevent rattling.

8. Valve stem snake—This little item saves my knuckles when I am threading the inner tube valve stem back through the rim after a repair. It's a simple screw that is the same thread size as the valve stem core with a wire or string attached. With some stiff sidewall tires, it can save half an hour of cursing. Again, trust me on this.

Non-tool essentials—These items are not tools per se, but are easy to carry and take up little space.

1. **Chain lubricant**—To get maximum wear from a drive chain, I try to lubricate it about every five hundred miles or every other fill-up. I carry the lubricant with me to use when I reach these points away from home.

2. **Spare handlebar levers** (front brake and clutch)—These cost less than $10 each, are lightweight, and pack small. Once I had to ride more than one hundred miles without a clutch when my bike tipped over and a lever broke off. Never again!

3. **Spare spark plug(s)**—I like to have these just in case.

4. **Inner tubes**—If I'm going on an overnight trip, I usually carry both front and rear tubes (each is a different size on my bike). If carrying only one, I carry the larger of the two sizes because it can be used temporarily in the smaller tire. Even if not carrying tubes, I always have a patch kit. A note here: once the glue tube in a patch kit has been opened, replace it. Otherwise, it will dry out and be useless.

5. **Spare fuses**—They are inexpensive, take up little space, and can mean the difference between riding and walking home.

6. **Cell phone**—Everybody has one these days.

7. **Tank and/or tail bag**—This holds odds and ends or items that I want to access easily. Also, most tank bags have a map window that allows me to glance down at a map while I ride rather than having to stop and look.

8. **Visor cleaner**—I use a small aerosol can that I keep in an old tube sock. The process is simple: remove the can from the sock, remove cap and spray onto visor, use sock to clean bugs and dirt from helmet visor, replace can into sock.

PACKING FOR THE RIDE

The bike I ride has a convenient compartment behind the rider's seat that holds all my tools, air compressor, spare levers, inner tube patch kit, tire irons, spark plug(s), headlight, tape, and epoxy putty stick, plus a few other odds and ends. All these items stay there all the time. Unless there's a problem, I never touch them, but it's nice knowing they're handy.

For day trips, typically I carry a small tail bag that mounts behind the seat and holds the chain lubricant and visor cleaner kit and has plenty of room for other items such as a rain suit, extra gloves, water, and snacks.

On multi-day trips when the side cases are mounted, I'll pack them with extra inner tubes (which are somewhat bulky) and spare clutch and throttle cables, along with the usual items needed on the road for camping and such.

Taking in the sunset on the Alabama River after a ride

PART II

RIDES IN NORTHEAST ALABAMA
Ride Loops 1–10

Paint Rock River and Monte Sano State Park Ride

Approximately 105 miles
Riding time 4–5 hours

Start/End Point GPS Coordinates:
34°42'41.92"N
86°32'03.84"W

THIS IS ONE OF MY FAVORITE RIDES in northeast Alabama. Beginning at the turn from U.S. Highway 431 toward Monte Sano State Park, the first leg carries you through the state park, north back down the mountain, and out to U.S. Highway 72 to the community of Paint Rock, where Highway 65 begins.

From here, the route follows Highway 65 through a lovely valley dotted with old buildings and varying between woodland, pasture, and even some twists along the banks of the Paint Rock River, which the road generally follows as it meanders through the valley. Most of the turns are smooth sweeps through gently rising and falling hills.

When Highway 65 forms a T with Highway 146, a right turn begins an ascent of nicely finished sweeps from the valley floor, through part of the Skyline Wildlife Management Area, up Jacobs Mountain, and finally to Alabama Highway 79, just about ten miles south of the Tennessee state line.

You could take an interesting side trip here to hike the Walls of Jericho area. If you turn left on Highway 79 for about nine miles instead of following the route to the right, the trailhead for the Walls is on the left just before the Alabama-Tennessee line. Be warned, however, that this hike is quite strenuous and will take several hours.

Back to the route, the next section of road comes off the mountain beginning where County Road 17 turns off Highway 79 at Skyline, and gets steeper and twistier after turning onto County Road 8 at Letcher. This road is great fun from either direction and includes a couple of horseshoe-type switchback turns. The road surface is good, but not all of it is silky-smooth asphalt.

After getting on County Road 63 at Woodville and crossing U.S. 72 again, you'll pass the entrance to Cathedral Caverns State Park before going up the mountain to Grant. The caverns boast one of the largest cave entrances in the world—large enough, in fact, to drive an eighteen-wheeler through. Tours of the caverns require an admission fee.

From Grant, my route takes a right for a more direct path through Bucksnort on Simpson Point Road; but, if the sun is setting, some riders might prefer a quicker route back to U.S. 431 by continuing straight for another 3.5 miles. It adds only a couple of miles, but requires more droning along the four-lane 431.

Twisting along County Road 8 in Jackson County on an autumn day

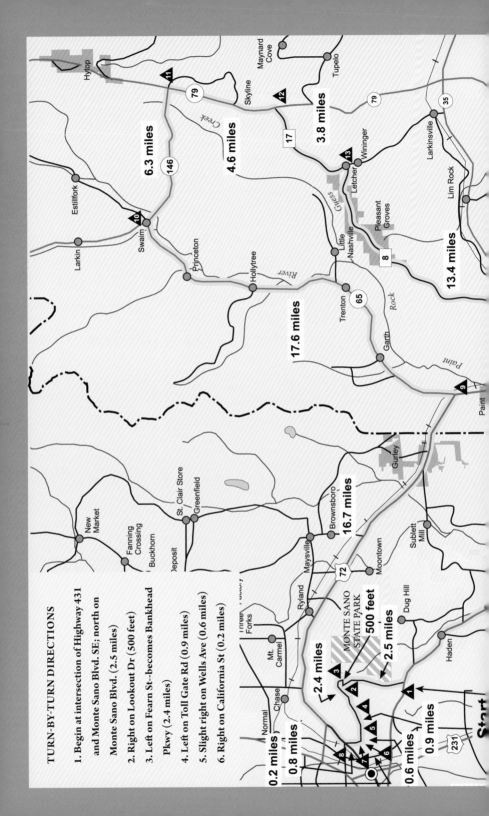

TURN-BY-TURN DIRECTIONS

1. Begin at intersection of Highway 431 and Monte Sano Blvd. SE; north on Monte Sano Blvd. (2.5 miles)

2. Right on Lookout Dr (500 feet)

3. Left on Fearn St--becomes Bankhead Pkwy (2.4 miles)

4. Left on Toll Gate Rd (0.9 miles)

5. Slight right on Wells Ave (0.6 miles)

6. Right on California St (0.2 miles)

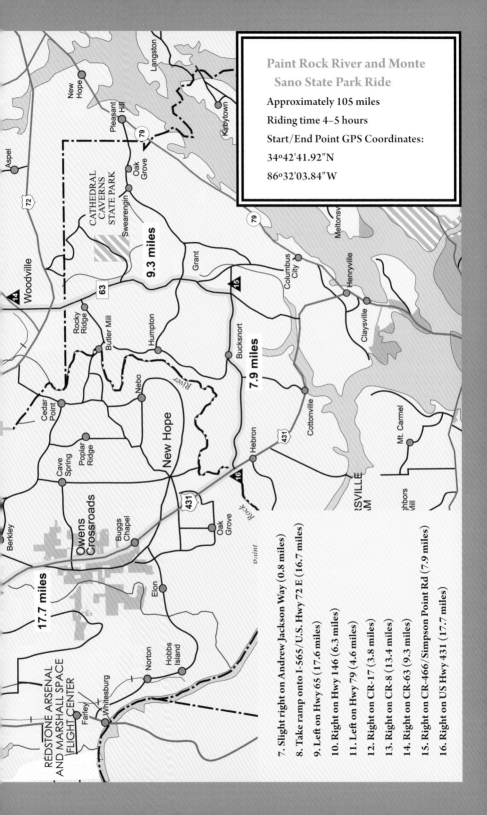

**Paint Rock River and Monte
Sano State Park Ride**

Approximately 105 miles

Riding time 4–5 hours

Start/End Point GPS Coordinates:

34º42'41.92"N

86º32'03.84"W

9.3 miles

7.9 miles

17.7 miles

7. Slight right on Andrew Jackson Way (0.8 miles)

8. Take ramp onto I-565/U.S. Hwy 72 E (16.7 miles)

9. Left on Hwy 65 (17.6 miles)

10. Right on Hwy 146 (6.3 miles)

11. Left on Hwy 79 (4.6 miles)

12. Right on CR-17 (3.8 miles)

13. Right on CR-8 (13.4 miles)

14. Right on CR-63 (9.3 miles)

15. Right on CR-466/Simpson Point Rd (7.9 miles)

16. Right on US Hwy 431 (17.7 miles)

Springville, Gallant, Oneonta, Remlap Ride

Approximately 78 miles
Riding time 3–4 hours

Start/End Point GPS Coordinates:
33°46'38.61"N
86°25'37.98"W

THIS SCENIC RURAL RIDE TOUCHES parts of St. Clair, Jefferson, Blount, and Etowah counties and features several switchback roads that traverse mountains northeast of the Birmingham metro area.

Beginning at Exit 156 on Interstate 59 in Springville, the first leg heads east toward Ashville on Highway 23, a quick-paced sweeping blacktop road.

Walker Gap switchback

About twelve miles into the ride comes the first tight, twisty ascent up Walker Gap Road, which climbs from the Crawford Cove valley floor almost two miles to the crest of Straight Mountain at County Road 24. This section is very tight and steep in places, and the switchback turns were not smooth asphalt as of this writing, so caution is advised, particularly if you are riding a long wheel-based cruiser.

After a few miles along the brow of Straight Mountain, the route dives back into a valley on U.S. Highway 231 South before turning onto Gallant Road. About two miles down Gallant Road, you'll pass the right-hand turn up Chandler Mountain to Horse Pens 40, a mountaintop cluster of rock formations that formed a natural "pen" where locals hid livestock from raiding parties during the Civil War.

Gallant Road meanders through a wide valley dotted with farms for the 8.4 miles between U.S. 231 and the turn for Tumlin Gap

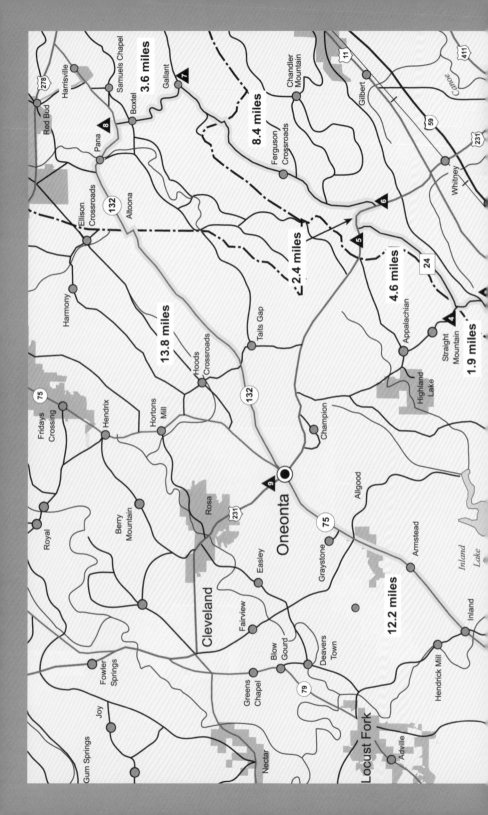

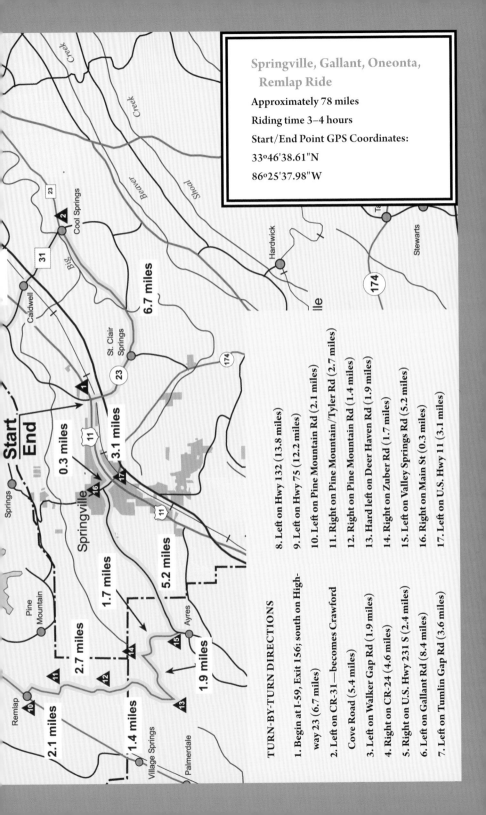

Springville, Gallant, Oneonta, Remlap Ride

Approximately 78 miles

Riding time 3–4 hours

Start/End Point GPS Coordinates:

33°46'38.61"N

86°25'37.98"W

TURN-BY-TURN DIRECTIONS

1. Begin at I-59, Exit 156; south on Highway 23 (6.7 miles)

2. Left on CR-31—becomes Crawford Cove Road (5.4 miles)

3. Left on Walker Gap Rd (1.9 miles)

4. Right on CR-24 (4.6 miles)

5. Right on U.S. Hwy 231 S (2.4 miles)

6. Left on Gallant Rd (8.4 miles)

7. Left on Tumlin Gap Rd (3.6 miles)

8. Left on Hwy 132 (13.8 miles)

9. Left on Hwy 75 (12.2 miles)

10. Left on Pine Mountain Rd (2.1 miles)

11. Right on Pine Mountain/Tyler Rd (2.7 miles)

12. Right on Pine Mountain Rd (1.4 miles)

13. Hard left on Deer Haven Rd (1.9 miles)

14. Right on Zuber Rd (1.7 miles)

15. Left on Valley Springs Rd (5.2 miles)

16. Right on Main St (0.3 miles)

17. Left on U.S. Hwy 11 (3.1 miles)

View from Walker Gap Road

Road. This ascending road has some tight turns as well, but they are neither as narrow nor extreme as those along Walker Gap.

From its connection with Highway 132, the route follows another valley through the town of Altoona in Etowah County back to Oneonta in Blount County, where it joins Highway 75 to follow the valley back toward Pinson to the town of Remlap and the third switchback ascent at Pine Mountain Road.

After climbing atop Pine Mountain, the route makes its way back

to Springville along the Jefferson-Blount county line, winding in and out of lakes and hills on scenic narrow lanes.

At Springville the route joins U.S. Highway 11/Main Street and takes you back to the start.

Along this route, Springville and Oneonta are the only two towns of significant size. Each has several offerings for dining, ranging from fast food to various sit-down restaurants. While there are few major towns on the route, fuel is available at numerous places along the way and shouldn't be a worry.

Brompton and St. Clair County Ride

Approximately 87 miles
Riding time 3–4 hours

Start/End Point GPS Coordinates:
33°34'41.58"N
86°28'33.52"W

ONCE YOU BEGIN THIS ROUTE at the Brompton Exit (number 147) off Interstate 20, within a mile the scenery becomes distinctly rural on the winding turns of Kelly Creek Road.

At the end of Kelly Creek Road, Highway 174 heads into Odenville, follows U.S. Highway 411 for about a mile, then turns north toward Springville.

The route leaves Highway 174 at Shanghi Road, a 2.2-mile cut-through road to Highway 23 that connects Springville and Ashville.

Highway 23 is a joy to ride, as you follow rolling hills through a valley and dart in and out of woodlands, all while enjoying quick-paced sweeping turns.

At the historic town of Ashville—where one of St. Clair County's two courthouses is located—Highway 23 becomes U.S. 411 and continues northeast. This part of the route follows a wide and open valley past farm after farm.

Just before reaching Neely Henry Lake, the route turns right at Greensport Road and travels through another valley back southwest. This section goes past the oldest house in St. Clair County—the John Looney Pioneer House Museum—on the right about 1.2 miles before the intersection with County Road 33. The old cabin

Crowd at Vintage Festival at Barber Motorsports Park in Leeds

and barn have been restored and furnished to reflect the period when they were constructed. This is also likely to be the oldest two-story dogtrot house in the entire state. The museum is open by appointment only (call 205-629-6897), with the exception of the second Saturday in October, when the St. Clair County Historical Society holds its Fall Festival.

From the Looney House, the route takes a left on County Road 33, and after two miles another left at County Road 26, which ascends Beaver Mountain and continues into Ragland. From Ragland, the route follows Highway 144 into Coal City and left on U.S. 231 back to Highway 174.

After about five miles on 174, the route turns left at Cook Springs Road and follows it almost five miles to Old U.S. Highway 78, crossing under Interstate 20 at Exit 152 and then traveling through an arched tunnel under a railroad at the town of Cook Springs.

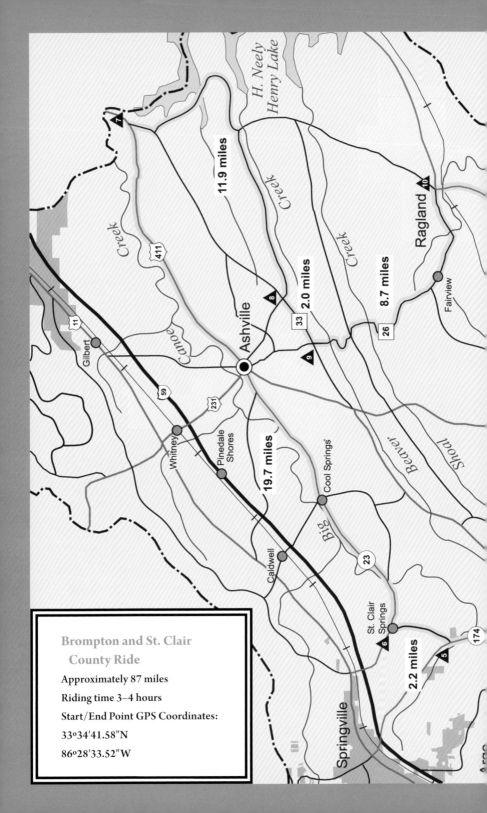

H. Neely
Henry Lake

11.9 miles

7

Creek

Creek

411

Ragland

10

Creek

8.7 miles

Ashville

8

33   2.0 miles

26

9

Fairview

11

Gilbert

59

231

Whitney

Pinedale
Shores

19.7 miles

Cool Springs

Beaver

Shoal

Canoe

Caldwell

Big

23

St. Clair
Springs

6

2.2 miles

5

174

Springville

**Brompton and St. Clair
County Ride**

Approximately 87 miles

Riding time 3–4 hours

Start/End Point GPS Coordinates:

33°34'41.58"N

86°28'33.52"W

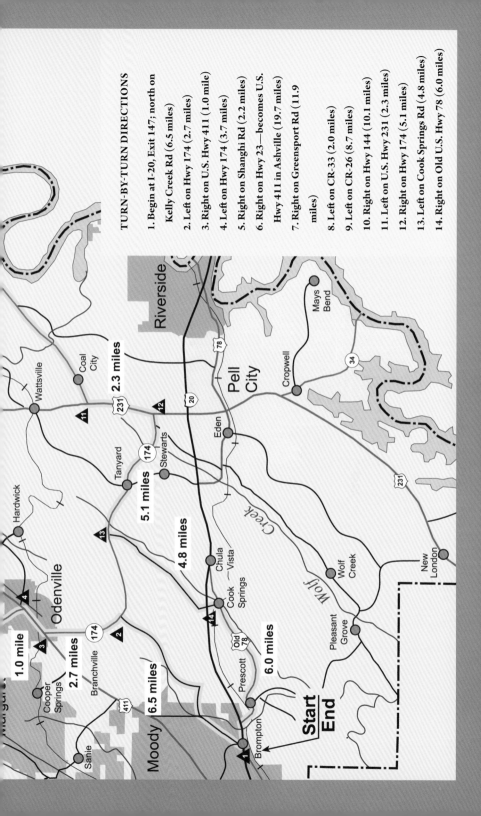

TURN-BY-TURN DIRECTIONS

1. Begin at I-20, Exit 147; north on Kelly Creek Rd (6.5 miles)
2. Left on Hwy 174 (2.7 miles)
3. Right on U.S. Hwy 411 (1.0 mile)
4. Left on Hwy 174 (3.7 miles)
5. Right on Shanghi Rd (2.2 miles)
6. Right on Hwy 23 — becomes U.S. Hwy 411 in Ashville (19.7 miles)
7. Right on Greensport Rd (11.9 miles)
8. Left on CR-33 (2.0 miles)
9. Left on CR-26 (8.7 miles)
10. Right on Hwy 144 (10.1 miles)
11. Left on U.S. Hwy 231 (2.3 miles)
12. Right on Hwy 174 (5.1 miles)
13. Left on Cook Springs Rd (4.8 miles)
14. Right on Old U.S. Hwy 78 (6.0 miles)

Riders have the option to take the interstate back to the start instead of winding the six miles of U.S. 78.

Just west of the start/end point for this route is the town of Leeds, where the Barber Vintage Motorsports Museum and Barber Motorsports Park are located. They are a must-see for any motorcycle enthusiast in the area.

The museum boasts the largest collection of vintage motorcycles in North America (possibly in the world), as well as a world-class road racing track and facilities. Approximately five hundred of the more than nine hundred vintage motorcycles in the collection are on display at any one time. For more information on the museum, visit its Web site at www.barbermuseum.org.

On Highway 227 at Lake Guntersville State Park

Lake Guntersville State Park, Sand Mountain, Langston Ride

Approximately 80 miles
Riding time 3–4 hours

Start/End Point GPS Coordinates:
34°22'56.22"N
86°11'53.90"W

THIS RIDE FOLLOWS LAKE GUNTERSVILLE on the Tennessee River for nearly twenty miles, then ascends Sand Mountain, and finally loops back to the start point. Traversing the Alabama Mountain Lakes region, the roads on this ride provide a good sense of why that name was chosen.

The start point at Lake Guntersville State Park offers a variety of lodging accommodations and a fine restaurant. In fact, although not on the route, the road that loops through the park is a worthwhile side trip for anyone who hasn't experienced it. It begins at the state park entrance intersection with Highway 227, goes past the lodge and golf course, and runs down along the lake and campground/beach/boat ramp areas and back around to the entrance. Be aware of the possibility of deer in the roadway in the park—and really throughout this entire area.

From the park entrance, Highway 227 follows the lake and becomes South Sauty Road/Highway 67 at Five Points.

At Langston, about two miles past a long causeway, County Road 38 or Langston Gap Road turns right to begin a steep ascent up Sand Mountain. This is a fun road with some horseshoe-turn switchbacks.

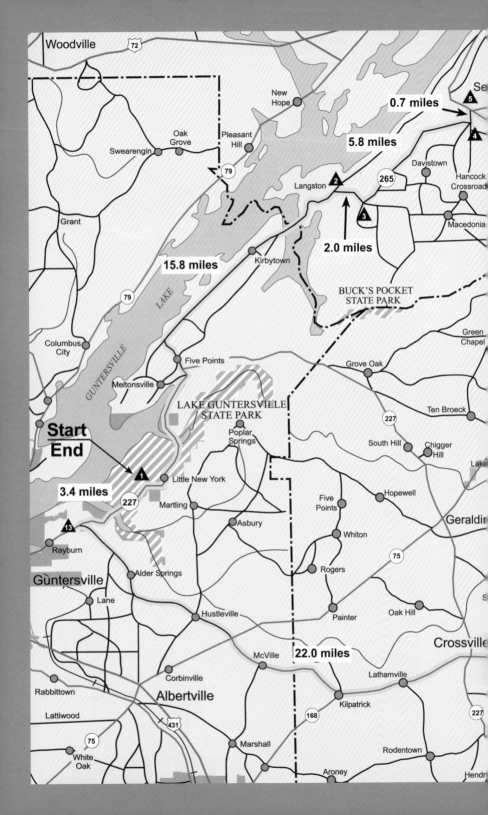

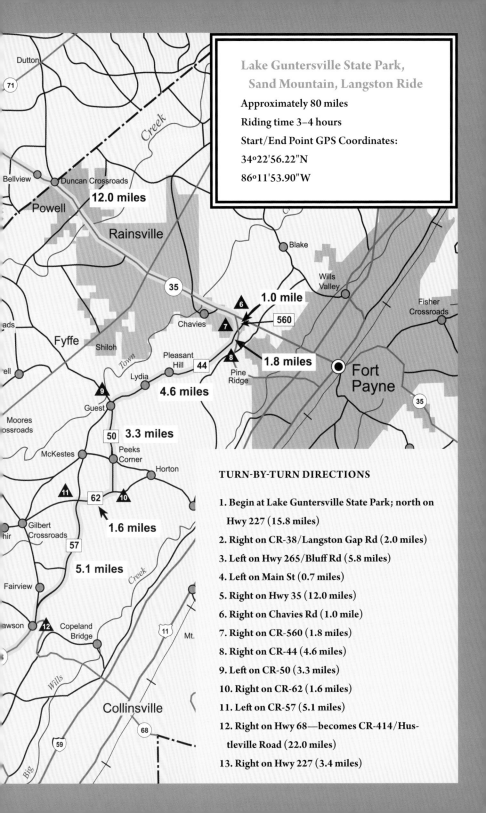

Lake Guntersville State Park,
Sand Mountain, Langston Ride

Approximately 80 miles

Riding time 3–4 hours

Start/End Point GPS Coordinates:

34º22'56.22"N

86º11'53.90"W

TURN-BY-TURN DIRECTIONS

1. Begin at Lake Guntersville State Park; north on Hwy 227 (15.8 miles)
2. Right on CR-38/Langston Gap Rd (2.0 miles)
3. Left on Hwy 265/Bluff Rd (5.8 miles)
4. Left on Main St (0.7 miles)
5. Right on Hwy 35 (12.0 miles)
6. Right on Chavies Rd (1.0 mile)
7. Right on CR-560 (1.8 miles)
8. Right on CR-44 (4.6 miles)
9. Left on CR-50 (3.3 miles)
10. Right on CR-62 (1.6 miles)
11. Left on CR-57 (5.1 miles)
12. Right on Hwy 68—becomes CR-414/Hustleville Road (22.0 miles)
13. Right on Hwy 227 (3.4 miles)

In winter, when the trees are bare, this section features some breath-taking views of the river below, looking to the northeast toward Scottsboro.

After a couple of miles, a left on Highway 265/Bluff Road leads to the town of Section on the brow of Sand Mountain.

An interesting side trip here is to not take that left and continue to nearby Buck's Pocket State Park, where legend has it that defeated politicians come to lick their electoral wounds. The park strides South Sauty Creek—a popular white-water run for canoes and kayaks in season—and offers camping and hiking trails. A geological quirk causes the creek to disappear underground in dryer months so

Camping at Lake Guntersville State Park

that the creek bed is completely dry where it passes the campground at Buck's Pocket. If there's sufficient water for the creek to be there, chances are that white-water paddlers will be as well.

If not going to Buck's Pocket, go on to Section, where the route joins Highway 35 for twelve miles of mostly four lanes past Rainsville to a right on Chavies Road and a section of smaller two-lane roads that generally follow the southeastern brow of Sand Mountain back to Highway 68 near Dawson.

From that point, Highway 68 becomes CR-414/Hustleville Road after crossing Highway 75, and then rejoins Highway 227 about 3.4 miles west of the start/end point at the state park.

Near Buck's Pocket State Park

Little River Canyon, Mentone, DeSoto State Park Ride

Approximately 82 miles
Riding time 4–5 hours

Start/End Point GPS Coordinates:
34°30'04.05"N
85°37'05.08"W

TRULY ONE OF THE PREMIERE rides in all of Alabama, the twenty-plus miles of this route that follow the rim of Little River Canyon feature breathtaking views at nearly every turn.

The mapped route for this ride begins at DeSoto State Park and picks up the rim road at the head of the canyon off Highway 35 near Little River Falls, then follows the river downstream to Canyon Mouth Picnic Area. From there it heads back northeast and briefly into the edge of Georgia before looping back through Mentone to the starting point.

DeSoto State Park offers both primitive and developed camping, as well as other lodging ranging from chalets to conventional rooms. There is also a restaurant with a tasty breakfast buffet and Sunday lunch buffet, along with conventional menu dining.

To begin, the route heads southwest from the park on the Lookout Mountain Parkway to Highway 35 above Fort Payne. From there it's about five miles to the beginning of the Little River Canyon Parkway/Highway 176.

Opposite: Little River Canyon

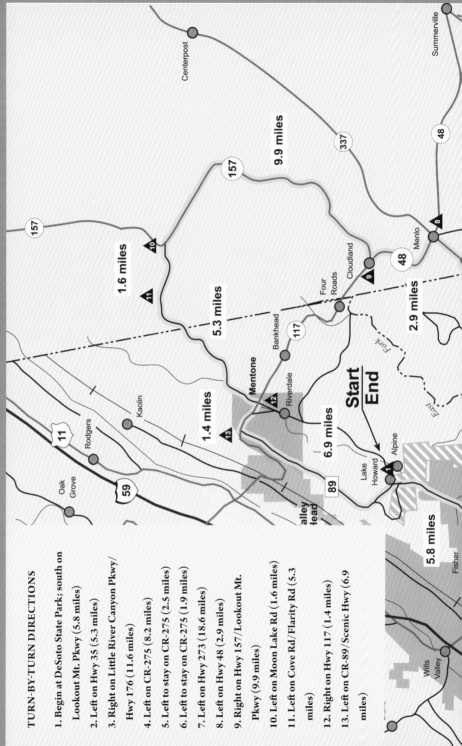

TURN-BY-TURN DIRECTIONS

1. Begin at DeSoto State Park; south on Lookout Mt. Pkwy (5.8 miles)

2. Left on Hwy 35 (5.3 miles)

3. Right on Little River Canyon Pkwy/ Hwy 176 (11.6 miles)

4. Left on CR-275 (8.2 miles)

5. Left to stay on CR-275 (2.5 miles)

6. Left to stay on CR-275 (1.9 miles)

7. Left on Hwy 273 (18.6 miles)

8. Left on Hwy 48 (2.9 miles)

9. Right on Hwy 157/Lookout Mt. Pkwy (9.9 miles)

10. Left on Moon Lake Rd (1.6 miles)

11. Left on Cove Rd/Flarity Rd (5.3 miles)

12. Right on Hwy 117 (1.4 miles)

13. Left on CR-89/Scenic Hwy (6.9 miles)

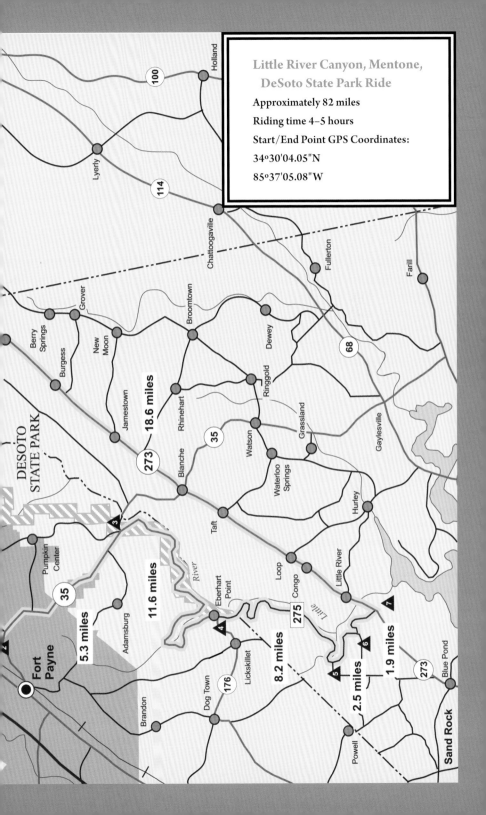

Little River Canyon, Mentone,
DeSoto State Park Ride

Approximately 82 miles

Riding time 4–5 hours

Start/End Point GPS Coordinates:

34o30'04.05"N

85o37'05.08"W

Little River Canyon Parkway

But for anyone who hasn't seen Little River Falls, I highly recommend continuing another quarter mile or so on Highway 35 past the Highway 176 turn to the parking area above the falls and make the short paved hike down to see it.

Back to the route, Turn 3 marks the beginning of the canyon drive. As of this writing, the first half of the ride was recently paved with a smooth asphalt surface, but the last half of the rim road—from Eberhart Point where Highway 176 veers away toward Dog Town—has noticeably rougher pavement, including at least two *very* steep downhill stretches at Johnnie's Creek and Canyon Mouth Picnic Area.

This first half of the ride features numerous pull-offs and developed overlooks with majestic views into the canyon. There's even one spot where a rock formation known as Mushroom Rock splits the road into two lanes. Tumbling off the southwestern wall of the side canyon formed by Bear Creek approaching Eberhart Point is Graces High Falls, which is most impressive following a hard rain.

Eberhart Point has the only paved hiking trail into the seven-hundred-foot-deep canyon. The path follows the old service road used in the 1960s when a chairlift used to descend into the canyon here. It's a good place to pause for lunch or take a rest-room break as well.

From Eberhart the canyon rim road enters Cherokee County and follows County Road 275 along the brow of the canyon (Turn 4). It twists for a bit over ten miles, crossing Johnnie's Creek—where another interesting waterfall can be seen—and finally coming down Lookout Mountain on a steep descent to Canyon Mouth Picnic Area, where picnic and rest-room facilities are available. Note that the final 0.7-mile descent to the park is one of the steepest inclines in Alabama, so use extreme caution here.

From Canyon Mouth Picnic Area, it's another mile or so to Highway 273, where the route turns northeast for almost nineteen miles into Menlo, Georgia. From there it follows Georgia Highway 48 to Cloudland to pick up Highway 157/Lookout Mountain Parkway.

An interesting side trip here is found about eight miles after you get on the parkway. A turn to the right on Dougherty Gap Road will take you off the mountain through some of the sharpest switchbacks I've seen anywhere. After a mile and a half, the road broadens into an open cove and is a good shortcut for points north and east in north Georgia and east Tennessee.

Getting back to the route, after 9.9 miles on the parkway, the route turns left at Moon Lake Road and again left on Cove Road.

This road pops out in the resort town of Mentone, still atop Lookout Mountain. Mentone and the surrounding areas offer a variety of accommodations and eateries and even Alabama's only ski resort, Cloudmont.

From Mentone, the route follows County Road 89/Scenic Highway back to DeSoto State Park, passing the turn for DeSoto Falls en route. The falls are about a mile off the route and worth making a side trip for those who haven't visited them. At over one hundred feet, they are among the highest in the state. An overlook for the falls is accessed via an easy paved footpath of a few hundred feet in length.

Mushroom Rock at Little River Canyon

Crossing Little River upstream of Alabama Highway 35

Bikes at Wolf Creek Overlook along the Little River Canyon Parkway

Union Bridge in DeKalb County

Biker passing on Little River Canyon Parkway

Horses wading in Little River in DeKalb County

One of the sharp switchbacks on Dougherty Gap Road, near Little River Canyon

Hammondville, Scottsboro, Stevenson Ride

Approximately 90 miles

Riding time 3–4 hours

Start/End Point GPS Coordinates:

34°35'38.90"N

85°38'28.56"W

BEGINNING AT THE FOOT OF Lookout Mountain, this ride climbs Sand Mountain, crosses the Tennessee River twice, and features some of the most winding and twisty stretches of roadway in the state.

The first leg of the ride begins at Exit 231 on Interstate 59 and takes Highway 40 all the way to its intersection with Highway 35 just south of the Tennessee River Bridge at Scottsboro.

It follows Highway 35 into the city of Scottsboro, where after 4.2 miles it becomes Tupelo Pike at East Willow Street as Highway 35

Rock Zoo on County Road 32 in Jackson County

branches off to the left. After 6.8 miles, Tupelo Pike forms a T with County Road 33, where you turn left (Turn 4).

The ascent up Crow Mountain on County Road 33 is a fun, tightly winding series of switchbacks until it reaches Moody Gap and flattens out eight hundred feet above the valley floor.

When you take Turn 5 to the right onto County Road 39, you'll first climb up, then steeply descend off of Crow Mountain with even steeper and sharper switchbacks than County Road 33 into Goshen Hollow and back through the Carns community, where Turn 6 takes a left onto County Road 42.

An off-route sight worth checking out via a 1.8-mile detour is the Rock Zoo on County Road 32. Here the landowner has painted rocks along the roadside to resemble a wide array of animals. To get there, at Carns turn right at County Road 42, and go south 0.6 miles, then right again on County Road 32 for 1.2 miles. You can't miss it.

Back on the route, after taking Turn 6 onto County Road 42, turn left on County Road 55 and then right on County Road 53 into Rash.

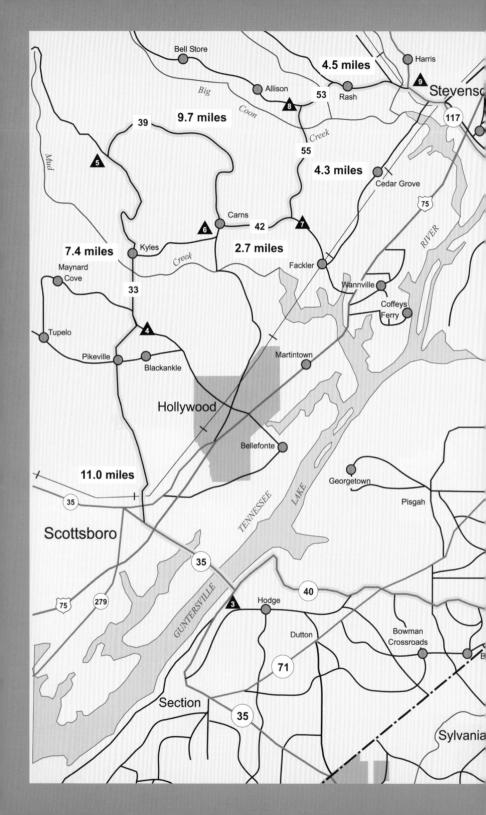

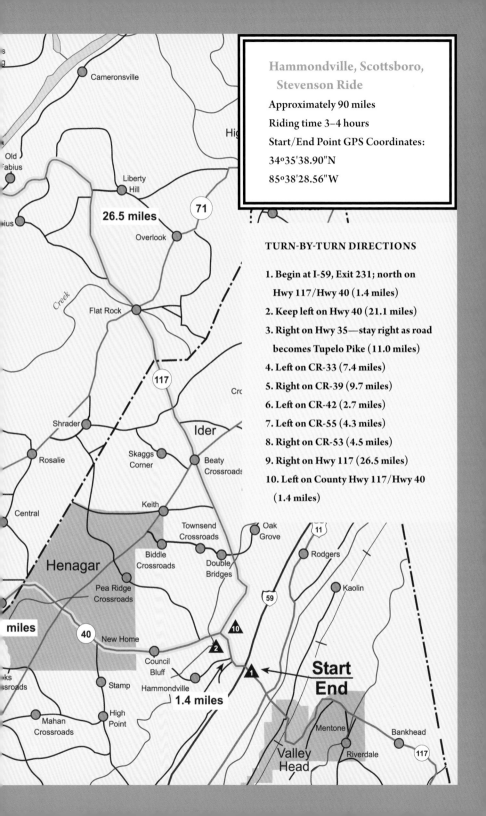

Hammondville, Scottsboro, Stevenson Ride

Approximately 90 miles
Riding time 3–4 hours
Start/End Point GPS Coordinates:
34°35'38.90"N
85°38'28.56"W

TURN-BY-TURN DIRECTIONS

1. Begin at I-59, Exit 231; north on Hwy 117/Hwy 40 (1.4 miles)
2. Keep left on Hwy 40 (21.1 miles)
3. Right on Hwy 35—stay right as road becomes Tupelo Pike (11.0 miles)
4. Left on CR-33 (7.4 miles)
5. Right on CR-39 (9.7 miles)
6. Left on CR-42 (2.7 miles)
7. Left on CR-55 (4.3 miles)
8. Right on CR-53 (4.5 miles)
9. Right on Hwy 117 (26.5 miles)
10. Left on County Hwy 117/Hwy 40 (1.4 miles)

Abandoned railroad station at Orme

The intersection of County Road 53 and Highway 117 in Rash has a busy railroad crossing, so be aware that seeing a train is not unusual.

If time permits, another off-route excursion turns left here on Highway 117 and travels up onto the Cumberland Plateau to Sewanee, Tennessee. Highway 117 becomes Sherwood Road after crossing into Tennessee and follows a beautiful valley before climbing the plateau. The detour will add almost sixty miles to the route if you go to Sewanee and back.

Back on route, it's less than a mile from the County Road 53/Highway 117 intersection (Turn 9) into Stevenson. The route then crosses the Tennessee River and goes back up and across Sand Mountain before reaching its intersection with Highway 40, where a left turn returns to the start point in 1.4 miles.

Falkville, Eva, Florette Ride

Approximately 83 miles
Riding time 3–4 hours

Start/End Point GPS Coordinates:
34º22'05.58"N
86º53'29.21"W

THIS RIDE OFFERS A REPRESENTATIVE sampling of north central Alabama's terrain, ranging from twisting mountain roads with views of the Tennessee River valley to wide expanses of pastureland and fertile cotton fields.

Beginning at Exit 322 on Interstate 65 at Falkville, the route heads east on Highway 55 toward Eva, passing numerous farms on a smooth blacktop road. After a slight zigzag to Eva Road via Nat Key Road and Gandy Cove Road, a left turn on Six-Mile Creek Road leads to a smooth asphalt switchback descent off a mountainside with several views to the north when leaves are off the trees.

The ascent back up Peck Mountain Road is just as entertaining, but the pavement isn't quite as smooth as it approaches Eva Road.

From Florette, which you reach at Turn 10, the route follows the scenic but fairly high-traffic Highway 67 for almost a dozen miles to its intersection with Highway 69. From there it's 6.7 miles to the next right turn (Turn 12) at Fairview and back toward Eva.

At Eva, a left turn on Eva Road heads southward, and after about 3.3 miles you'll see a quite unique sight. The owner of a convenience store and gas station in the Enon community has placed a 1930s air-

TURN-BY-TURN DIRECTIONS

1. Begin at I-65, Exit 322; east on Hwy 55 E (2.9 miles)
2. Left on Nat Key Rd (0.3 miles)
3. Right on Gandy Cove Rd (3.5 miles)
4. Left on Eva Rd (1.1 miles)
5. Left on Six-Mile Creek Rd (3.9 miles)
6. Right on Six-Mile Rd (1.0 mile)
7. Right on Peck Hollow Rd (2.1 miles)
8. Right on Peck Mountain Rd (1.8 miles)
9. Left on Eva Rd (2.4 miles)
10. Right on Hwy 67 (11.7 miles)
11. Right on Hwy 69 (6.7 miles)
12. Right on Wesley Ave (7.8 miles)
13. Left on Eva Rd (10.8 miles)
14. Right on Hwy 157 (13.4 miles)
15. Right on CR-25 (1.8 miles)
16. Left on Burney Mountain Rd (3.4 miles)
17. Right on W Lacon Rd (2.5 miles)
18. Left on Old Hwy 31 (0.8 miles)
19. Left on U.S. Hwy 31 (2.3 miles)
20. Right on Hwy 55 (1.0 mile)

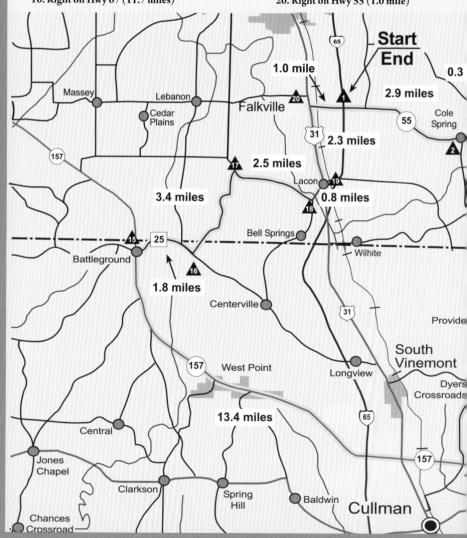

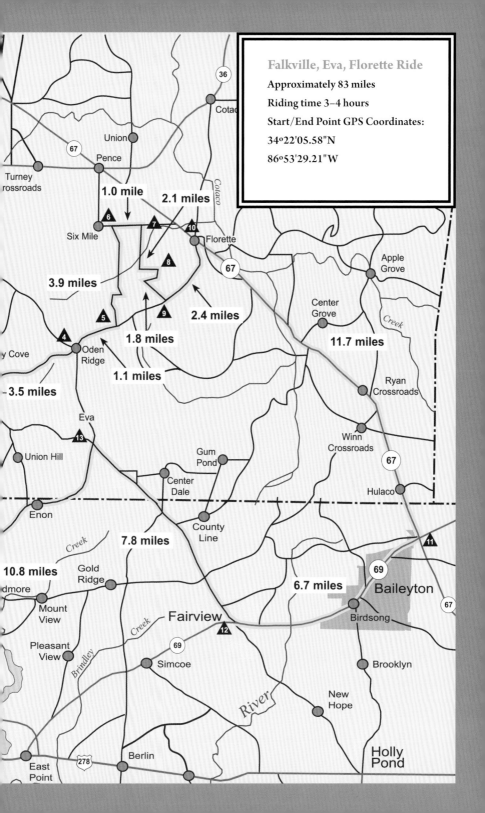

Falkville, Eva, Florette Ride
Approximately 83 miles
Riding time 3–4 hours
Start/End Point GPS Coordinates:
34º22'05.58"N
86º53'29.21"W

North Alabama countryside

liner atop a pole to attract attention for his store. And of course it works! Who could pass by without at least a second look?

At Turn 14, the route follows Highway 157 north to Battleground and then east back to U.S. Highway 31 at Lacon, where a popular flea market is held on weekends. From Lacon, the start point is about three miles north.

Enon's one-of-a-kind convenience store

Heflin, Piedmont, Talladega National Forest Dual-Sport Ride

Approximately 77 miles
Riding time 4–6 hours

Start/End Point GPS Coordinates:
33°37'18.03"N
85°35'44.95"W

THIS SEVENTY-SEVEN-MILE RIDE more or less circumnavigates the part of the Talladega National Forest that lies north of U.S. Highway 78, alternating between well-maintained gravel forest service roads and choice bits of paved roads.

Because of the gravel and the numerous places for stopping to sightsee, plan on this ride taking the better part of a day. While all of the gravel roads on the route are generally well maintained by the forest service, there will sometimes be places with muddy spots after a hard rain or loose gravel immediately after road maintenance where fresh gravel has been put down.

Although most any motorcycle could ride this route, it will be the most fun on a dual-sport bike that's designed for this kind of riding. That said, I used to ride with a buddy who had a midsize cruiser—750cc V-twin, low to the ground, long and heavy (six hundred pounds without a rider)—who would ride it all over these roads. But he had to go very slow, put his feet down in the loose gravel sections, and use other precautions.

I'd like to offer one more caution about riding in or around national forests in Alabama. From time to time the forest service has

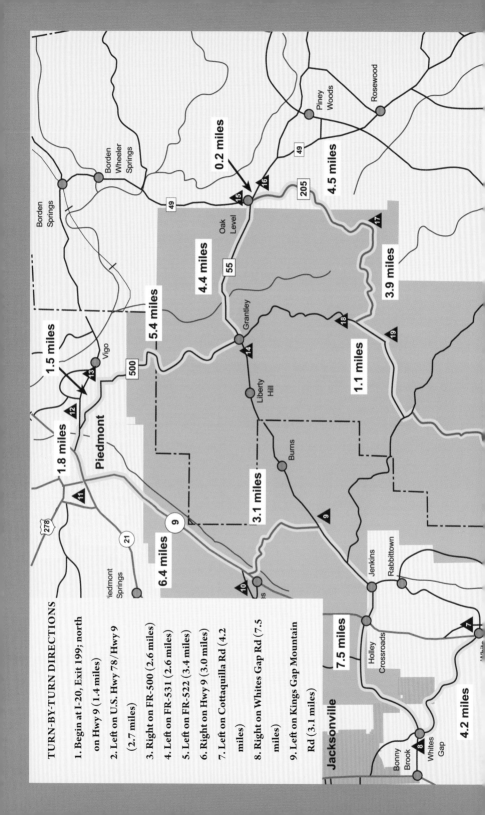

TURN-BY-TURN DIRECTIONS

1. Begin at I-20, Exit 199; north on Hwy 9 (1.4 miles)
2. Left on U.S. Hwy 78/Hwy 9 (2.7 miles)
3. Right on FR-500 (2.6 miles)
4. Left on FR-531 (2.6 miles)
5. Left on FR-522 (3.4 miles)
6. Right on Hwy 9 (3.0 miles)
7. Left on Cottaquilla Rd (4.2 miles)
8. Right on Whites Gap Rd (7.5 miles)
9. Left on Kings Gap Mountain Rd (3.1 miles)

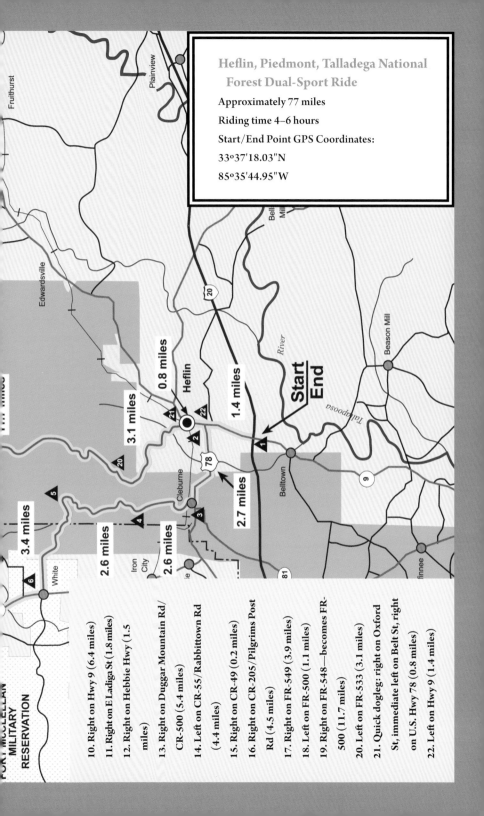

Heflin, Piedmont, Talladega National Forest Dual-Sport Ride

Approximately 77 miles

Riding time 4–6 hours

Start/End Point GPS Coordinates:

33º37'18.03"N

85º35'44.95"W

10. Right on Hwy 9 (6.4 miles)

11. Right on E Ladiga St (1.8 miles)

12. Right on Hebbie Hwy (1.5 miles)

13. Right on Duggar Mountain Rd/ CR-500 (5.4 miles)

14. Left on CR-55/Rabbittown Rd (4.4 miles)

15. Right on CR-49 (0.2 miles)

16. Right on CR-205/Pilgrims Post Rd (4.5 miles)

17. Right on FR-549 (3.9 miles)

18. Left on FR-500 (1.1 miles)

19. Right on FR-548—becomes FR-500 (11.7 miles)

20. Left on FR-533 (3.1 miles)

21. Quick dogleg: right on Oxford St, immediate left on Belt St, right on U.S. Hwy 78 (0.8 miles)

22. Left on Hwy 9 (1.4 miles)

A wooded lane

controlled burns to eliminate volatile underbrush from the forest floor. During these burns, the smoke can be obnoxious at best and noxious to your health at worse. Before I plan a ride, I usually check the USDA Forest Service's Web site (www.fs.fed.us/r8/alabama) for any planned burns in the area.

This ride begins and ends at Exit 199 on Interstate 20 near Heflin, and approximately two-thirds of the loop is on gravel roads.

From I-20, the route follows Highway 9 to the northern terminus of the Skyway Motorway (Highway 281) at its intersection with Highway 9 and U.S. Highway 78. This is the scenic parkway that goes through Cheaha State Park and the highest point in the state.

The first section of gravel road—Forest Service Road 500—is really just an unpaved continuation of the Skyway heading north toward Piedmont. My route leaves Forest Service Road 500 (Turn 4) and makes its way back to Highway 9 and a few miles of pavement.

At Turn 7—Cottaquilla Road—the route winds up and over a mountain on what I consider one of the best five-mile stretches of pavement for motorcycling in the state. After the twisty Cottaquilla Road, Whites Gap Road (Turn 8) goes back over a mountain before the route takes Kings Gap Mountain Road (Turn 9) to rejoin Highway 9 near Nances Creek.

The route also rejoins pavement at Highway 9 near Nances Creek and heads northeast into Piedmont. This will be one of the last gas/rest room/snack stops on the route and marks about the halfway point in terms of riding time.

At Turn 13 the route is back on gravel for about five miles into Grantley and a few miles of pavement on Rabbittown Road over to County Road 49.

Turn 16 puts the route back onto gravel, and it stays mostly off pavement until back in Heflin at Turn 21, just a couple of miles from the starting point. Forrest roads are often changed and rerouted. Please pay close attention to signage as there may be some quick doglegs to stay on the same numbered road.

Camping is available at two developed campgrounds in this part of the Talladega National Forest: Coleman Lake has full hookups and showers and can be accessed via paved roads. From this route, access is just after Turn 19 off Forest Service Road 548 (follow signs).

Pine Glen—located off this route on Forest Service Road 500— is a more primitive campground with only chemical rest rooms and no showers or hookups. To get to Pine Glen, which is beside Shoal Creek in a hollow, follow Forest Service Road 500 another 5.3 miles past Forest Service Road 531 (Turn 4).

An Alabama back road

Blount County Covered Bridges Ride

Approximately 78 miles
Riding time 3–4 hours

Start/End Point GPS Coordinates:
33°52'36.34"N
86°52'03.82"W

BLOUNT COUNTY HAS THE LAST three covered bridges still open to traffic for daily use in the state of Alabama. All built in the 1930s, these three are but a fraction of the covered bridges that used to dot the landscape in Blount County.

All three bridges—Horton Mill, Swann, and Easley—are relatively close to one another. Covered bridges were thought to prevent horses from becoming spooked when crossing moving water, and these three bridges all span streams where the water's motion can be both seen and heard, especially after a hard rain. The bridges probably owe their longevity to the fact that their timbers are not exposed to the weather. Because of their age, the bridges are sometimes closed for renovations or repairs.

This route begins and ends at Rickwood Caverns State Park near Warrior and Hayden in the far western edge of Blount County. I tried to include roads that offer a representative sampling of the Blount County landscape, which includes miles of rolling countryside through family farms as well as deep hollows and woodlands.

In the first leg of the ride, County Highway 5 (Turn 2) crosses Interstate 65 and sets the mood for this ride as it meanders beside cascades on Murphy Creek in its last half mile before intersecting with U.S. Highway 31 at Blount Springs.

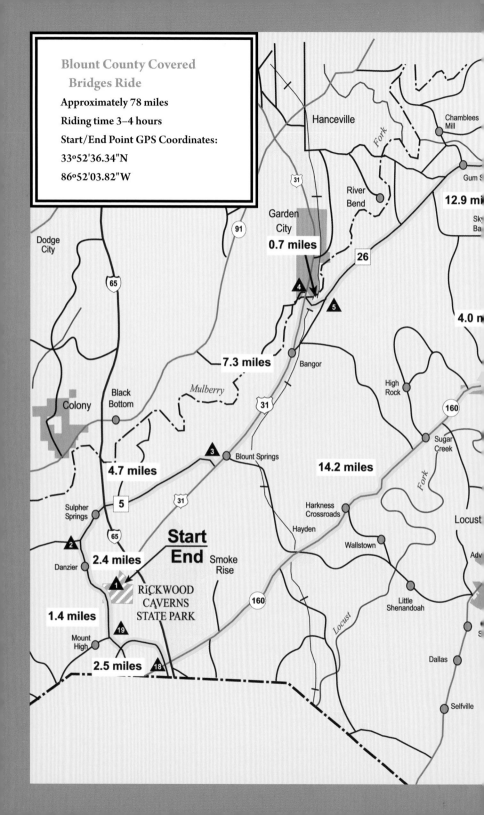

**Blount County Covered
Bridges Ride**

Approximately 78 miles

Riding time 3–4 hours

Start/End Point GPS Coordinates:

33º52'36.34"N

86º52'03.82"W

Hanceville

Chamblees
Mill

Gum S

12.9 mi

River
Bend

Sk
Ba

Garden
City

0.7 miles

26

4

5

4.0 m

Dodge
City

91

65

Mulberry

7.3 miles

Bangor

High
Rock

160

Black
Bottom

Colony

31

3

Blount Springs

14.2 miles

Sugar
Creek

4.7 miles

Harkness
Crossroads

Locust

Sulpher
Springs

5

31

Hayden

2

65

Wallstown

Adv

Danzier

2.4 miles

**Start
End** Smoke
Rise

RICKWOOD
CAVERNS
STATE PARK

160

Little
Shenandoah

1.4 miles

1

19

Mount
High

Dallas

2.5 miles

18

Selfville

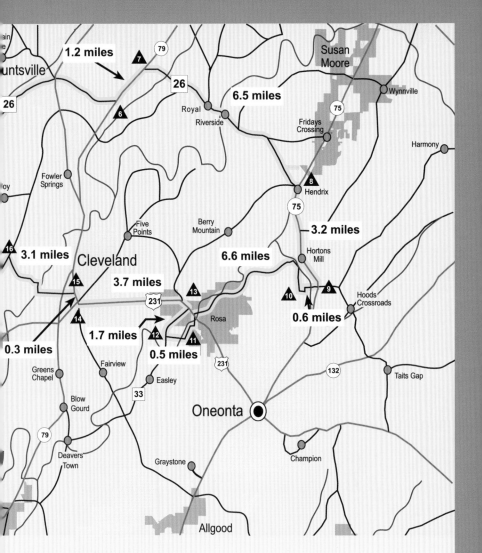

TURN-BY-TURN DIRECTIONS

1. Begin at Rickwood Caverns State Park; north on Rickwood Caverns Rd (2.4 miles)
2. Right on CR-5 (4.7 miles)
3. Left on U.S. Hwy 31 (7.3 miles)
4. Right on 3rd St SE (0.7 miles)
5. Right on CR-26 (12.9 miles)
6. Left on Hwy 79 N (1.2 miles)
7. Right on CR-26 (6.5 miles)
8. Right on Hwy 75 S (3.2 miles)
9. Right on Covered Bridge Circle (0.6 miles)
10. Right on Horton Mill Rd—becomes Ebell Rd (6.6 miles)
11. Right on Easley Bridge Rd (0.5 miles)
12. Right on CR-33 (1.7 miles)
13. Left on U.S. Hwy 231 (3.7 miles)
14. Right on U.S. Hwy 231 (0.3 miles)
15. Left on Swann Bridge Rd (3.1 miles)
16. Left on Joy Rd (4.0 miles)
17. Right on Hwy 160 (14.2 miles)
18. Right on Skyline Dr (2.5 miles)
19. Right on Rickwood Caverns Rd (1.4 miles)

Easley Bridge, the shortest of Blount County's three remaining covered bridges

As it's in my backyard, I can highly recommend the Top Hat BBQ in Blount Springs for some home-style hickory-cooked barbecue.

From Blount Springs, the route follows Highway 31 to Garden City, where it turns east on County Road 26 through Blountsville and finally to Highway 75, which is 3.2 miles north of the first covered bridge—Horton Mill, the highest bridge of its construction in the world. Unfortunately, at the time of this writing, the bridge is temporarily closed to traffic due to damage from vandals. However, Blount County plans to make repairs and reopen the bridge.

For this reason, my route detours past the bridge on Highway 75 and adds about 2.8 miles to the trip versus crossing the bridge from Highway 75.

From the western side of Horton Mill Bridge, the route follows Ebell Road to cross U.S. Highway 231 at Rosa and continue 1.2 miles to the second bridge—Easley, the shortest of the three bridges.

After crossing Easley, the route takes County Road 33 back to U.S. 231 and to Cleveland, where a left turn (Turn 15) joins Swann Bridge Road 1.5 miles from the longest covered bridge in the state.

If making this ride in the springtime or on most any weekend following a soaking rain, look to see canoes and kayaks at Swann Bridge, as it's the center point of one of the most popular white-water runs in Alabama—the Locust Fork of the Warrior River.

I'd like to note here that the floorboards of a covered bridge are often irregular and worn. Crossing such a bridge in a four-wheeled vehicle is seldom a problem, but I've seen motorcycles adversely affected as the wheels track over the irregular surface. Just go slowly and use caution.

From Swann Bridge, the road climbs out of the Locust Fork

Swann Bridge, the longest covered bridge in Alabama

gorge on a road that often has dogs wanting to chase motorcycles. At Joy Road (Turn 16) the route stays on a hilltop for a few miles, offering expansive views of the back side of Straight Mountain to the south.

The final leg of the ride along Highway 160 crosses Interstate 65 near Hayden and takes you back to the starting point at Rickwood Caverns State Park.

Camping is available at Rickwood Caverns State Park, and hotel accommodations can be found in Oneonta or in the towns of Hanceville and Cullman, which are off-route north on Interstate 65.

Riding inside the enclosed Swann Bridge

RIDE LOOP 10
Blount County Covered Bridges Dual-Sport Ride

Approximately 96 miles
Riding time 4–5 hours

Start/End Point GPS Coordinates:
33°54'42.14"N
86°51'54.38"W

THIS RIDE CAN BE MADE with any motorcycle, so long as you don't mind getting your bike a bit dusty or muddy. The shorter Blount County Covered Bridges Ride in Ride Loop 9 visits the same three bridges in Blount County but never goes off the asphalt.

With this route I tried to find the gravel roads and less-than-perfect tar-and-gravel back roads that are ideally suited for dual-sport machines. All roads on the ride are public streets, but in general are twistier and a bit more nitty-gritty than the pavement-only ride.

This route begins at Exit 289 on Interstate 65 and heads west out County Road 5 toward Arkadelphia. This formerly gravel road section has now been paved.

The route leaves Highway 91 at Turn 5 onto County Road 509 and follows the Mulberry Fork of the Warrior River into Garden City. About 2.5 miles into the County Road 509 leg, you'll come to the site of an annual canoe and kayak slalom race on the Mulberry Fork that's held on the last weekend of February or in the first week of March. The river is only a one-hundred-yard walk from the road here, and if time permits, the setting is worth a stop to look at the rapids from atop a forty-foot-high bluff.

At Garden City, the route turns south on U.S. Highway 31 (Turn

Autumn color on Guinns Cove Road

7) and continues into Bangor, where the Blount County courthouse was once located. After 2.1 miles on County Road 9, the route turns left onto Guinns Cove Road; the last 1.5 miles of that road is gravel down to County Road 26 (Turn 11).

After 5.4 miles on County Road 26 is another gravel section—Johns Road, a two-mile connecting road traversing a ridge to Joy Road.

From Joy Road, it's 2.7 miles to Swann Bridge Road and another 1.6 miles down to the bridge across the Locust Fork, which is another popular canoeing and kayaking area. Swann is the longest covered bridge in Alabama and one of the longest covered bridges in the world that's still in daily use.

Five Points Road that begins in Cleveland (Turn 17) has about

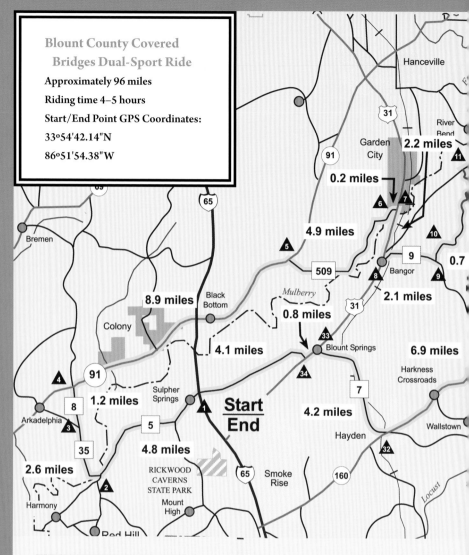

Blount County Covered Bridges Dual-Sport Ride

Approximately 96 miles

Riding time 4–5 hours

Start/End Point GPS Coordinates:

33º54'42.14"N

86º51'54.38"W

Hanceville

31

River Bend

Garden City   2.2 miles

91   0.2 miles

4.9 miles

509   *Mulberry*

8.9 miles   Black Bottom   0.8 miles

Colony   33   Blount Springs

4.1 miles   34

6.9 miles

Harkness Crossroads

4   91   1.2 miles   Sulpher Springs   **Start End**   7

8   4.2 miles   Wallstown

Arkadelphia   3   5   Hayden   32

35   4.8 miles

2.6 miles   RICKWOOD CAVERNS STATE PARK   65   Smoke Rise   160   *Locust*

Harmony   2   Mount High

Red Hill

Bremen   65   69

Bangor   9   0.7   10   11   9   2.1 miles

TURN-BY-TURN DIRECTIONS

1. Begin at I-65, Exit 289; west on CR-5 W (4.8 miles)

2. Right on Arkadelphia Rd—becomes CR-35 (2.6 miles)

3. Right on CR-8 (1.2 miles)

4. Right on Hwy 91 (8.9 miles)

5. Right on CR-509 (4.9 miles)

6. Right on Short St (0.2 miles)

7. Right on U.S. Hwy 31 (2.2 miles)

8. Left on CR-9 (2.1 miles)

9. Left on Guinns Cove Rd (0.7 miles)

10. Right on Guinns Cove Rd (3.6 miles)

11. Right on CR-26 (5.4 miles)

12. Right on Johns Rd (2.0 miles)

13. Right on Joy Rd (2.7 miles)

14. Left on Swann Bridge Rd (2.6 miles)

15. Left on Hwy 79 (0.3 miles)

16. Right on Park Rd (0.8 miles)

17. Left on Five Points Rd (7.9 miles)

18. Left on CR-57 (0.8 miles)

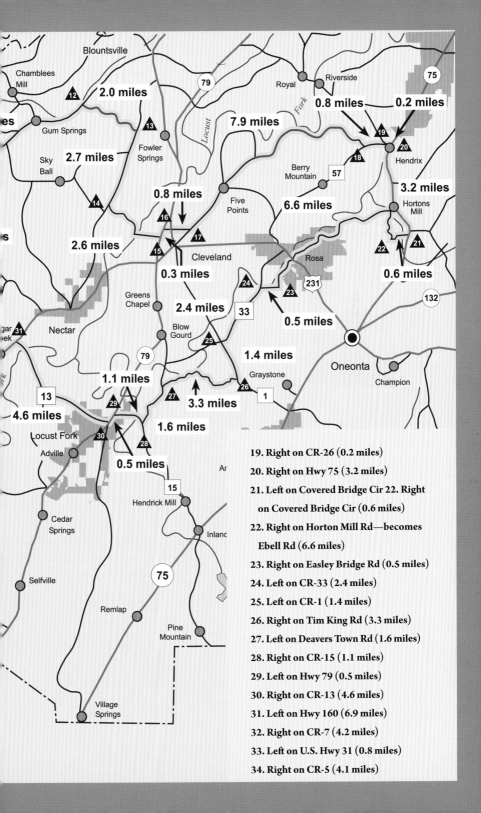

19. Right on CR-26 (0.2 miles)
20. Right on Hwy 75 (3.2 miles)
21. Left on Covered Bridge Cir 22. Right on Covered Bridge Cir (0.6 miles)
22. Right on Horton Mill Rd—becomes Ebell Rd (6.6 miles)
23. Right on Easley Bridge Rd (0.5 miles)
24. Left on CR-33 (2.4 miles)
25. Left on CR-1 (1.4 miles)
26. Right on Tim King Rd (3.3 miles)
27. Left on Deavers Town Rd (1.6 miles)
28. Right on CR-15 (1.1 miles)
29. Left on Hwy 79 (0.5 miles)
30. Right on CR-13 (4.6 miles)
31. Left on Hwy 160 (6.9 miles)
32. Right on CR-7 (4.2 miles)
33. Left on U.S. Hwy 31 (0.8 miles)
34. Right on CR-5 (4.1 miles)

Blount County's Horton Mill Bridge, the highest covered bridge over water in the United States

House Road Bridge, located off County Road 15 near Hendrick Mill

1.7 miles of gravel before intersecting with County Road 57. On this gravel section, you'll see a picturesque spot, where a bend in the Locust Fork of the Warrior River comes almost up to the roadway, that's always cool and shady in summer.

After County Road 57 and a brief 0.2-mile stretch of County Road 26, the route turns south on Highway 75 about two miles from the second covered bridge—Horton Mill, which is the highest covered bridge over water in the country.

As of this writing, Horton Mill Bridge is temporarily closed to traffic. Because of this, my route includes a 2.8-mile detour to the opposite side of the bridge (Turns 21 and 22).

After passing the bridge, Ebell Road crosses U.S. Highway 231 at Rosa and continues on to the third and smallest covered bridge of the three, Easley Bridge.

From Easley the route makes a couple of left turns, first on County Road 33, then on County Road 1, and finally onto what is probably the most crooked road in Blount County if not in all of North Alabama—Tim King Road, 3.3 miles of tight and twisting tar and gravel usually sprinkled with gravel in the curves. It can be fun on a dual-sport bike, but be careful here.

After Tim King Road, the route passes through the town of Locust Fork and across the river again to Nectar, Hayden, and past Blount Springs. The final 4.1 miles to the starting point on County Road 5 offer some fun curves along Murphy Creek. After leaving the creek it's not uncommon to see deer on this road, so, again, be careful!

PART III

RIDES IN NORTHWEST ALABAMA
Ride Loops 11–20

Bankhead National Forest Dual-Sport Ride

Approximately 130 miles
Riding time 6–7 hours

Start/End Point GPS Coordinates:
33°57'07.81"N
87°36'58.89"W

THE BANKHEAD NATIONAL FOREST in northwest Alabama offers a great variety of recreational activities, and touring the area on a dual-sport motorcycle is one of the best ways to experience the forest.

A longtime favorite destination for hikers, horseback riders, and canoeists, the forest and the Sipsey Wilderness Area that lies within its boundaries boast hundreds of waterfalls, the beautiful Sipsey River Gorge, and secluded hiking and camping spots. This is also one of the few places in Alabama where hemlock trees thrive. All these elements combine for an outdoor experience unlike any other in this part of the world.

Of course, the wilderness area is off-limits to motorized vehicles, including motorcycles, but it is possible to ride the forest service roads that surround the wilderness, which was one of my goals when planning this route.

Some riders may wish to divide this long ride—130 miles—into two days, especially if you have to travel a significant distance to reach the starting point, Exit 39, on the new Corridor X/Highway 78—future Interstate 22—that will eventually link Memphis and Birmingham. Lodging can be found in nearby Jasper, Moulton, or Haleyville, but only camping facilities are directly within this route.

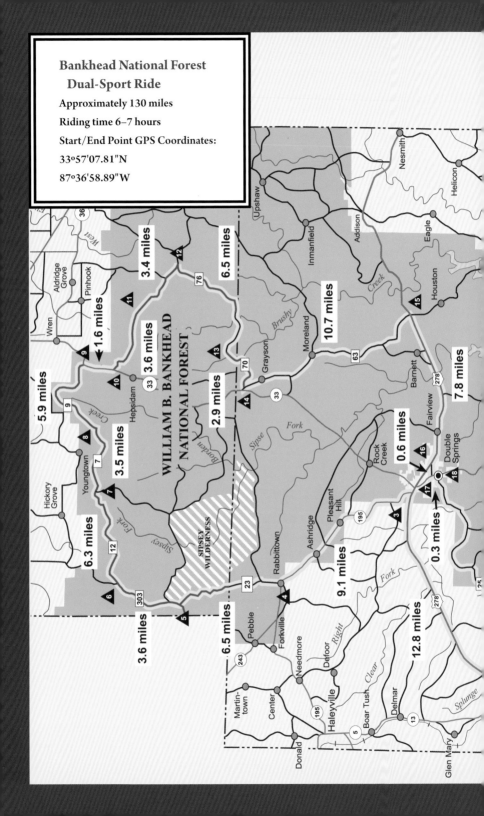

**Bankhead National Forest
Dual-Sport Ride**

Approximately 130 miles

Riding time 6–7 hours

Start/End Point GPS Coordinates:

33°57'07.81"N

87°36'58.89"W

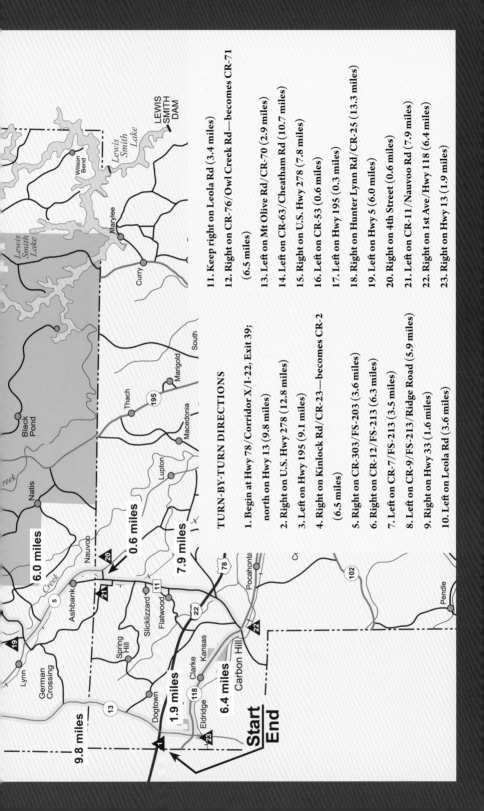

TURN-BY-TURN DIRECTIONS

1. Begin at Hwy 78 / Corridor X / I-22, Exit 39; north on Hwy 13 (9.8 miles)
2. Right on U.S. Hwy 278 (12.8 miles)
3. Left on Hwy 195 (9.1 miles)
4. Right on Kinlock Rd / CR-23 — becomes CR-2 (6.5 miles)
5. Right on CR-303 / FS-203 (3.6 miles)
6. Right on CR-12 / FS-213 (6.3 miles)
7. Left on CR-7 / FS-213 (3.5 miles)
8. Left on CR-9 / FS-213 / Ridge Road (5.9 miles)
9. Right on Hwy 33 (1.6 miles)
10. Left on Leola Rd (3.6 miles)
11. Keep right on Leola Rd (3.4 miles)
12. Right on CR-76 / Owl Creek Rd — becomes CR-71 (6.5 miles)
13. Left on Mt Olive Rd / CR-70 (2.9 miles)
14. Left on CR-63 / Cheatham Rd (10.7 miles)
15. Right on U.S. Hwy 278 (7.8 miles)
16. Left on CR-53 (0.6 miles)
17. Left on Hwy 195 (0.3 miles)
18. Right on Hunter Lynn Rd / CR-25 (13.3 miles)
19. Left on Hwy 5 (6.0 miles)
20. Right on 4th Street (0.6 miles)
21. Left on CR-11 / Nauvoo Rd (7.9 miles)
22. Right on 1st Ave / Hwy 118 (6.4 miles)
23. Right on Hwy 13 (1.9 miles)

Winston County courthouse in Double Springs

Inside the national forest, primitive camping is permitted except where No Camping signs are posted. There is one developed forest service campground on the route at Brushy Lake. This is typical of the basic forest service campground—very scenic with a picturesque lake built in the 1930s and campsites along the lake's shoreline as well as a camp loop. You won't find showers, but there are water faucets (except in winter) and chemical toilets. For a backwoods site, I've always found it well maintained and clean. And the fishing is not bad here either.

For the ride itself, from the start point of the ride route near Eldridge the first thirty-two miles or so are on major roads—Highway 13 to Natural Bridge, U.S. Highway 278 to Double Springs, and Highway 195 to Rabbittown.

After turning on Kinlock Road in Rabbittown, you'll be on pavement for another 2.5 miles before the road turns to gravel (between Turns 4 and 5). All the gravel sections are well-maintained forest service or county roads that can be ridden on most kinds of motorcycles, though they would be much more enjoyable on a dual-sport bike.

On this section of the trip, you'll pass a popular swimming hole—Kinlock Falls—within a mile after the road turns to gravel.

From there, it's about twenty miles of all gravel to Turn 9 at Highway 33 near Wren.

At this point, an off-route detour of 2.3 miles north on Highway 33 will take you to Lamar Marshall's Warrior Mountains Trading Company and Indian Museum in Wren. It's the first possible stop for gas, sandwiches, or snacks and has an interesting inventory of merchandise, much of which is dedicated to enjoying the forest. The town of Moulton lies a few more miles up Highway 33, where more dining and lodging choices are available.

Back on route, from Turn 9 you'll be on paved road for just 1.6 miles before turning onto Leola Road and another 13.5 miles of gravel road before reaching Mt. Olive Road (Turn 13). At this turn,

Brushy Lake campground, one of the more developed and scenic camping spots along this ride loop

Riding through the Bankhead National Forest on a dual-sport bike

consider making a right on County Road 70/Pine Torch Road for another off-route detour. The Pine Torch Church—named for the pine-knot torches used to light the building in the early days—is about a mile off route on a paved road. The log church is the oldest structure in the forest and was built sometime before 1850. Up this road you will also find signs directing you to Brushy Lake, where the National Forest has a campground.

Back on route, the last gravel section (between Turns 13 and 14) is about three miles to the intersection of Mt. Olive Road and Highway 63.

For an alternate route that bypasses all of the gravel roads between Turns 9 and 14, continue on Highway 33 from Turn 11, turning left at Highway 63 after 9.4 miles.

At the time of this writing, Highway 63 had just been repaved with fresh asphalt, so the 10.7-mile section between turns 14 and 15 is simply a delight to experience on a motorcycle, with easy sweeping turns bobbing up and down rolling hills through farm and pasture land.

From Turn 15, the route heads west on U.S. Highway 278 back to Double Springs, then south on Hunter Lynn Road, making several turns at Lynn and Nauvoo, two of the oldest towns in northwest Alabama.

At Nauvoo the route turns south again (Turn 21) and continues south to Carbon Hill and a final 8.3 miles back to the start.

Lewis Smith Lake and Bankhead National Forest Ride

Approximately 113 miles
Riding time 4–5 hours

Start/End Point GPS Coordinates:
34º03'17.35"N
86º51'58.98"W

THIS 113-MILE LOOP PROVIDES a great way to tour both Lewis Smith Lake and parts of the Bankhead National Forest in a single day. In fact, it crosses parts of the lake or its feeder streams seven times.

Beginning at Dodge City (Exit 299 on Interstate 65), the first leg follows Highway 69 to Bremen before joining County Road 222 and heading for the first lake crossing at "Big Bridge," where both food and lodging are available.

At the next left (Turn 3) at Trade, the road narrows to a small country lane and twists and turns through farmland for 7.4 miles, crossing the lake again near the confluence of Crooked Creek and Rock Creek.

The next leg of the route crosses the lake again at Rock Creek before connecting briefly with County Road 41 at Arley (Turn 5).

After 0.9 miles, the route takes a left onto County Road 63 (Turn 6) and hits an eighteen-mile stretch of some of the best motorcycle road in this part of the state. The road again crosses the lake in this section, this time at Brushy Creek.

Cruising Highway 33 through the Bankhead National Forest

Note here that County Road 63 makes a slight left-then-right dogleg when crossing U.S. Highway 278 at Houston.

About a mile after crossing U.S. Highway 278, look on the right for a small pullout and parking area. This national forest recreation area has a half-mile walking trail out to a "natural bridge" rock formation. There are also restroom facilities here.

About eleven miles north of Highway 278 (Turn 7), the route turns right on Highway 33 and stays in the national forest for another 11.6 miles to Highway 36 at Wren (Turn 8).

The next twenty-two miles on Highway 36 and Highway 157 are regrettably on fast two- and four-lane roadways but offer some in-

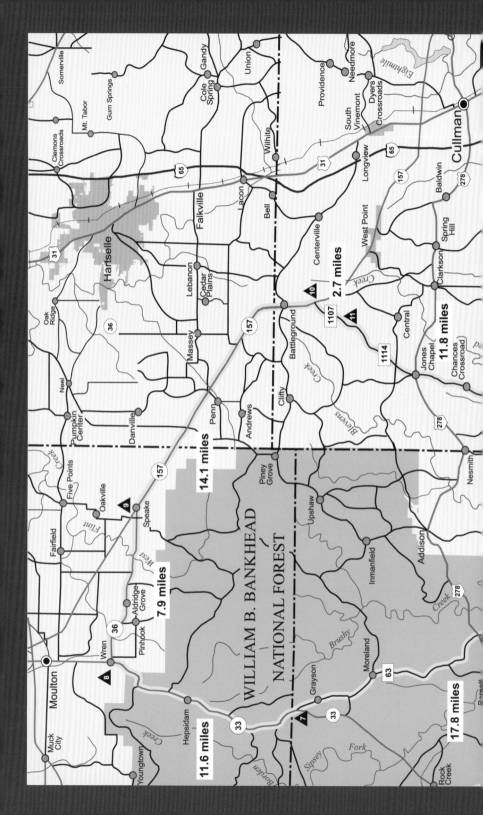

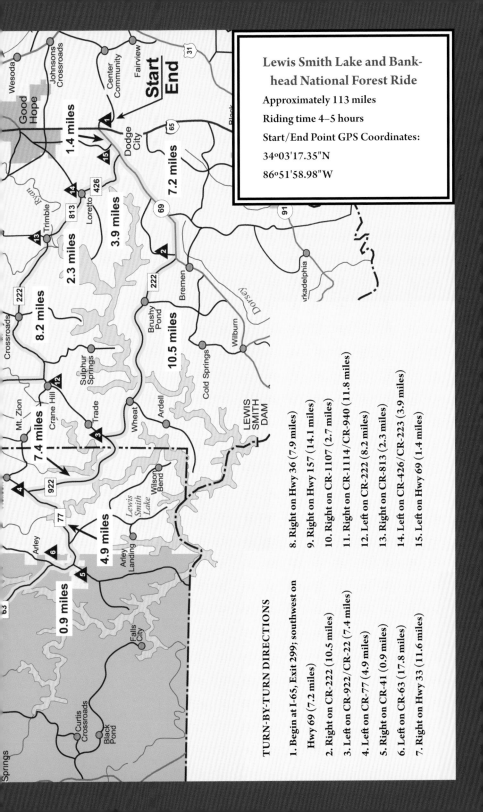

Lewis Smith Lake and Bank-head National Forest Ride

Approximately 113 miles

Riding time 4–5 hours

Start/End Point GPS Coordinates:

34º03'17.35"N

86º51'58.98"W

TURN-BY-TURN DIRECTIONS

1. Begin at I-65, Exit 299; southwest on Hwy 69 (7.2 miles)

2. Right on CR-222 (10.5 miles)

3. Left on CR-922/CR-22 (7.4 miles)

4. Left on CR-77 (4.9 miles)

5. Right on CR-41 (0.9 miles)

6. Left on CR-63 (17.8 miles)

7. Right on Hwy 33 (11.6 miles)

8. Right on Hwy 36 (7.9 miles)

9. Right on Hwy 157 (14.1 miles)

10. Right on CR-1107 (2.7 miles)

11. Right on CR-1114/CR-940 (11.8 miles)

12. Left on CR-222 (8.2 miles)

13. Right on CR-813 (2.3 miles)

14. Left on CR-426/CR-223 (3.9 miles)

15. Left on Hwy 69 (1.4 miles)

teresting sights. Just north of Turn 9 at Speake are the Jesse Owens Museum and Oakville Indian Mounds Park.

Turn 10 at Battleground puts the route back on two-lane roads heading toward Smith Lake, crossing U.S. Highway 278 again at Jones Chapel and continuing south to Crane Hill and County Road 222.

The next leg of the route crosses the lake again at Rock Creek on County Road 222 and again at Ryan Creek just after Turn 13 at Trimble.

The entrance for Smith Lake Park is 0.9 miles after Turn 13. This county-operated park offers camping, cabins, swimming, and boating facilities.

From here the route crosses the lake one more time between Turns 14 and 15 at the backwater where Simpson Creek enters Smith Lake. The final 1.4–mile stretch of this ride backtracks on Highway 69 to the start point at Dodge City.

Hamilton, Natchez Trace, Florence Ride

Approximately 145 miles
Riding time 5–6 hours

Start/End Point GPS Coordinates:
34°10'02.70"N
88°03'47.96"W

The Natchez Trace Parkway is a national scenic highway spanning the 444 miles between Nashville, Tennessee, and Natchez, Mississippi.

Native Americans used the "Trace" as a pathway for thousands of years. After lands along the Mississippi, Ohio, and Tennessee rivers were settled by Europeans and Americans, this path became a primary return route north for boatmen who floated merchandise down the Mississippi to Natchez or New Orleans.

In an age before steam-powered riverboats, river travel in wooden flatboats was a one-way endeavor, meaning that the boatmen—known collectively as "Kaintucks"—had to get back to their homes on foot or horseback. The almost five-hundred-mile trip from Natchez to Nashville took about thirty-five days on foot or about ten days fewer on horseback. According to the National Park Service, which oversees the parkway, in the year 1810 alone more than ten thousand Kaintucks made their way back home via the Trace.

I'd like to caution riders that speeding on the parkway is typically not tolerated by the Park Service officers, and anything over the posted speed limits will likely bring out their ticket books.

About thirty-three miles of the parkway slice through the extreme

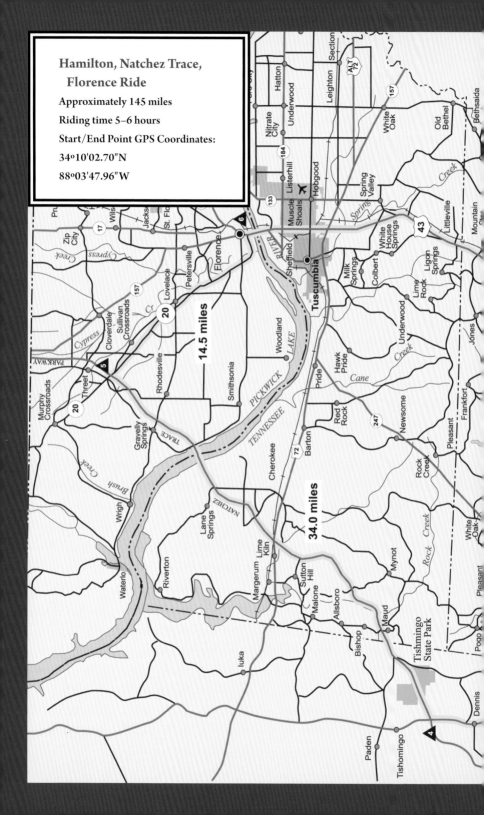

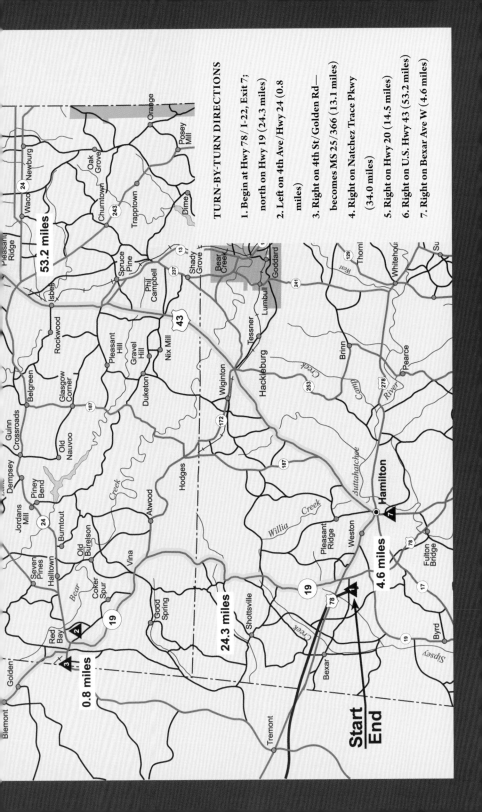

TURN-BY-TURN DIRECTIONS

1. Begin at Hwy 78 / I-22, Exit 7; north on Hwy 19 (24.3 miles)

2. Left on 4th Ave / Hwy 24 (0.8 miles)

3. Right on 4th St / Golden Rd— becomes MS 25 / 366 (13.1 miles)

4. Right on Natchez Trace Pkwy (34.0 miles)

5. Right on Hwy 20 (14.5 miles)

6. Right on U.S. Hwy 43 (53.2 miles)

7. Right on Bexar Ave W (4.6 miles)

Motorcyclists at Colbert Ferry Landing on the Natchez Trace Parkway

northwestern corner of Alabama, and this route begins seven miles south of the state line in Mississippi and leaves the Trace five miles before reaching the Tennessee line.

But even though the Alabama section represents less than eight percent of the total mileage of the Trace, it has its notable points: the Trace crosses the Tennessee River in Alabama, and the highest elevation of the entire road is found here.

As I was planning this route within the parameters for this book—ensuring that each loop begins and ends at an interstate exit or state park, and limiting every route length to 150 miles—the Trace's location in the extreme northwest corner of the state presented a unique challenge. I selected the route here in order to meet the above criteria and make a complete loop. However, some riding this loop may choose to eliminate parts of the mapped route, depending on their

Motorcyclists at the Tennessee River on the Natchez Trace Parkway

start point and ultimate destination. All the routes are designed so a rider can join them anywhere and still follow the turn-by-turn directions for the remainder of the loop or the parts that are most practical for his or her situation.

This route begins at Exit 7 off of Highway 78 —future Interstate 22—just north and west of Hamilton. From there it follows Highway 19 for 24.3 miles into Red Bay. This first section is a fun ride on a motorcycle and consists of swift, sweeping curves over well-maintained pavement for most of the way.

Just outside Red Bay, the route goes into Mississippi for about eleven miles more before connecting with the Natchez Trace Parkway near Tishomingo State Park, and the first 6.2 miles of the Trace on this route are actually inside Mississippi. In creating this ride loop, I found a couple of ways to get on the parkway and also stay within

A stop for lunch at the Tennessee River along the Natchez Trace Parkway

Alabama's borders, but each one meant several miles of gravel road and, because this is not recommended as a dual-sport ride, I decided to go with the Mississippi route.

In all, this route contains about thirty-four miles of the Trace, including some of the most interesting spots on the parkway. Fortunately, the Alabama section includes some of the more hilly—and therefore curvy—terrain on the Trace.

At Milepost 317 is the Freedom Hills Overlook, the highest point on the Natchez Trace.

Just before crossing the Tennessee River at Colbert Ferry (Milepost 327), you'll reach a parkway ranger's office. Picnic areas on both

Tom Hendrix's rock wall honoring his Native American great-grandmother, found at Milepost 338 along the Natchez Trace

Prayer circle in Tom Hendrix's rock wall

sides of the river offer panoramic views. This area would be a good choice for a picnic lunch or restroom break.

A few miles north of the river at Milepost 330, a self-guiding nature trail at Rock Spring includes a shady, winding pathway beside a beaver pond. In fact, the last time I was there I watched a young beaver swim all the way across the pond.

This ride loop leaves the Trace at Milepost 336 on Highway 20. But if you want to see Tom Hendrix's rock wall, just proceed a bit farther to Milepost 338 and take a right on Lauderdale County Road 8. This phenomenal dry rock wall was built by hand, stone by stone, to honor Hendrix's great-grandmother, a Native American woman who walked back from the Oklahoma territory after removal on the Trail of Tears.

Highway 20 heads southeast into Florence, where it joins Highway 43 (Turn 6), crosses the Tennessee River again, and continues south a total of fifty-three miles, all the way to Hamilton and back to the start.

Joe Wheeler State Park, Lexington, Cairo Ride

Approximately 78 miles

Riding time 3–4 hours

Start/End Point GPS Coordinates:

34°49'53.78"N

87°19'09.22"W

THIS SEVENTY-EIGHT-MILE LOOP begins and ends at Joe Wheeler State Park near Rogersville and tours the rolling hills and countryside of extreme north Alabama, crossing the Elk River twice.

A variety of lodging choices is available at Wheeler State Park, including conventional rooms, lakefront cottages, and camping. The park also has a restaurant and marina.

The loop's first 9.4 miles on U.S. Highway 72 from the park to Briggs Road feature the only four-lane section in the route.

At Turn 2 the fun begins, where the route heads north toward Lexington. The character of the ride from here on varies between twisty two-lane winding roads through wooded, shaded hollows and open sweepers in big-sky agricultural country.

At Lexington (Turns 5 and 6), the route follows Highway 64 east for four miles before turning south on Betty Highway toward Anderson.

Be sure to watch for a small gristmill just before the community of Salem on Highway 99. The first time I rode this route, I didn't even notice the mill because I was traveling in the opposite direction from the route shown here. From that direction, the mill building conceals the mill's dam and steel overshot wheel until you've passed

Joe Wheeler State Park, Lexington, Cairo Ride

Approximately 78 miles

Riding time 3–4 hours

Start/End Point GPS Coordinates:

34º49'53.78"N

87º19'09.22"W

TURN-BY-TURN DIRECTIONS

1. Begin at Joe Wheeler State Park; west o
   U.S. Hwy 72 (9.4 miles)
2. Right on Briggs Rd (2.1 miles)
3. Right on Grave Rd/Hwy 71 (3.3 miles)
4. Left on Hwy 71 (5.3 miles)
5. Left on Hwy 101 (0.3 miles)
6. Right on Hwy 64 (4.0 miles)
7. Right on Betty Hwy (2.5 miles)
8. Left on Hwy 52 (1.8 miles)

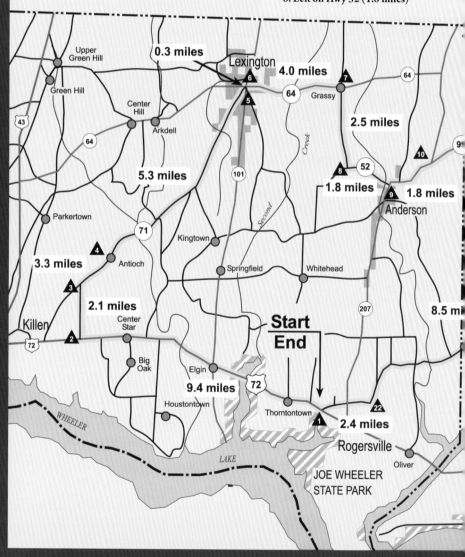

9. Left on Hwy 207 (1.8 miles)

10. Right on Hwy 99 (7.6 miles)

11. Left on Salem Minor Hill Rd (0.9 miles)

12. Right on Easter Ferry Rd (3.4 miles)

13. Sharp left on Leggtown Rd (1.4 miles)

14. Right on Leggtown Rd (2.1 miles)

15. Right on Leggtown Rd Valley (1.4 miles)

16. Right on Hwy 127 (5.9 miles)

17. Right on Witty Mill Rd (2.7 miles)

18. Left on Easter Ferry Rd (0.5 miles)

19. Right on Ft Hampton Rd—becomes Elk River Mills Rd (6.8 miles)

20. Right on Elk River Mills Rd (3.3 miles)

21. Left on Stinnett Hollow Rd—becomes Snake Rd (8.5 miles)

22. Right on Rose St (2.4 miles)

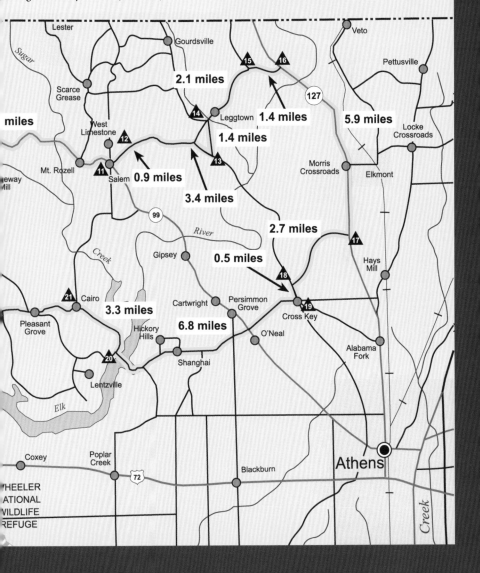

it. But when you approach from the west, the red wheel really stands out against the green foliage. Later I discovered that the woman who owns the mill was born and raised here and that her parents had to sell the wheel to pay the doctor's bill when she was born in 1938. It took her more than fifty years, but she finally bought back the mill wheel from the subsequent owners.

After Salem, the route continues eastward through a series of turns passing near the town of Elkmont, turning back southeast at Highway 127 just north of the Elk River (Turn 16).

Leaving Highway 127 at Turn 17, the remainder of the loop heads west through Shanghai, crosses the Elk River again, runs through Cairo, and finally follows Snake Road back into Rogersville. This road is a delightful mixture of fast sweeps interspersed with twisty sections through hills and hollows. The road follows the Elk River backwater for a good distance before crossing, and there are numerous places to pull off and take in the view.

The ride eventually terminates back at Rogersville on the north side of U.S. Highway 72, across from the Wheeler State Park main entrance.

Opposite: Historic gristmill in Salem

Left: Bike beside the Salem Mill

Lake Lurleen State Park Ride

Approximately 79 miles
Riding time 3–4 hours

Start/End Point GPS Coordinates:
33°17'45.35"N
87°40'36.62"W

THIS RELATIVELY QUICK SEVENTY-NINE-MILE loop follows two roads of almost identical length over dramatically different terrain, beginning and ending at Lake Lurleen State Park.

The northward leg of the route follows the hilly and twisty Highway 159 for almost twenty-eight miles toward Fayette, then turns back south to follow the Sipsey River valley for twenty-eight miles of mostly bottomland on Highway 171. Most of the route runs through rural areas and stands of timber.

Leaving the state park, which offers boat and canoe rental as well as camping, the initial three miles goes south on Columbus and Sam Sutton roads before joining U.S. Highway 82 at Turn 4.

After 14.5 miles heading west on U.S. Highway 82, the northward leg begins at the town of Gordo (Turn 5) onto Highway 159. In my opinion, this is one of the most enjoyable stretches of pavement in west Alabama. The road dips in and out of hollows and ridges with plenty of gentle, sweeping turns. There are few, if any, service stations in this section, so I'd advise you to gas up before leaving Gordo. Highway 159 does dogleg at 4th Avenue in Gordo, but the signage clearly shows the way to stay on route.

Just a few miles out of Fayette, the route takes a right at Highway

64 (Turn 6) to cut through to Highway 171, only about a half mile away.

Turn 7 onto Highway 171 begins the southward leg of the trip. Generally straighter and flatter than Highway 159 to the west, Highway 171 features numerous lakes and streams visible from the road. But the last few miles before turning onto Mount Olive Road (Turn 8) keep the ride interesting with some nice sweeping curves.

Once on Mount Olive Road, it's only about four miles back to the Lake Lurleen State Park entrance. At Mount Olive Church, take the right arm of the Y (Lake Lurleen Road) to skirt the back side of the park.

Townley rest area

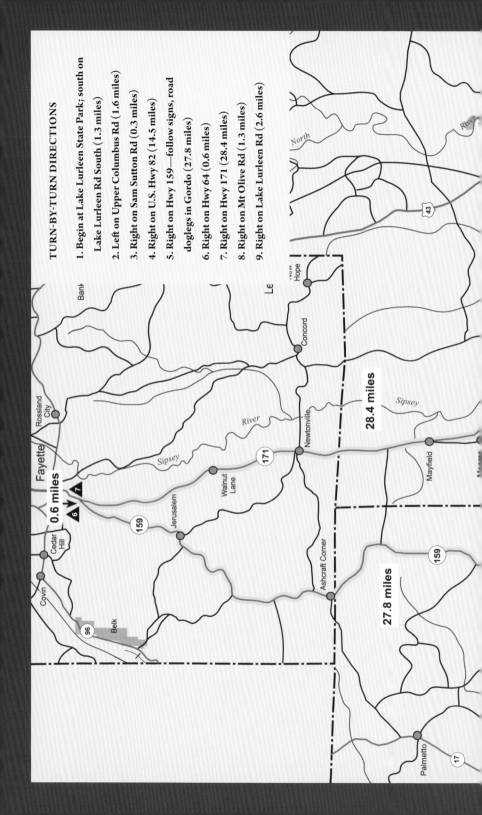

TURN-BY-TURN DIRECTIONS

1. Begin at Lake Lurleen State Park; south on Lake Lurleen Rd South (1.3 miles)

2. Left on Upper Columbus Rd (1.6 miles)

3. Right on Sam Sutton Rd (0.3 miles)

4. Right on U.S. Hwy 82 (14.5 miles)

5. Right on Hwy 159—follow signs, road doglegs in Gordo (27.8 miles)

6. Right on Hwy 64 (0.6 miles)

7. Right on Hwy 171 (28.4 miles)

8. Right on Mt Olive Rd (1.3 miles)

9. Right on Lake Lurleen Rd (2.6 miles)

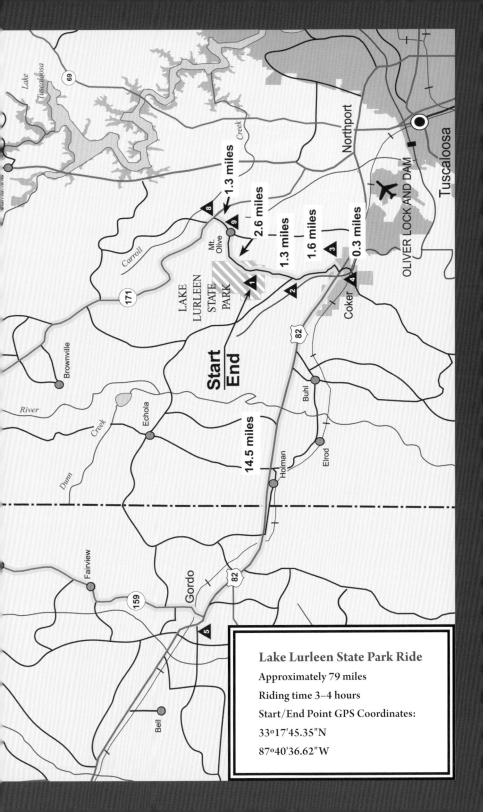

Lake Lurleen State Park Ride

Approximately 79 miles

Riding time 3–4 hours

Start/End Point GPS Coordinates:

33°17'45.35"N

87°40'36.62"W

Eutaw, Aliceville, Gainesville Ride

Approximately 97 miles
Riding time 4–5 hours

Start/End Point GPS Coordinates:
32°52'07.70"N
87°55'27.34"W

TOTALING NEARLY ONE HUNDRED MILES, this loop passes remnants of the elegant antebellum South as well as evidence of the extreme poverty of Alabama's Black Belt region in mostly rural Greene, Sumter, and Pickens counties.

Beginning at Exit 40 on Interstate 20/59 in Greene County, the city of Eutaw is less than three miles into the ride. Eutaw has several antebellum homes that have been restored and converted into bed-and-breakfast lodgings, including the Kirkwood Mansion in downtown Eutaw. Nearby is another pre–Civil War mansion, Twin Oaks, that is also on the National Register of Historic Places.

In Eutaw, be sure to follow the signs to get on U.S. Highway 11 north toward Knoxville. About nineteen miles from Exit 40, the route takes a sharp left turn at Ralph Loop Road, then goes northwest to Highway 2 at Jena (Turn 7) and westward into the Pickens County city of Aliceville.

In Aliceville—named for the wife of railroad magnate John T. Cochrane—there are a few fast-food places and more antebellum-era homes in varying states of restoration. From Aliceville the route turns southwest on Highway 17 (Turn 11) for 8.4 miles before going south on County Road 85/Warsaw Road at Cochrane toward

Gainesville. The almost twenty miles in this section are generally in good shape, but my last ride had places with some nasty potholes, mostly on the northern third of the road. County Road 85 follows the western banks of the Tombigbee River to Warsaw and through farms and forested wetlands to the Sumter County town of Gainesville, where a few more stately old homes and churches can still be found.

About two miles after Turn 14 at Gainesville on Highway 39, look to the right to see a lock and dam that are part of the Tennessee-Tombigbee Waterway. From here it's about fifteen miles back to the start point.

Lock on Tombigbee River near Gainesville

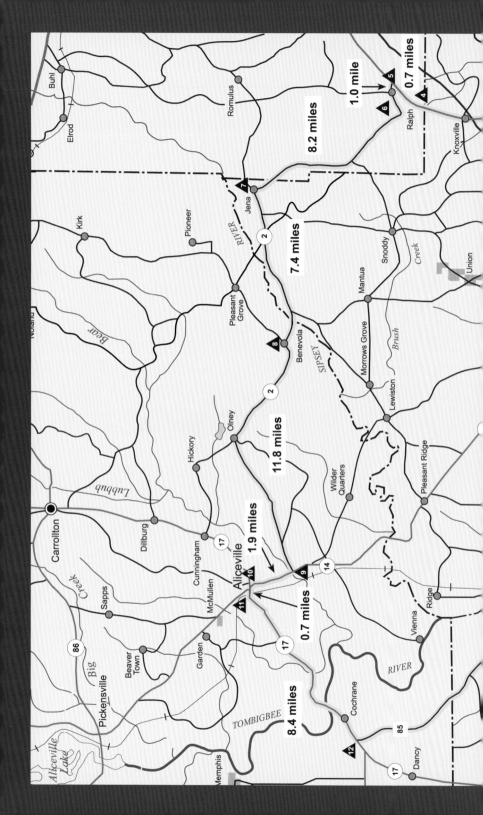

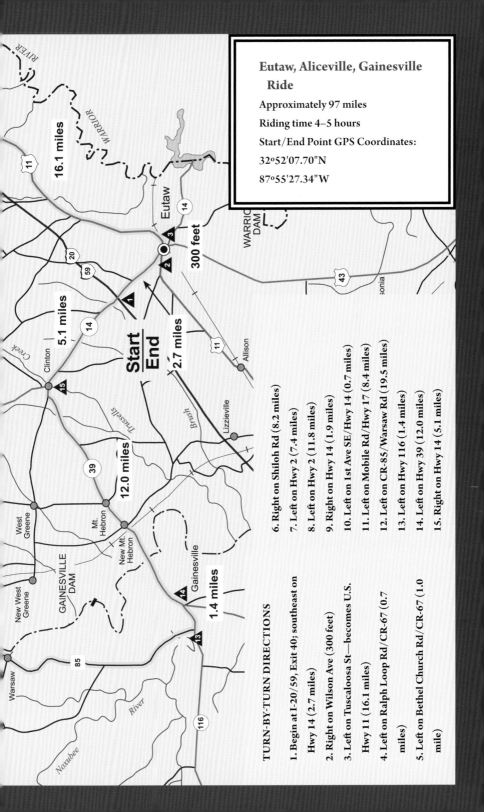

Eutaw, Aliceville, Gainesville Ride

Approximately 97 miles

Riding time 4–5 hours

Start/End Point GPS Coordinates:

32º52'07.70"N

87º55'27.34"W

16.1 miles

5.1 miles

300 feet

2.7 miles

12.0 miles

1.4 miles

Start / End

WARRIOR RIVER

Eutaw

WARRIOR DAM

Allison

Lizzieville

Clinton

Creek

Trussels

Brush

West Greene

Mt. Hebron

New Mt. Hebron

Gainesville

GAINESVILLE DAM

New West Greene

Warsaw

River

Noxubee

sonia

TURN-BY-TURN DIRECTIONS

1. Begin at I-20/59, Exit 40; southeast on Hwy 14 (2.7 miles)

2. Right on Wilson Ave (300 feet)

3. Left on Tuscaloosa St—becomes U.S. Hwy 11 (16.1 miles)

4. Left on Ralph Loop Rd/CR-67 (0.7 miles)

5. Left on Bethel Church Rd/CR-67 (1.0 mile)

6. Right on Shiloh Rd (8.2 miles)

7. Left on Hwy 2 (7.4 miles)

8. Left on Hwy 2 (11.8 miles)

9. Right on Hwy 14 (1.9 miles)

10. Left on 1st Ave SE/Hwy 14 (0.7 miles)

11. Left on Mobile Rd/Hwy 17 (8.4 miles)

12. Left on CR-85/Warsaw Rd (19.5 miles)

13. Left on Hwy 116 (1.4 miles)

14. Left on Hwy 39 (12.0 miles)

15. Right on Hwy 14 (5.1 miles)

Brilliant, Haleyville, Bear Creek, Hackleburg Ride

Approximately 98 miles

Riding time 3–4 hours

Start/End Point GPS Coordinates:
34°00'44.73"N
87°50'04.67"W

THIS NINETY-EIGHT-MILE RIDE offers a tour of typical northwest Alabama countryside as it alternates between hills, hollows, and creek beds through both farmland and forests.

Beginning at Exit 26 on Highway 78—the future Interstate 22— the first part of the ride climbs steadily through Brilliant, White- house, and Haleyville, starting at around six hundred feet of eleva- tion and rising to over nine hundred feet at Haleyville, to just over one thousand at Phil Campbell.

Between Haleyville and Phil Campbell, the route crosses Bear Creek just below the dam for the Bear Creek Reservoir. This is a popular canoe run in summer months because the Tennessee Valley Authority (TVA) makes scheduled water releases from the lake after most other streams in north Alabama have dried up.

At Isbell (Turn 5), Highway 36 offers some fun curves before con- necting with Highway 24 for two miles (Turn 6). At Belgreen (Turn 7), the route begins its southward leg and Highway 187 provides a smorgasbord of motorcycling fun as it winds for more than twelve miles through valleys of pastureland, crossing creeks and bobbing in and out of woodland with smooth, sweeping turns.

After a cut-through road (Turns 8 and 9) just outside of Hodges, the route follows Highway 172 into Hackleburg, then turns south for twenty-five more twisty miles on Highway 253 and a return to Highway 44 and the starting point (Turn 11).

Enjoying a straightaway on a northwest Alabama roadway

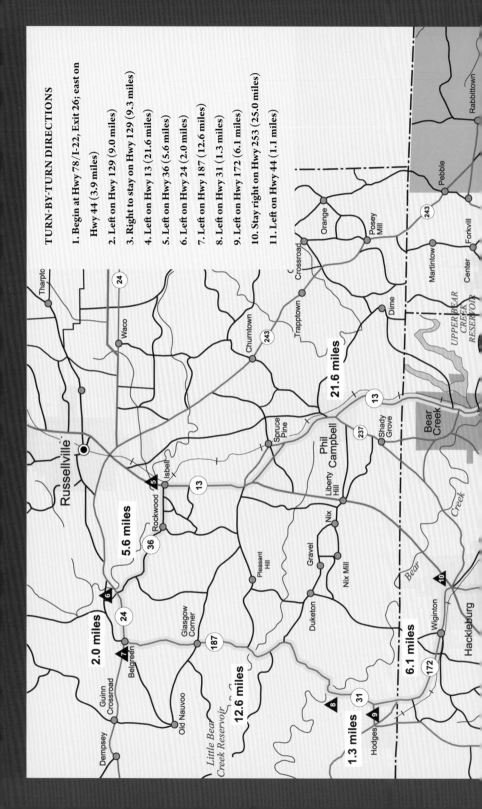

TURN-BY-TURN DIRECTIONS

1. Begin at Hwy 78/I-22, Exit 26; east on Hwy 44 (3.9 miles)
2. Left on Hwy 129 (9.0 miles)
3. Right to stay on Hwy 129 (9.3 miles)
4. Left on Hwy 13 (21.6 miles)
5. Left on Hwy 36 (5.6 miles)
6. Left on Hwy 24 (2.0 miles)
7. Left on Hwy 187 (12.6 miles)
8. Left on Hwy 31 (1.3 miles)
9. Left on Hwy 172 (6.1 miles)
10. Stay right on Hwy 253 (25.0 miles)
11. Left on Hwy 44 (1.1 miles)

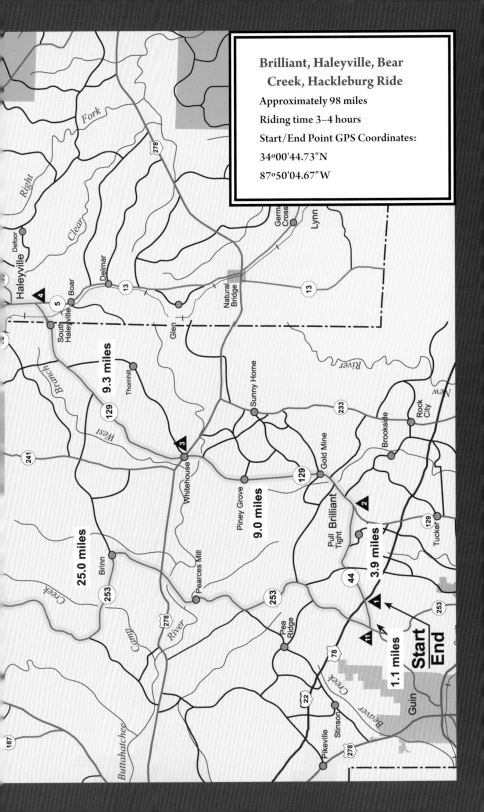

Brilliant, Haleyville, Bear Creek, Hackleburg Ride

Approximately 98 miles

Riding time 3–4 hours

Start/End Point GPS Coordinates:

34°00'44.73"N

87°50'04.67"W

Warrior, Arkadelphia, Maytown Ride

Approximately 97 miles
Riding time 4–5 hours

Start/End Point GPS Coordinates:
33°48'40.93"N
86°49'38.06"W

THIS ROUTE INCLUDES LOTS of semi-rough but paved back roads interspersed with sections of smooth blacktop and provides a snap-shot tour of coal mining country in parts of Walker and Jefferson counties. The ride also touches parts of Blount and Cullman counties as well.

Beginning at Exit 282 on Interstate 65 at Warrior, the first leg parallels the interstate northward to Skyline Drive.

Alabama Highway 91 near Arkadelphia

At the next stop sign, it turns right toward the old town of Arkadelphia, where a building once used as a Confederate infirmary still stands and Mr. Swann's general store is the only business in town—and a good place to take a break.

At Arkadelphia the route turns onto Highway 91 for 8.3 miles. This section was recently paved as of this writing and includes some fun sweeping turns and one very tight hairpin curve. Be careful, because it's not uncommon for gravel to wash into the road after heavy rains.

In Bug Tussle (also known as Wilburn), take a left turn onto Highway 69 (Turn 5), and after 7.3 miles the route goes back left onto Abe Myers Road (Turn 6) for about the same distance into the Lynns Park Community, where the route takes a right onto River Road (Turn 7).

River Road crosses U.S. Highway 78 after 0.7 miles, then follows the river into Cordova, where the route turns left onto Cordova-

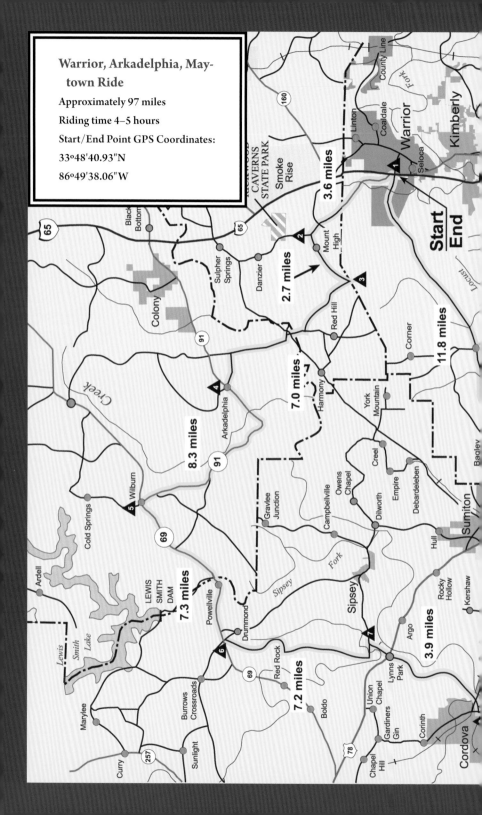

Warrior, Arkadelphia, May-town Ride

Approximately 97 miles

Riding time 4–5 hours

Start/End Point GPS Coordinates:

33°48'40.93"N

86°49'38.06"W

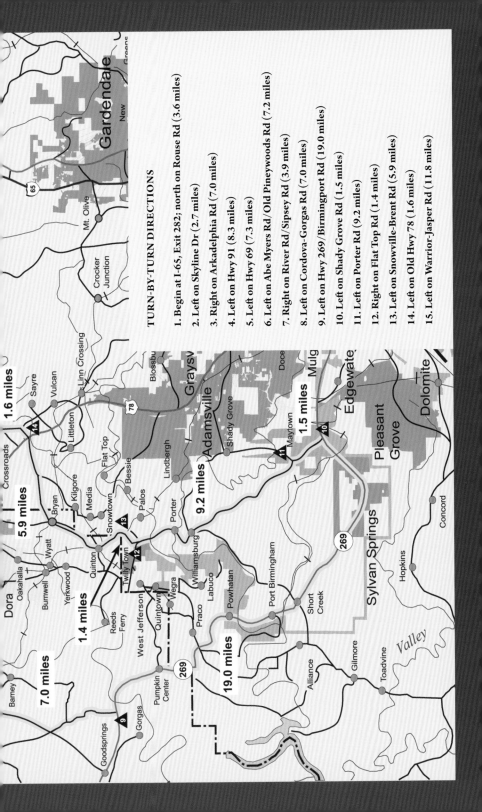

TURN-BY-TURN DIRECTIONS

1. Begin at I-65, Exit 282; north on Rouse Rd (3.6 miles)
2. Left on Skyline Dr (2.7 miles)
3. Right on Arkadelphia Rd (7.0 miles)
4. Left on Hwy 91 (8.3 miles)
5. Left on Hwy 69 (7.3 miles)
6. Left on Abe Myers Rd/Old Pineywoods Rd (7.2 miles)
7. Right on River Rd/Sipsey Rd (3.9 miles)
8. Left on Cordova-Gorgas Rd (7.0 miles)
9. Left on Hwy 269/Birmingport Rd (19.0 miles)
10. Left on Shady Grove Rd (1.5 miles)
11. Left on Porter Rd (9.2 miles)
12. Right on Flat Top Rd (1.4 miles)
13. Left on Snowville-Brent Rd (5.9 miles)
14. Left on Old Hwy 78 (1.6 miles)
15. Left on Warrior-Jasper Rd (11.8 miles)

Above the James H. Miller Jr. Electric Generating Plant

Gorgas Road (Turn 8). After crossing Highway 78—the future Interstate 22—the road follows ridges through reclaimed strip mines until forming a T with Highway 269/Birmingport Road (Turn 9).

The nineteen miles on Birmingport Road crosses both the Mulberry and Locust forks of the Black Warrior River before turning back north at Maytown on Shady Grove Road (Turn 10).

Again, it will be obvious that you're in coal country after turning left on Porter Road as it follows ridges past several working strip mine operations. For the first few miles of Porter Road, the pavement is somewhat rough, so use caution. After about eight miles on Porter Road the massive cooling towers of the James H. Miller Jr. Electric Generating Plant appear, and the road winds its way past the huge facility before crossing future Interstate 22 again and back to turn left on Old U.S. Highway 78 (Turn 14). Then take a right onto the Warrior-Jasper Road (Turn 15), and travel 11.8 miles back to the start.

RIDE LOOP 19
Brookwood, Windham Springs, Tuscaloosa Ride

Approximately 98 miles
Riding time 4–5 hours

Start/End Point GPS Coordinates:
33°11'19.70"N
87°18'04.63"W

THIS LOOP CARRIES YOU OVER the Black Warrior River in two places. The first half of this ninety-eight-mile ride winds its way through the coal fields of Tuscaloosa, Walker, and West Jefferson counties before reaching Highway 69. From there the route follows a beautiful two-lane highway into first Northport and then Tuscaloosa before going back to the start.

Beginning at Exit 86 of Interstate 20/59, the route heads north on Covered Bridge Road, which winds 5.7 miles through mostly residential areas before intersecting with Highway 216 at Brookwood (Turn 2).

There will be no doubt you're in coal-mining country about a mile after turning onto Lock 17 Road (Turn 3). For nearly a mile, the route passes the Jim Walter No. 4 Mine, a huge underground mining operation with multiple conveyors sprinkling black dust into mountains of coal. It takes more than a mile just to ride past the mine.

The terrain along Lock 17 Road for the next twelve miles or so passes other evidence of mining—both underground and surface mining—as well as stretches of woodland and even some family farms.

The landscape abruptly becomes more wooded at Groundhog

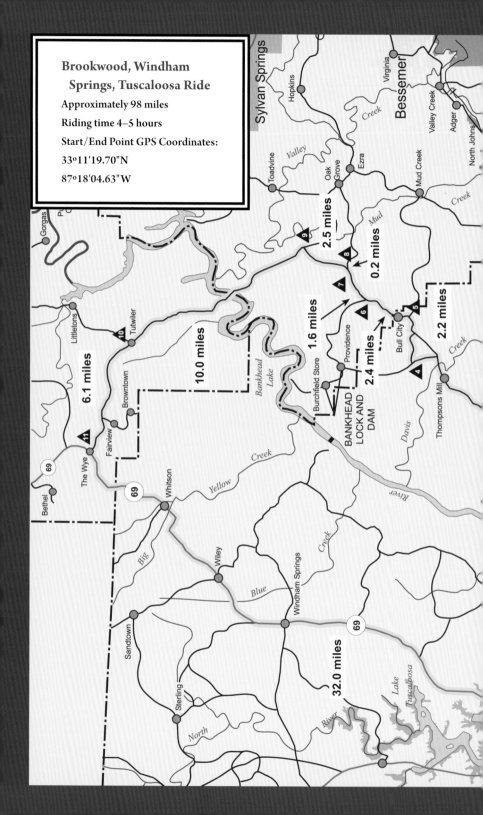

**Brookwood, Windham
Springs, Tuscaloosa Ride**
Approximately 98 miles
Riding time 4–5 hours
Start/End Point GPS Coordinates:
33o11'19.70"N
87o18'04.63"W

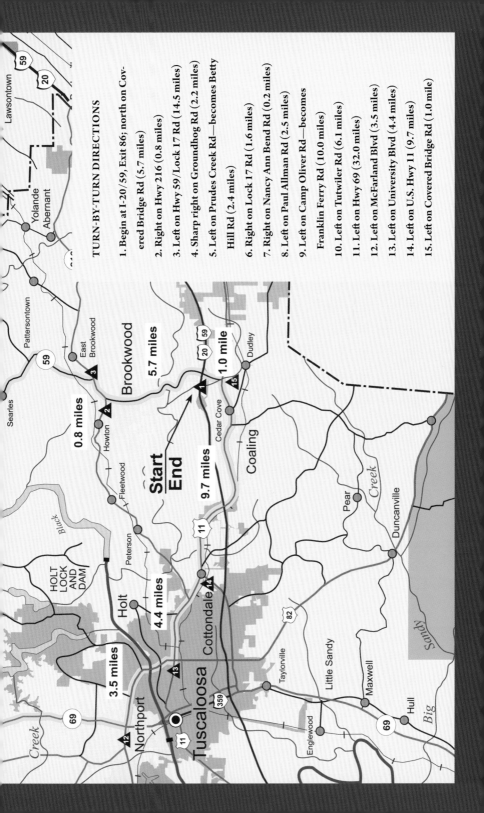

TURN-BY-TURN DIRECTIONS

1. Begin at I-20/59, Exit 86; north on Covered Bridge Rd (5.7 miles)
2. Right on Hwy 216 (0.8 miles)
3. Left on Hwy 59/Lock 17 Rd (14.5 miles)
4. Sharp right on Groundhog Rd (2.2 miles)
5. Left on Prudes Creek Rd—becomes Betty Hill Rd (2.4 miles)
6. Right on Lock 17 Rd (1.6 miles)
7. Right on Nancy Ann Bend Rd (0.2 miles)
8. Left on Paul Allman Rd (2.5 miles)
9. Left on Camp Oliver Rd—becomes Franklin Ferry Rd (10.0 miles)
10. Left on Tutwiler Rd (6.1 miles)
11. Left on Hwy 69 (32.0 miles)
12. Left on McFarland Blvd (3.5 miles)
13. Left on University Blvd (4.4 miles)
14. Left on U.S. Hwy 11 (9.7 miles)
15. Left on Covered Bridge Rd (1.0 mile)

Road (Turn 4), and even more so at Betty Hill Road (Turn 5), where the road descends several hundred feet in a series of a dozen tight turns along the shoulder of a hill. Expect much fun here!

From Betty Hill, the route rejoins Lock 17 Road for 1.6 miles (Turn 6), then turns right on Nancy Ann Bend Road for 0.2 miles (Turn 7), before taking Paul Allman Road northward (Turn 8) to cut through to Camp Oliver Road (Turn 9). (If you take the short detour left on Nancy Ann Bend Road, the road climbs onto a high ridgeline that offers a panoramic view north to the Black Warrior River valley and south to the diminishing horizons of the coastal plain).

In mid-straightaway, Camp Oliver Road becomes Franklin Ferry Road and crosses the Black Warrior River, just downstream of where the Locust and Mulberry forks of the river join.

About 5.5 miles after the river, the route goes left on Tutwiler Road (Turn 10) for 6.1 miles to Highway 69 (Turn 11).

The next thirty-two miles of Highway 69 to Northport are a steady series of sweeping turns on good blacktop roadway, bobbing up and down rolling hills through both farm- and pastureland and forested areas—a very nice motorcycling road. At about the halfway mark, a left turn well marked by signage will take you to Deerlick Creek Park on the Black Warrior River, a well-maintained campground run by the Army Corps of Engineers (open annually from May 1 to November 1).

The route passes some congested traffic areas through Northport and Tuscaloosa. After crossing the Black Warrior River after Turn 12, stay in the right lane and bear right on an exit ramp off Highway 82/McFarland Boulevard to a left turn (Turn 13) onto University

Boulevard/Highway 217, and proceed through the many lights of Alberta City to join Highway 11 beyond Five Points. The final 7.5 miles south of I-20/59 (Turns 14 and 15) are more open and rural.

Abandoned dragline in Walker County

Lacon, Hartselle, Addison, Clarkson Ride

Approximately 76 miles
Riding time 3–4 hours

Start/End Point GPS Coordinates:
34°18'59.53"N
86°54'02.64"W

THIS RIDE COVERS SEVENTY-SIX MILES of north Alabama countryside that varies between wide-open pastureland and densely wooded hollows and passes a historic covered bridge. The majority of the ride runs over fairly fast roadways, so it can be easily done in an afternoon.

The loop begins at Exit 318 on Interstate 65 at Lacon and follows U.S. Highway 31 north for 9.1 miles to Hartselle, where it heads northwest on Vaughn Bridge Road (Turn 2).

From here the route meanders north and west (Turns 3 to 6) through open farmland and woodlands with pleasantly sweeping curves until the intersection of Mud Tavern Road and Kirby Bridge Road (Turn 7).

From Turn 7 to the intersection of Danville Road and Highway 157, the terrain opens up into long, straight sections through open farms and pasture.

For the fifteen miles south of Highway 157, Danville Road/Highway 41 ascends and descends rolling hills and has numerous fast, sweeping turns that are quite entertaining on a motorcycle.

At Addison (Turn 9), the route heads back east on the Sardis-Airport Road, which parallels U.S. Highway 278 for 13.2 miles. This section varies between deep wooded hollows and farmland and passes the old Clarkson/Legg Covered Bridge at Crooked Creek. Cullman County operates a park there, and both picnic and restroom facilities are available.

The next section heads north first on Battleground Road, which becomes County Road 1127, and then on County Road 1141 back to Highway 157 (Turns 10 to 12).

At Highway 157, cruiser or sport-bike riders may wish to turn right and follow Highway 157 the 7.6 miles south to I-65 for a faster return to the starting point, rather than taking the route on the map. The mapped route (Turns 13 to 18) has numerous turns on somewhat rough county roads but does offer a more intimate tour of the terrain.

Clarkson/Legg Covered Bridge in Cullman County

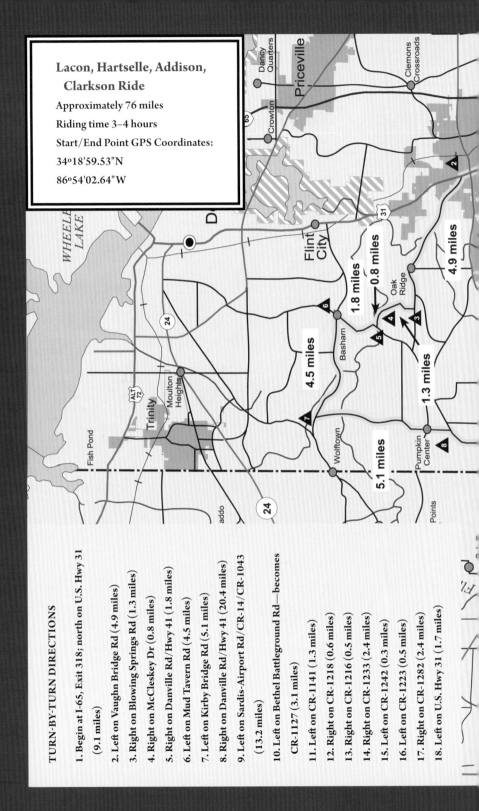

Lacon, Hartselle, Addison, Clarkson Ride

Approximately 76 miles

Riding time 3–4 hours

Start/End Point GPS Coordinates:

34º18'59.53"N

86º54'02.64"W

TURN-BY-TURN DIRECTIONS

1. Begin at I-65, Exit 318; north on U.S. Hwy 31 (9.1 miles)
2. Left on Vaughn Bridge Rd (4.9 miles)
3. Right on Blowing Springs Rd (1.3 miles)
4. Right on McCleskey Dr (0.8 miles)
5. Right on Danville Rd/Hwy 41 (1.8 miles)
6. Left on Mud Tavern Rd (4.5 miles)
7. Left on Kirby Bridge Rd (5.1 miles)
8. Right on Danville Rd/Hwy 41 (20.4 miles)
9. Left on Sardis-Airport Rd/CR-14/CR-1043 (13.2 miles)
10. Left on Bethel Battleground Rd—becomes CR-1127 (3.1 miles)
11. Left on CR-1141 (1.3 miles)
12. Right on CR-1218 (0.6 miles)
13. Right on CR-1216 (0.5 miles)
14. Right on CR-1233 (2.4 miles)
15. Left on CR-1242 (0.3 miles)
16. Left on CR-1223 (0.5 miles)
17. Right on CR-1282 (2.4 miles)
18. Left on U.S. Hwy 31 (1.7 miles)

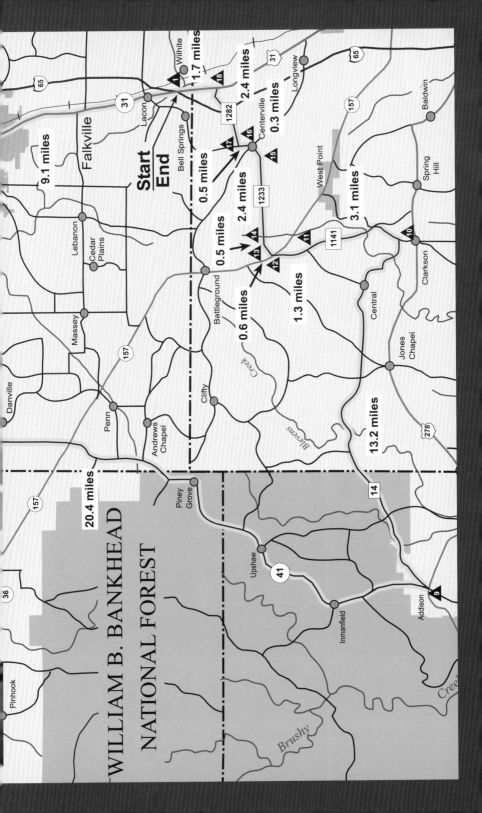

Old bridge near Addison

PART IV

RIDES IN EAST-CENTRAL ALABAMA
Ride Loops 21–30

Alabama-Georgia State Line Ride

Approximately 112 miles
Riding time 4–5 hours

Start/End GPS Coordinates:
33°39'13.09"N
85°24'49.21"W

MILE FOR MILE, THIS RIDE probably has the most spectacular views found anywhere in the state of Alabama. It follows a high ridgeline that hugs the Alabama-Georgia state line southward from Exit 210 on Interstate 20 to the city of Roanoke, then turns north on scenic U.S. Highway 431, and finally returns to the start via small winding farm roads.

The first forty miles of the route stay high as the road steadily climbs on County Road 49 through Ranburne (here you have to jog right 250 feet and then left to stay on County Road 49) and reaches a maximum elevation of more than 1,500 feet.

Once atop this ridge, the western side is mostly open; and for miles the road offers spectacular views of the Talladega Mountains—including Alabama's highest point at Mount Cheaha—thirty miles to the west.

County Road 49 becomes County Road 87 at the county line (marked by the bridge over Little Tallapoosa River) and gradually descends south of Omaha to about eight hundred feet in elevation by the time it terminates into Highway 22 at Roanoke (Turn 4). From there the route begins its northward leg on U.S. Highway 431. This stretch of highway is an enjoyable and easy series of sweeping turns and changing scenery.

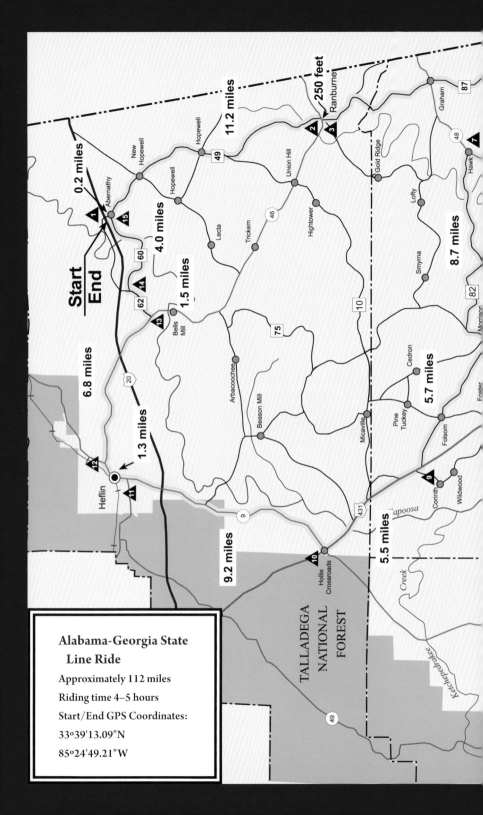

Start
End

0.2 miles

250 feet
Ranburne

11.2 miles

4.0 miles

1.5 miles

6.8 miles

1.3 miles

9.2 miles

8.7 miles

5.7 miles

5.5 miles

Hopewell
New Hopewell
Abernathy
Hopewell
Lecta
Trickem
Union Hill
Hightower
Gold Ridge
Lofty
Smyrna
Graham
Hawk
Bells Mill
Arbacoochee
Beason Mill
Micaville
Pine Tuckey
Cedron
Folsom
Foster
Morrison
Corinth
Wildwood
Heflin
Hollis Crossroads

Tallapoosa

Creek

Ketchepedrakee

49

15

60

62

44

43

20

9

2

3

49

46

10

75

82

48

87

431

42

11

10

9

TALLADEGA NATIONAL FOREST

Alabama-Georgia State Line Ride

Approximately 112 miles

Riding time 4–5 hours

Start/End GPS Coordinates:

33°39'13.09"N

85°24'49.21"W

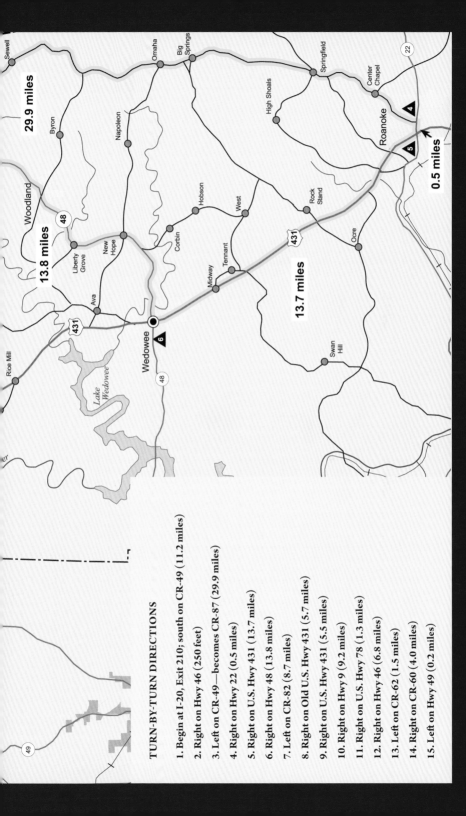

TURN-BY-TURN DIRECTIONS

1. Begin at I-20, Exit 210; south on CR-49 (11.2 miles)
2. Right on Hwy 46 (250 feet)
3. Left on CR-49—becomes CR-87 (29.9 miles)
4. Right on Hwy 22 (0.5 miles)
5. Right on U.S. Hwy 431 (13.7 miles)
6. Right on Hwy 48 (13.8 miles)
7. Left on CR-82 (8.7 miles)
8. Right on Old U.S. Hwy 431 (5.7 miles)
9. Right on U.S. Hwy 431 (5.5 miles)
10. Right on Hwy 9 (9.2 miles)
11. Right on U.S. Hwy 78 (1.3 miles)
12. Right on Hwy 46 (6.8 miles)
13. Left on CR-62 (1.5 miles)
14. Right on CR-60 (4.0 miles)
15. Left on Hwy 49 (0.2 miles)

Breaking up the mostly rural landscape is the town of Wedowee with its downtown business district that still looks much as it did in the mid-twentieth century. After leaving U.S. Highway 431 at Highway 48 in Wedowee (Turn 6), the route heads northeast through woodland and small farms into the Hawk community at Turn 7 and works its way back to the west on County Road 82 to join a scenic piece of Old U.S. Highway 431 and finally merge again with the new 431 at Turn 9.

After a few miles on U.S. Highway 431, the ride turns right onto Highway 9 at Turn 10 and follows this gently winding road to cross I-20 into Heflin, before it picks up Highway 46 (Turn 12) to cross I-20 again.

Less than a mile after you cross the interstate, Turn 13 takes a left onto County Road 62; then you will head back eastward, paralleling I-20 on County Road 60 (Turn 14) through country lanes that cross the Tallapoosa River just before rejoining Highway 49 (Turn 15), just 0.2 miles south of the start point.

Looking toward the Talladega Mountains from Randolph County Road 112

Wetumpka, Weogufka, Clanton, Pine Level Ride

Approximately 120 miles
Riding time 4–5 hours

Start/End GPS Coordinates:
32°32'58.89"N
86°27'27.99"W

THE 120 MILES INCLUDED in this loop either cross or stay within sight of the lower three lakes on the Coosa River—Lay, Mitchell, and Jordan—before the river joins with the Tallapoosa to form the Alabama River just north of Montgomery.

The route also includes thirty miles of one of the prettiest roads in central Alabama: County Road 29 from U.S. Highway 231 in Elmore County to Weogufka in Coosa County.

Starting at Interstate 65, Exit 186, the route begins by heading north on U.S. Highway 31 for 2.2 miles to Highway 40. The route briefly joins Highway 143 at Deatsville (Turn 3), and then heads southeast into Wetumpka on Highway 111, following Jordan Lake and the Coosa River for most of the 14.9 miles.

At Wetumpka you'll cross the Coosa on one of the most picturesque bridges in the state. Bibb Graves Bridge, named for an Alabama governor, was built in 1937 and features four sweeping concrete arches. The bridge connects the east and west sides of the city of Wetumpka; the old downtown section of the east side is stereotypical small-town Americana, so much so that it's been chosen as a location backdrop for several Hollywood feature films, including Tim Burton's 2003 *Big Fish*. Just after crossing the bridge, you'll find

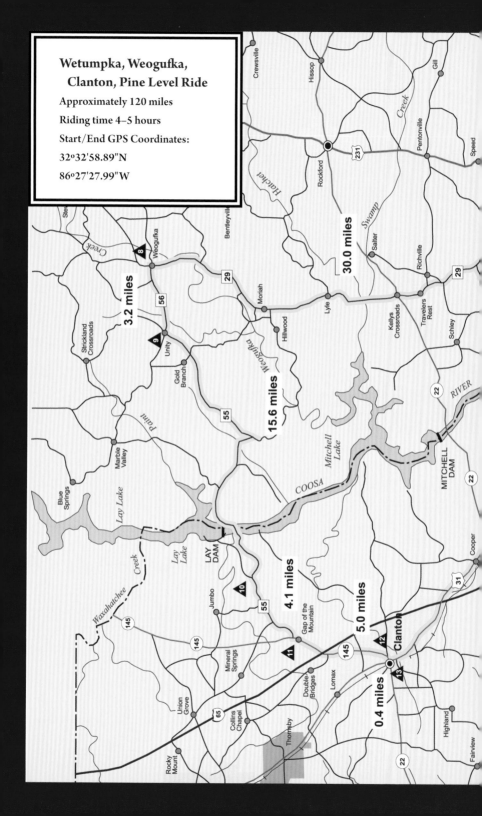

**Wetumpka, Weogufka,
Clanton, Pine Level Ride**

Approximately 120 miles

Riding time 4–5 hours

Start/End GPS Coordinates:

32º32'58.89"N

86º27'27.99"W

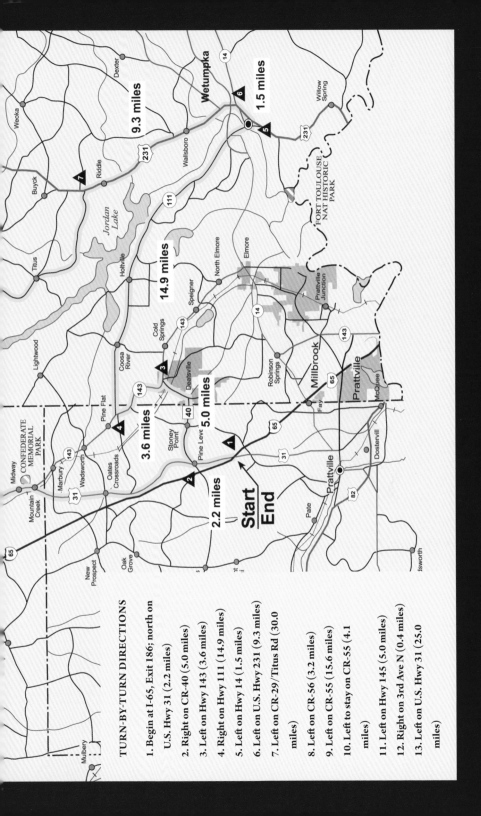

TURN-BY-TURN DIRECTIONS

1. Begin at I-65, Exit 186; north on U.S. Hwy 31 (2.2 miles)

2. Right on CR-40 (5.0 miles)

3. Left on Hwy 143 (3.6 miles)

4. Right on Hwy 111 (14.9 miles)

5. Left on Hwy 14 (1.5 miles)

6. Left on U.S. Hwy 231 (9.3 miles)

7. Left on CR-29/Titus Rd (30.0 miles)

8. Left on CR-56 (3.2 miles)

9. Left on CR-55 (15.6 miles)

10. Left to stay on CR-55 (4.1 miles)

11. Left on Hwy 145 (5.0 miles)

12. Right on 3rd Ave N (0.4 miles)

13. Left on U.S. Hwy 31 (25.0 miles)

Cyclists parked outside the one-of-a-kind Caperton's Old South Store in Weogufka

a parking area to the left and a boardwalk that crosses beneath the bridge for a nice view.

From Wetumpka, the route turns north on U.S. Highway 231 (Turn 6) for 9.3 miles before turning left onto County Road 29/ Titus Road (Turn 7).

For about the first half of the thirty miles of County Road 29 on this route—the part south of Kellys Crossroads on Highway 22— the road winds through a landscape ranging from farmland to forested bottomlands.

From Kellys Crossroads north to Weogufka in Coosa County, the terrain feels much more remote and wild. As one of the most sparsely populated counties in the state, Coosa County can give the impression of going back in time fifty years. In Weogufka, the Caperton's Old South Store is a unique experience offering one-stop shopping for guns or beer.

At Weogufka the route turns west on County Road 56 for 3.2 miles to another left at County Road 55 (Turns 8 and 9), and then continues west to cross the Coosa again just downstream of Lay Dam. This stretch to the dam passes through an even more remote part of Coosa County that includes the Coosa Wildlife Management Area and the Weogufka State Forest.

After crossing the river, the route begins its southward leg, joining Highway 145 and crossing I-65 into Clanton, before continuing south on U.S. Highway 31 (Turn 13) for twenty-five miles to the starting point.

Wind Creek State Park, Lake Martin Ride

Approximately 88 miles

Riding time 3–4 hours

Start/End GPS Coordinates:

32°51'31.73"N

85°56'08.91"W

BEGINNING AT AND LOOPING BACK to Wind Creek State Park, this eighty-eight-mile ride would make an ideal day trip for someone staying at the park, which offers both camping and cabins. This ride circumnavigates Lake Martin on the Tallapoosa River and also passes by the Horseshoe Bend National Military Park between Dadeville and New Site.

Leaving Wind Creek State Park, the route first turns south for 11.7 miles on Highway 63 and crosses the lake at Kowaliga Bridge. A driveway to the right after you cross the bridge takes you past the marina to Sinclair's Restaurant, where the original wooden Indian that inspired Hank Williams's song "Kowaliga" resides.

About 3 miles after turning onto Hwy 229 (Turn 3), the road becomes Highway 50 at Red Hill. The road is also called Martin Dam Road, because after about 5.5 miles the route crosses the Tallapoosa River outflow just downstream from Martin Dam at Cherokee Bluffs. When the Alabama Power Company built this dam in the 1920s— the first of four dams the company built on the Tallapoosa River—it created the world's largest artificial body of water.

From the dam, the route continues to follow Highway 50 through

Stopping at Horseshoe Bend National Military Park

Dudleyville General Store

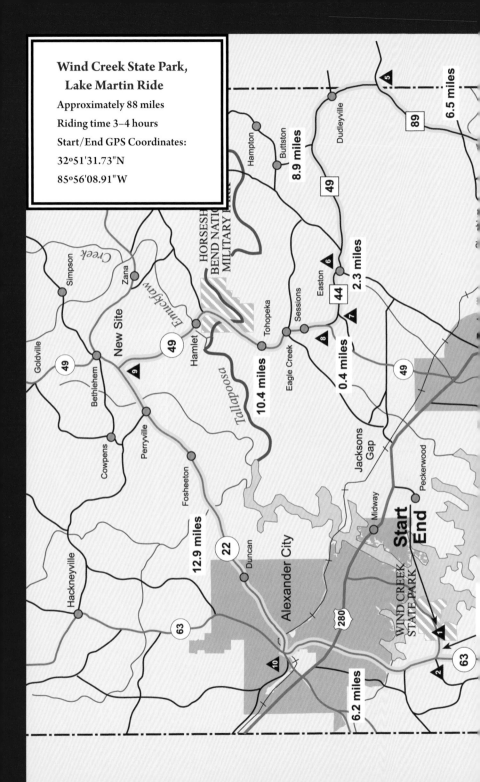

Wind Creek State Park, Lake Martin Ride

Approximately 88 miles

Riding time 3–4 hours

Start/End GPS Coordinates:

32°51'31.73"N

85°56'08.91"W

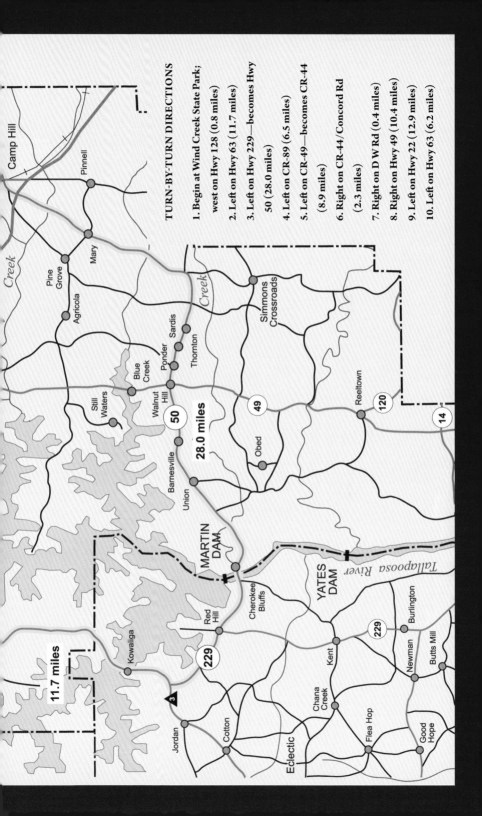

TURN-BY-TURN DIRECTIONS

1. Begin at Wind Creek State Park; west on Hwy 128 (0.8 miles)
2. Left on Hwy 63 (11.7 miles)
3. Left on Hwy 229—becomes Hwy 50 (28.0 miles)
4. Left on CR-89 (6.5 miles)
5. Left on CR-49—becomes CR-44 (8.9 miles)
6. Right on CR-44/Concord Rd (2.3 miles)
7. Right on D W Rd (0.4 miles)
8. Right on Hwy 49 (10.4 miles)
9. Left on Hwy 22 (12.9 miles)
10. Left on Hwy 63 (6.2 miles)

Walnut Hill at the intersection with Highway 49, and Camp Hill after an intersection with U.S. Highway 280.

Just northeast of Camp Hill, the route turns left at County Road 89 and continues on County Road 49 toward Dudleyville (Turns 4 and 5). From Dudleyville, Turns 6 and 7 take the route to Highway 49 near Sessions (Turn 8).

About six miles north on Highway 49 is the entrance to the Horseshoe Bend National Military Park. In 1814, the decisive battle with the Creek Indians took place at this location named for the shape of a bend in the Tallapoosa River, when Andrew Jackson's army defeated the Red Sticks. In fact, the battle saw the most Native

Entrance to Wind Creek State Park

American deaths (more than eight hundred) in a single battle in the entire history of the United States. The defeat led to the surrender of the Creeks to Jackson four months later and opened the way toward settlement of present-day Alabama. The park has numerous interactive exhibits, picnic areas, and hiking trails, as well as a drive-through tour of the battlefield. Living-history events are also held at the park from time to time. For more information, visit the park's Web site at www.nps.gov/hobe.

North of Horseshoe Bend, the route turns southwest on Highway 22 and passes through Alexander City, where it rejoins Highway 63 (Turn 10) and takes you back to the starting point.

Historic Lake Martin Dam

RIDE LOOP 24
Lanett, Wadley, Horseshoe Bend Ride

Approximately 118 miles
Riding time 4–5 hours

Start/End GPS Coordinates:
32°50'52.41"N
85°11'08.14"W

THIS 118-MILE RIDE WILL LIKELY take the better part of a day and includes two sections (Highway 77 and Highway 49) that seem to have been expressly designed for riding on two wheels.

Beginning at Exit 79 of Interstate 85 near the Alabama-Georgia state line at Lanett, the first leg winds northwest through rural countryside on the Fredonia Highway to Five Points, where it joins U.S. Highway 431 (Turn 4).

After about four miles, a right turn on County Road 114 cuts through from U.S. Highway 431 to Highway 77 at Penton (Turns 5 and 6).

Here begins a 24.2-mile section over rolling hills with sweeping curves that are a joy to experience on a motorcycle.

At Mellow Valley, the route turns back south on Highway 49 for twenty-nine more miles of great motorcycling. On this stretch you pass the Horseshoe Bend National Military Park (discussed in detail in Ride Loop 23, the Wind Creek State Park, Lake Martin Ride).

Horseshoe Bend marks about the halfway point and would be a good place to stop for lunch or a restroom break.

After Horseshoe Bend, the route turns southeast on U.S. High-

Downtown Goodwater

way 280 at Dadeville (Turn 8) and then east on Highway 50 near Camp Hill (Turn 9).

The final thirty-two miles on Highway 50 pass through mostly rural countryside, except for the town of LaFayette, which is about eighteen miles out of Camp Hill.

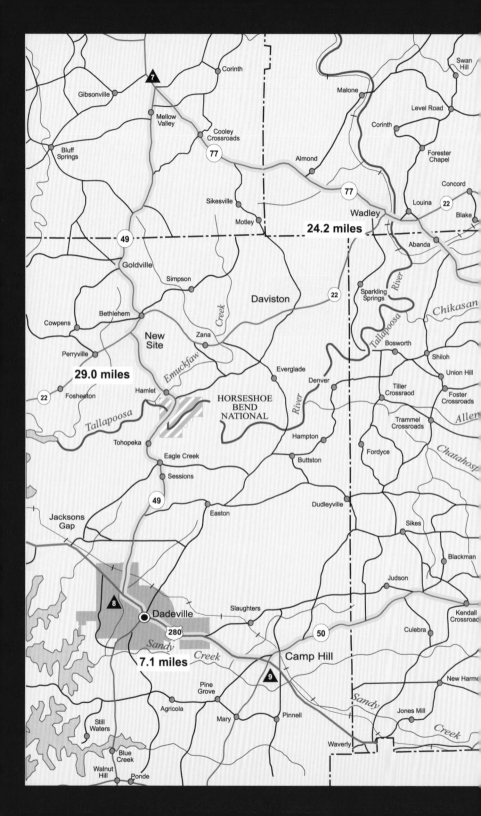

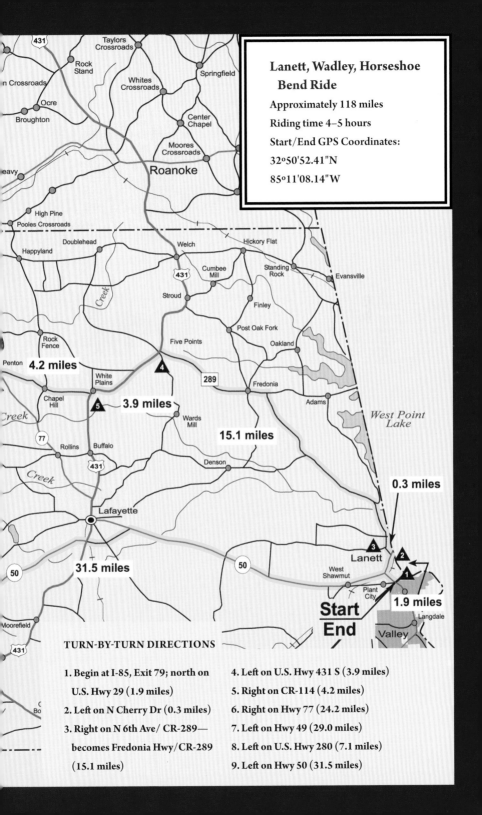

Lanett, Wadley, Horseshoe Bend Ride

Approximately 118 miles
Riding time 4–5 hours
Start/End GPS Coordinates:
32°50'52.41"N
85°11'08.14"W

TURN-BY-TURN DIRECTIONS

1. Begin at I-85, Exit 79; north on U.S. Hwy 29 (1.9 miles)
2. Left on N Cherry Dr (0.3 miles)
3. Right on N 6th Ave/ CR-289— becomes Fredonia Hwy/CR-289 (15.1 miles)
4. Left on U.S. Hwy 431 S (3.9 miles)
5. Right on CR-114 (4.2 miles)
6. Right on Hwy 77 (24.2 miles)
7. Left on Hwy 49 (29.0 miles)
8. Left on U.S. Hwy 280 (7.1 miles)
9. Left on Hwy 50 (31.5 miles)

Cook Springs, Logan Martin Dam, Highway 25 Ride

Approximately 76 miles
Riding time 3–4 hours

Start/End GPS Coordinates:
33º35'44.57"N
86º23'43.98"W

THIS SEVENTY-SIX-MILE LOOP can easily be done in an afternoon from anywhere in the vicinity of Birmingham and could be combined with a visit to the Barber Vintage Motorsports Museum in Leeds for riders from outside the Birmingham area.

Beginning at Exit 152 on Interstate 20 at Cook Springs, the first section on Cook Springs Road passes beneath a railroad through an arched tunnel to pop out at the Cook Springs post office.

The route continues south across Old U.S. Highway 78 following twisty and narrow back roads through hilly farmland and woodland to Wolf Creek Road (Turns 2, 3, and 4); it then takes Camp Creek Road over to U.S. Highway 231 (Turn 6).

The 7.5-mile stretch of U.S. Highway 231 follows the western shoreline of Logan Martin Lake to Cropwell, just south of Pell City, before heading east on Highway 34 (Turn 7).

After about four miles the route crosses the lake at Stemley Bridge, and after another two miles it turns south on Cove Access Road (Turn 8).

The farmland/woodland landscape continues onto Howells Cove

Road (Turn 9) and Renfroe Road (Turn 10), until the route makes a right turn at Logan Martin Dam Road (Turn 11).

Less than a half mile after crossing the dam, Kelly Creek Road turns sharply left down a hill (Turn 12).

After crossing U.S. Highway 231 at Vincent (Kelly Creek Road is now Highway 60) the route joins Highway 25. The next 17.5 miles of Highway 25 are some of the most frequently traveled by motorcyclists in the state. Some call this section of Highway 25 the "Tail of the Lizard," a nickname that refers to the "Tail of the Dragon" at Deal's Gap in North Carolina.

Entering a kudzu-covered tunnel at Cook Springs

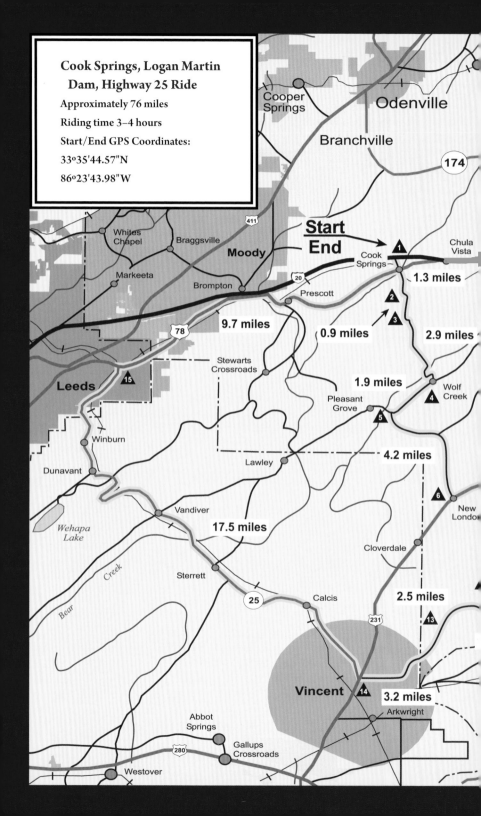

TURN-BY-TURN DIRECTIONS

1. Begin at I-20, Exit 152; south on Cook Springs Rd (1.3 miles)
2. Left to stay on Mountain Top Loop (0.9 miles)
3. Left on Cook Springs Cutoff (2.9 miles)
4. Right on Wolf Creek Rd (1.9 miles)
5. Left on Camp Creek Rd (4.2 miles)
6. Left on U.S. Hwy 231 (7.5 miles)
7. Right at Hwy 34 (6.4 miles)
8. Right on Cove Access Rd (3.1 miles)
9. Right on Howells Cove Rd (5.2 miles)
10. Right on Renfroe Rd (6.8 miles)
11. Right on Logan Martin Dam Rd (1.8 miles)
12. Sharp left on Kelly Creek Rd (2.5 miles)
13. Left to stay on Kelly Creek Rd—becomes Hwy 60 (3.2 miles)
14. Right on Hwy 25 (17.5 miles)
15. Right on U.S. Hwy 78 (9.7 miles)

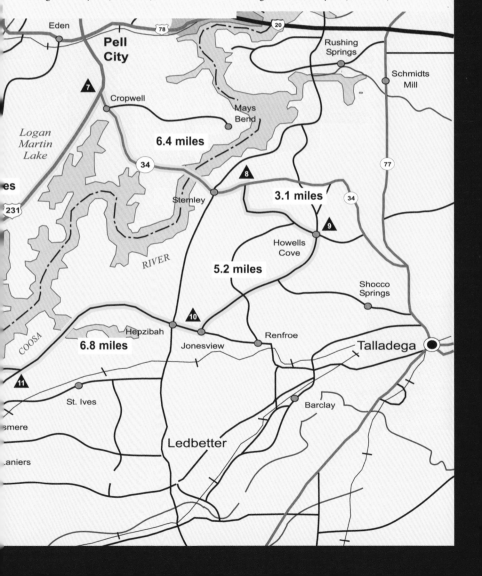

From this direction, the road becomes progressively curvy through the towns of Sterett and Vandiver before getting downright tight and twisty through Dunavant and on into Leeds.

Legend has it that the train tunnel that passes through Coosa Mountain was the one immortalized by the character in the folk song "John Henry." Henry apparently died after defeating a steam drill in a man-against-machine competition. Historians dispute whether or not this is the same tunnel where the steam drill contest took place, but anyone who has ridden Highway 25 across the mountain will appreciate it as one of the best motorcycling roads in the state.

At Leeds, Highway 25 intersects with Old U.S. Highway 78. The route turns right (Turn 15) to complete the loop ride back to Cook Springs.

If you turn left instead, the Barber Vintage Motorsports Museum lies approximately five miles down the road.

Cheaha State Park Dual-Sport Ride

Approximately 85 miles
Riding time 4–5 hours

Start/End GPS Coordinates:
33°28'37.72"N
85°48'29.72"W

IN MY OPINION, THE Talladega National Forest, both north and south of Cheaha State Park, offers the best concentration of motorcycling variety fun in the state. Whether you're on a big twin cruiser, sport bike, or dual-sport bike, the area is teeming with great rides. For this book I have included three rides that in one way or another touch the Cheaha area. One is strictly for street bikes, and the other two—one easy and one more challenging—are for dual-sport bikes.

As the easy ride for dual-sport bikes, this ride represents the middle ground of the three. Actually, all the roads on this ride—paved and well-maintained gravel—can be ridden on just about any motorcycle, although some would not be much fun on a street-oriented machine.

This eighty-five-mile route begins and ends at Cheaha State Park, which offers cabins, camping, and even a hotel for lodging. It also has a restaurant on the mountaintop with a panoramic view.

The first thirty miles of this route involves all road riding, followed by five miles of easy gravel, then twenty-one miles of pavement, about eight more miles of gravel, and finally seventeen miles

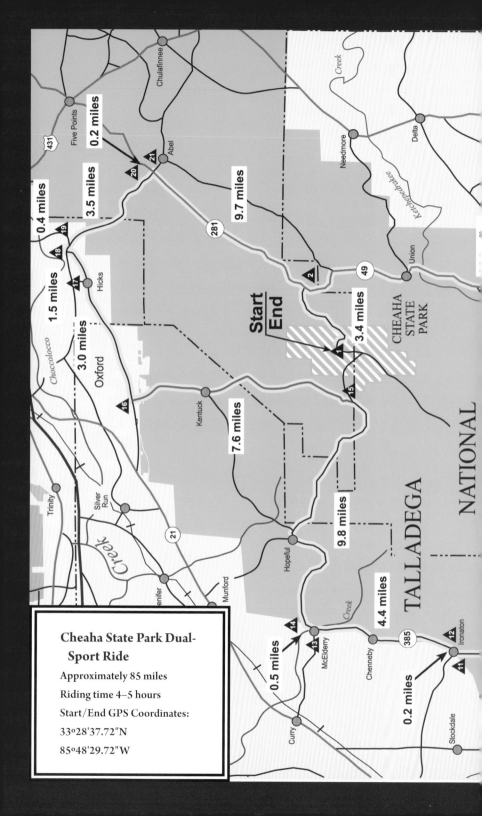

Cheaha State Park Dual-Sport Ride

Approximately 85 miles

Riding time 4–5 hours

Start/End GPS Coordinates:

33º28'37.72"N

85º48'29.72"W

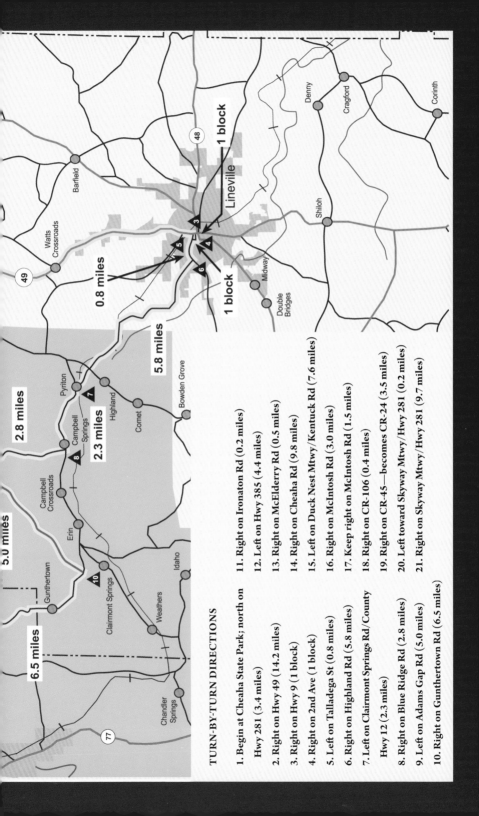

TURN-BY-TURN DIRECTIONS

1. Begin at Cheaha State Park; north on Hwy 281 (0.2 miles)

2. Right on Hwy 49 (14.2 miles)

3. Right on Hwy 9 (1 block)

4. Right on 2nd Ave (1 block)

5. Left on Talladega St (0.8 miles)

6. Right on Highland Rd (5.8 miles)

7. Left on Clairmont Springs Rd/County Hwy 12 (2.3 miles)

8. Right on Blue Ridge Rd (2.8 miles)

9. Left on Adams Gap Rd (5.0 miles)

10. Right on Gunthertown Rd (6.5 miles)

11. Right on Ironaton Rd (0.2 miles)

12. Left on Hwy 385 (4.4 miles)

13. Right on McElderry Rd (0.5 miles)

14. Right on Cheaha Rd (9.8 miles)

15. Left on Duck Nest Mtwy/Kentuck Rd (7.6 miles)

16. Right on McIntosh Rd (3.0 miles)

17. Keep right on McIntosh Rd (1.5 miles)

18. Right on CR-106 (0.4 miles)

19. Right on CR-45—becomes CR-24 (3.5 miles)

20. Left toward Skyway Mtwy/Hwy 281 (0.2 miles)

21. Right on Skyway Mtwy/Hwy 281 (9.7 miles)

Stone bridge near Cheaha State Park

of asphalt. So, only about thirteen miles of the total ride takes place off pavement.

The first leg leaves the parking lot of the park's camp store and descends the mountain on Highway 281 for 3.4 miles to Highway 49 (Turn 2). The first mile or so off the ridge contains many enjoyable banked turns as the elevation drops off rapidly. For the next thirteen miles into the Clay County town of Lineville, the road snakes its way through pastureland and wooded sections and past several roads leading to various popular hiking trailheads.

In Lineville the route turns west onto Highway 9 for just a block, then immediately back north on Second Avenue for a block, and then onto Talladega Street northwest for 0.8 miles before joining Highland Road at Turn 6. After 5.8 miles, the route turns left at

Clairmont Springs Road/County Highway 12 (Turn 7) for 2.3 miles before taking a right onto Blue Ridge Road at Turn 8.

As of this writing, Blue Ridge Road had been recently paved but, due to the steepness of the incline, had numerous potholes and wash-outs, making it as rough or perhaps rougher than the gravel roads on this loop. So be careful on the 2.8 miles up the mountain.

Blue Ridge Road ends at the southern terminus of Highway 281 (also known as Skyway Motorway) at Adams Gap. The left turn here (Turn 9) marks the first, five-mile-long gravel section. This road was reworked by the Forest Service in 2007, and in 2008 it was still in great shape. It follows the ridgelines with occasional panoramic views southeastward into Clay County before intersecting with Gunthertown Road (Turn 10).

The next 6.5 miles on Gunthertown Road are quite scenic as the road descends the mountain. After the dogleg right at Ironaton Road, then left onto Highway 385 (Turns 11 and 12), the route follows the edge of the mountain and the edge of the national forest for another 4.4 miles.

At McElderry Road (Turn 13), the route goes just 0.5 miles before Turn 14 onto Cheaha Road begins to climb back up the mountain. The next 9.8 miles of Cheaha Road—which is simply one tight curve after another—had several potentially dangerous spots due to loose gravel on the roadway at the time of this writing, so be careful here.

About 8.5 miles up Cheaha Road is the right-hand turn down to Lake Chinnabee (closed in winter). If the gate is open, it's a nice 1.5-mile side trip off the route to a lake built by the Civilian Conservation Corps in the 1930s. Chinnabee has both a picnic area and a small self-service, semi-primitive campground. From the picnic area, the Silent Warrior Trail follows Cheaha Creek upstream for an easy half mile, fifteen-minute hike to Devils Den Waterfalls, which are among the most beautiful in the state.

Back on the route, the next turn at Duck Nest Motorway is only about a mile past the turn to Chinnabee (Turn 15). This well-maintained gravel road connects to McIntosh Road after 7.6 miles and is the last gravel road on this ride. For ATVs and dirt bikes only, the Kentuck ORV (Off-Road Vehicle) Area can be accessed from this road.

Adams Gap, in the Mount Cheaha area

After turning right at McIntosh Road (Turn 16), after three miles keep right to stay on McIntosh. This is followed by two quick right turns onto County Road 106/Friendship Road for 0.4 miles, then onto County Road 45, which becomes County Road 24 when entering Cleburne County. After 3.5 miles the route turns left toward Highway 281. The remaining 9.7 miles back to Cheaha State Park on Highway 281 skirt along one of the highest ridges in the state.

Cruising through the Talladega National Forest

Cheaha State Park, Talladega National Forest Road Ride

Approximately 94 miles
Riding time 4–5 hours

Start/End GPS Coordinates:
33°28'37.72"N
85°48'29.72"W

AS MENTIONED IN THE PREVIOUS ride loop (Ride Loop 26: Cheaha State Park Dual-Sport Ride), the areas in and around Mount Cheaha provide a smorgasbord of motorcycling pleasures for any kind of bike or rider. This ninety-four-mile loop is aimed at riders of street-oriented motorcycles and covers some of the best roads that Alabama has to offer.

Starting at the camp store parking lot at Cheaha State Park, the fun begins immediately when you head north on Highway 281, which follows the ridgelines of the Talladega Mountains.

After about ten miles, the route leaves Highway 281 and goes 0.4 miles east on Highway 24 before turning back south on Abel Road (Turns 2, 3, and 4). Turn 2 is onto a loop-around off the scenic motorway that connects to 24 after 0.2 miles. Abel Road parallels Highway 281 back to Highway 49 (Turn 5).

An alternate route would be to turn off Highway 281 after the first 3.4 miles onto Highway 49 to ride the fun and steep curving descent 1.2 miles back to Abel Road. Take a left on Abel Road and follow it to Highway 24, then back on Highway 281 to Highway 49, and ride one of the best segments of Highway 49 a second time.

Highest point in Alabama in Cheaha State Park

Once at the intersection of Abel Road and Highway 49, you'll almost due south for 12.9 miles into Lineville over very well-maintained asphalt with lots of swift, sweeping turns as the route bobs in and out of hills and woodland.

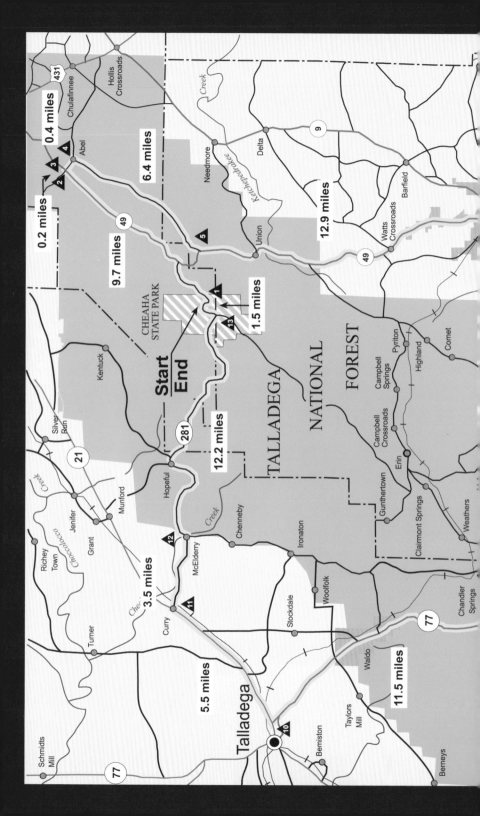

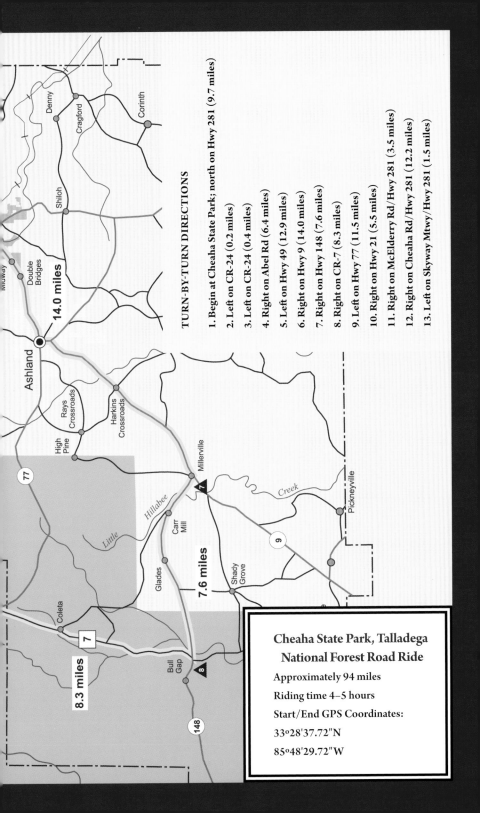

TURN-BY-TURN DIRECTIONS

1. Begin at Cheaha State Park; north on Hwy 281 (9.7 miles)
2. Left on CR-24 (0.2 miles)
3. Left on CR-24 (0.4 miles)
4. Right on Abel Rd (6.4 miles)
5. Left on Hwy 49 (12.9 miles)
6. Right on Hwy 9 (14.0 miles)
7. Right on Hwy 148 (7.6 miles)
8. Right on CR-7 (8.3 miles)
9. Left on Hwy 77 (11.5 miles)
10. Right on Hwy 21 (5.5 miles)
11. Right on McElderry Rd/Hwy 281 (3.5 miles)
12. Right on Cheaha Rd/Hwy 281 (12.2 miles)
13. Left on Skyway Mtwy/Hwy 281 (1.5 miles)

Cheaha State Park, Talladega National Forest Road Ride

Approximately 94 miles

Riding time 4–5 hours

Start/End GPS Coordinates:

33o28'37.72"N

85o48'29.72"W

Mount Cheaha overlook

At Lineville (Turn 6), the route joins Highway 9 for fourteen miles, passing through the Clay County seat at Ashland, where a picturesque courthouse square has been preserved.

Turn 7 at Millerville puts you on Highway 148 for 7.6 miles to just below Bull Gap on Rebecca Mountain, where County Road 7 intersects 148 (Turn 8).

From there, Highway 7 follows the foot of Horn Mountain 8.3 miles to Highway 77 at Turn 9. After about six miles on Highway 77, you'll pass a restaurant just before crossing Talladega Creek; behind the restaurant is what remains of the old Waldo Covered Bridge. It still sits on its foundations, but the roadway approaches have been removed.

Traveling a stretch of Alabama Highway 281 near Cheaha State Park

From there, Highway 77 goes into the city of Talladega, where the route turns northeast for 5.5 miles on Highway 21 (Turn 10). The next turn, McElderry Road/Highway 281, connects to Cheaha Road/Highway 281 and ascends the western flank of Mount Cheaha over 12.2 miles of extremely crooked road.

Unfortunately, at the time of this writing, the road had recently been given a coat of tar and gravel (not asphalt) surface, and it's not uncommon for loose gravel to be in turns at inopportune moments, so be careful!

Cheaha Road joins the Skyway Motorway/Highway 281 just 1.5 miles south of the starting point at the state park.

Mount Cheaha Ridges Dual-Sport Ride

Approximately 86 miles
Riding time 5–6 hours

Start/End GPS Coordinates:
33°28'37.72"N
85°48'29.72"W

I'M ALWAYS AMAZED AT THE variety of great motorcycling roads in the Mount Cheaha/Talladega National Forest areas. This is the third route in this book that begins and ends at Cheaha State Park, and each of the three offers a distinctly unique experience.

This all-day, eighty-six-mile route should be attempted only by those with true dual-sport motorcycles and a bit of experience riding over rough terrain. If making this ride after a hard rain, I would highly recommend knobby tires.

Whereas the other dual-sport ride for this area (Ride Loop 26: Cheaha State Park Dual-Sport Ride) included about thirteen miles of unpaved road over its eighty-five-mile length, this ride stays off the pavement for more than fifty of the eighty-six total miles.

Leaving the state park on Highway 281, this route continues straight after seven miles where the pavement ends at Adams Gap and Forest Service Road 602 begins.

The first three sections of gravel road stay up high on ridges of the Talladega Mountains and then Horn Mountain.

The first five miles of gravel are very mild because the road was reworked by the Forest Service in 2007. But after crossing Gunthertown Road at Clairmont Gap, the next five miles to Uniontown Road

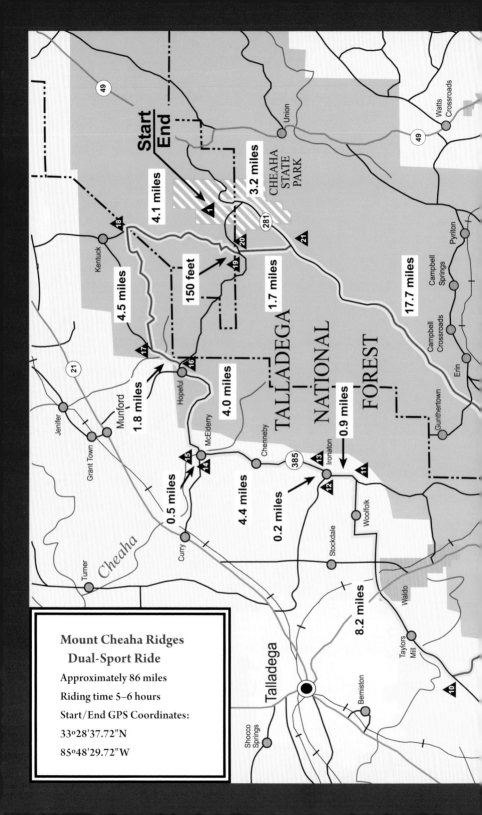

Start
End

4.1 miles

3.2 miles

CHEAHA STATE PARK

4.5 miles

150 feet

1.7 miles

17.7 miles

1.8 miles

4.0 miles

TALLADEGA NATIONAL FOREST

0.9 miles

0.5 miles

4.4 miles

0.2 miles

8.2 miles

Mount Cheaha Ridges
Dual-Sport Ride
Approximately 86 miles
Riding time 5–6 hours
Start/End GPS Coordinates:
33°28'37.72"N
85°48'29.72"W

Union
Watts Crossroads
49
49
281
21
Kentuck
18
20
19
16
17
Hopeful
Munford
21
Jenifer
Grant Town
McElderry
15
14
Chenneby
385
13
Ironaton
11
12
Woolfolk
Curry
Turner
Cheaha
Stockdale
Bemiston
Waldo
Talladega
Taylors Mill
10
Shocco Springs
Pyriton
Campbell Springs
Campbell Crossroads
Erin
Gunthertown

TURN-BY-TURN DIRECTIONS

1. Begin at Cheaha State Park; south on Hwy 281 (17.7 miles)—pavement ends after 7miles and becomes FS-602
2. Right on Horn Mtn Rd (1.4 miles)
3. Right on Hwy 77 (400 feet)
4. Left on Horn Mtn Rd/Skyway Mtwy/CR-6000-1 (13.9 miles)
5. Right on Hwy 148 (150 feet)
6. Right on Rocky Mt Church Rd/FS-616 (0.8 miles)
7. Right on New Rocky Mt Church Rd/FS-615 (5.6 miles)
8. Right to stay on New Rocky Mt Church Rd/FS-615 (3.2 miles)
9. Right on Germany Mtn Rd/CR-234 (7.1 miles)
10. Right on Berney Station Rd/FS-303—becomes Woolfolk Rd (8.2 miles)
11. Left on Cemetery Mtn Rd (0.9 miles)
12. Right on Ironaton Rd (0.2 miles)
13. Left on Hwy 385 (4.4 miles)
14. Right on McElderry Rd (0.5 miles)
15. Right on Cheaha Rd (4.0 miles)
16. Left on Salt Creek Rd (1.8 miles)
17. Right to stay on Salt Creek Rd (4.5 miles)
18. Right on Duck Nest Mtwy (4.1 miles)
19. Left on Cheaha Rd (150 feet)
20. Right on Skyway Mtwy/FS-603 (1.7 miles)
21. Left on Hwy 281 (3.2 miles)

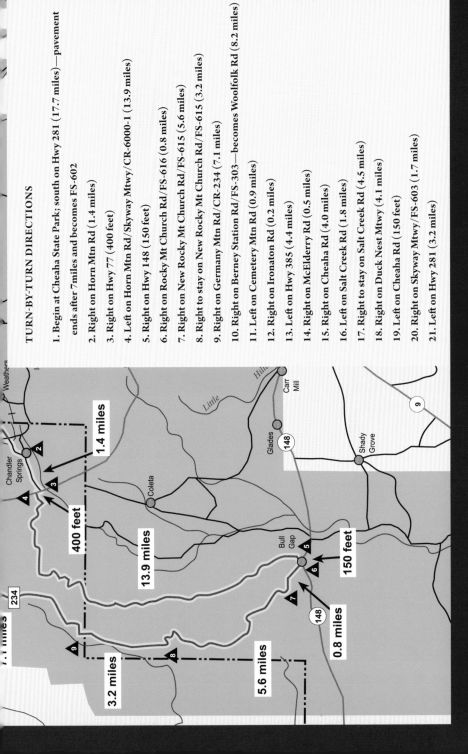

at Chandler Springs are noticeably rougher and have numerous ruts and exposed rocks.

At Turn 2 there's about 1.4 miles of pavement over to Highway 77, where the route crosses to Horn Mountain Road. Turns 3 and 4 indicate a short offset where you have to about four hundred feet north on Highway 77 before going left on Horn Mountain Road/ Skyway Motorway/County Road 6000-1.

The section across Horn Mountain is almost fourteen miles on the Skyway Motorway from Highway 77 to Highway 148, mostly atop the high ridge of the mountain. After 3.6 miles, there is a rocky overlook to the right facing west that's actually a very nice campsite. Sunsets can be beautiful from here.

At the 5.1-mile mark on Skyway Motorway, the turn for an old fire-spotting tower occurs. The access road is gated, and every time but one that I've been there the gate has been open; but if closed, I'd strongly advise not riding around it, as the authorities frown on such behavior. When open, this is a nice place for a lunch break, and even though the abandoned fire tower is fenced off, there's a restored log pavilion—originally built by the Civilian Conservation Corps (CCC)—and great views toward Sylacauga, Winterboro, and Talladega from a vantage point of nearly two thousand feet, the highest for miles around.

Within a few miles after passing the fire tower, the road condition deteriorates to include ruts that must be maneuvered carefully as well as deep and long mud holes after a few days of rain. This is probably the trickiest section of the entire loop.

A note here: when groups are making this ride, and one or more riders aren't sure about traveling the Horn Mountain section, an alternate route for those riders can be either Horn's Valley Road (grav-

Above: A gravel road on the Mount Cheaha Ridges Dual-Sport Ride

Left: Camping on Horn Mountain

el) or County Road 7 (paved), both of which parallel the mountain's eastern side. Then those riders can meet up with the rest of the group at Bull Gap, where the Skyway Motorway comes out of the woods briefly before descending the west side of the mountain on Rocky Mount Church Road (Turns 6 and 7) to begin another gravel road section of 16.7 miles northward.

After just 0.8 miles on Rocky Mount Church Road, the route turns right onto New Rocky Mount Church Road (Turn 7) and right again after 5.6 miles to stay on the same road (Turn 8).

In another 3.2 miles, the route takes a right turn at Germany Mountain Road/County Road 234 (Turn 9) and follows it 7.1 miles to Berney Station Road.

After crossing Highway 77, Berney Station Road becomes Woolfolk Road before intersecting into Cemetery Mountain Road at Turn 11.

From here to Cheaha Road (Turns 12 to 15), the route follows the western boundary of the national forest at the foot of Mount Cheaha on paved roads.

After four miles on Cheaha Road, the final twelve-mile stretch of gravel begins at Salt Creek Road (Turn 16) and continues on Duck Nest Motorway (Turn 18) back to the Skyway Motorway and Highway 281 (Turn 21) and 3.2 miles of pavement back to the state park starting point.

Sunrise over a campsite in the Talladega National Forest

Oak Mountain, Highway 25, Montevallo Ride

Approximately 130 miles

Riding time 3–4 hours

Start/End GPS Coordinates:

33º20'12.49"N

86º46'46.94"W

BEGINNING AND TERMINATING AT Exit 246 on Interstate 65 near Oak Mountain State Park, this 130-mile ride includes more than sixty miles of Highway 25 through the middle of Alabama, then crosses the Cahaba River, passes near Tannehill State Park, and returns to the start.

The first leg of this route heads northeast 18.1 miles on Highway 119 and, after 5.8 miles, passes an entrance to Oak Mountain State Park on the right.

Just before Leeds, the route turns right on Elliot Lane (Turn 2), and after 1.6 miles joins Highway 25 (Turn 3).

As mentioned earlier in the description of Ride Loop 25: Cook Springs, Logan Martin Dam, Highway 25 Ride, this first part of Highway 25 is sometimes called the "Tail of the Lizard" because it has sections of tight turns reminiscent of the Tail of the Dragon on U.S. Highway 129 at Deal's Gap, in North Carolina—a world-famous motorcycling road and destination. The first seven miles into Vandiver have the greatest concentration of twisty curves as Highway 25 climbs and crosses Coosa Mountain at Wyatt's Gap. Over the next seven miles, the landscape flattens out and the road becomes a series of nice sweepers through mostly farmland into Vincent.

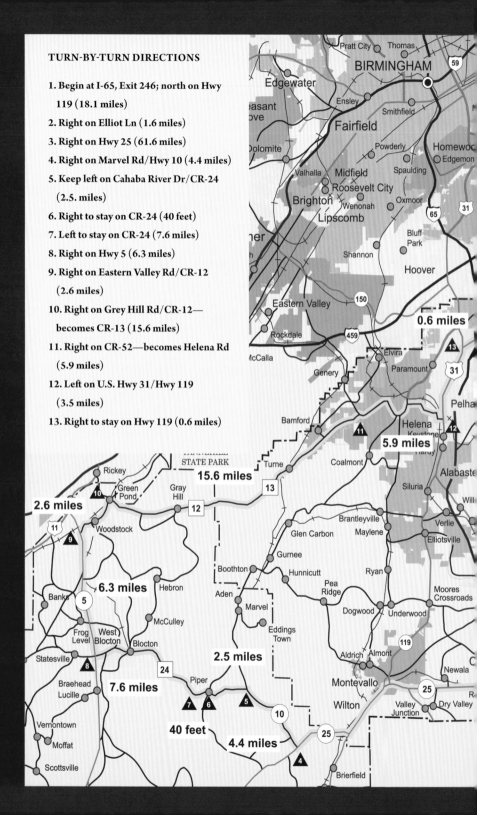

TURN-BY-TURN DIRECTIONS

1. Begin at I-65, Exit 246; north on Hwy 119 (18.1 miles)
2. Right on Elliot Ln (1.6 miles)
3. Right on Hwy 25 (61.6 miles)
4. Right on Marvel Rd/Hwy 10 (4.4 miles)
5. Keep left on Cahaba River Dr/CR-24 (2.5. miles)
6. Right to stay on CR-24 (40 feet)
7. Left to stay on CR-24 (7.6 miles)
8. Right on Hwy 5 (6.3 miles)
9. Right on Eastern Valley Rd/CR-12 (2.6 miles)
10. Right on Grey Hill Rd/CR-12— becomes CR-13 (15.6 miles)
11. Right on CR-52—becomes Helena Rd (5.9 miles)
12. Left on U.S. Hwy 31/Hwy 119 (3.5 miles)
13. Right to stay on Hwy 119 (0.6 miles)

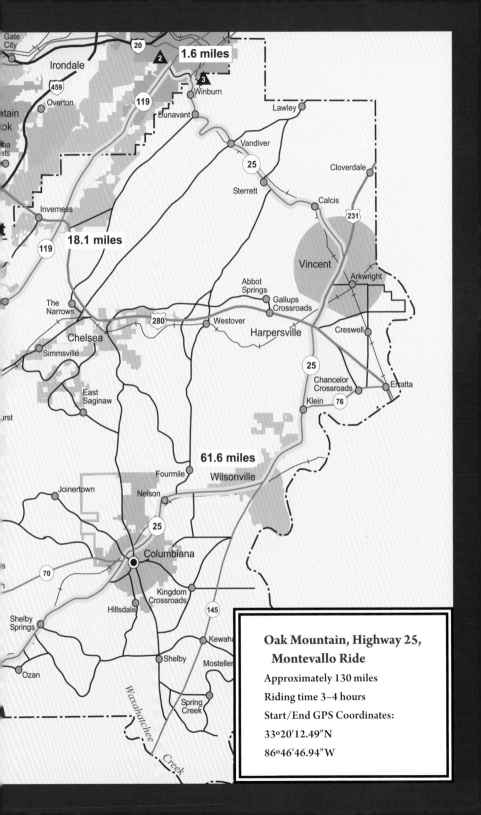

1.6 miles

18.1 miles

61.6 miles

Gate City
Irondale
Overton
Winburn
Lawley
Dunavant
Vandiver
Cloverdale
Sterrett
Calcis
Inverness
Vincent
Arkwright
Abbot Springs
Gallups Crossroads
The Narrows
Westover
Harpersville
Creswell
Chelsea
Simmsville
East Saginaw
Chancelor Crossroads
Klein
Erratta
Fourmile
Wilsonville
Joinertown
Nelson
Columbiana
Kingdom Crossroads
Hillsdale
Kewaha
Shelby Springs
Shelby
Mosteller
Ozan
Spring Creek

Waxahatchee Creek

Oak Mountain, Highway 25, Montevallo Ride

Approximately 130 miles

Riding time 3–4 hours

Start/End GPS Coordinates:

33º20'12.49"N

86º46'46.94"W

Entrance to the Cahaba River National Wildlife Refuge, especially worth visiting in late spring

The next forty-five miles of Highway 25 cuts south and west through Wilsonville, Columbiana, Calera, and Montevallo to Turn 4 at Marvel Road. Especially in the towns, pay special attention to signs to stay on Highway 25.

After 4.4 miles, the route turns left on Cahaba River Drive/County Road 24 (Turn 5), and after 4.8 miles—just after crossing the Cahaba River—you'll see a sign marking the entrance for the Cahaba River National Wildlife Refuge.

If riding this route from mid-May to mid-June, you may want to take a left on the gravel road that begins at the sign. After 0.3 miles, the road follows the Cahaba River for about 1.4 miles, and in late spring the shoals are full of blooming Cahaba lilies, which are found only in this and a few other similar streams in the Southeast. The gravel road is usually well kept but could be a challenge after a hard rain for some larger or heavier street bikes.

Coke ovens that helped power the mining/steel industry in the West Blocton area

Overgrown coke oven batteries near West Blocton

Back on route, continue another 5.3 miles to Highway 5 at West Blocton (Turn 8). At 3.7 miles after crossing the Cahaba River, on the right is a road that goes out to some abandoned coke oven batteries that were part of the mining/steel industry in the West Blocton area.

After traveling Highway 5 for 6.3 miles, the ride begins its final sections at turns 10 and 11, turning east at Green Pond (just south of Tannehill State Park) and following Grey Hill Road, which becomes County Road 13, for 15.6 miles, and then County Road 52 for 5.9 miles back to U.S. Highway 31/Highway 119 at Alabaster (Turn 12). At that turn, you have only a final four miles to get back to the starting point.

Chilton, Talladega, Coosa Counties Ride

Approximately 94 miles
Riding time 4–5 hours

Start/End GPS Coordinates:
32°48'06.98"N
86°34'48.79"W

THIS NINETY-FOUR-MILE RIDE makes a loop tour of eastern Chilton, western Coosa, and southern Talladega counties, crossing the Coosa River twice just downstream but within sight of both Mitchell and Lay dams.

Except for the initial and final few miles around Clanton, where there will be moderate traffic, the majority of the ride passes through some of the least populated areas in Alabama.

Beginning at Exit 205 on Interstate 65, the ride follows Highway 22/S. Highway 31 for four miles before turning left on Highway 22. After six miles you'll cross the Coosa River just below Mitchell Dam and enter into Coosa County for another 6.8 miles to Kellys Crossroads at County Road 29 (Turn 3).

Riding County Road 29, it's not hard to imagine going back in time to the 1950s as the road winds over rolling hills through pine and hardwood forests toward Weogufka. Along this section, nature has slowly reclaimed a number of abandoned farmhouses and covered them in vines. Be particularly watchful for deer along this road. I have found on my rides through this area that it's almost a surprise *not* to see a deer or several deer crossing the road.

The tiny town of Weogufka is a fine example of a crossroads with

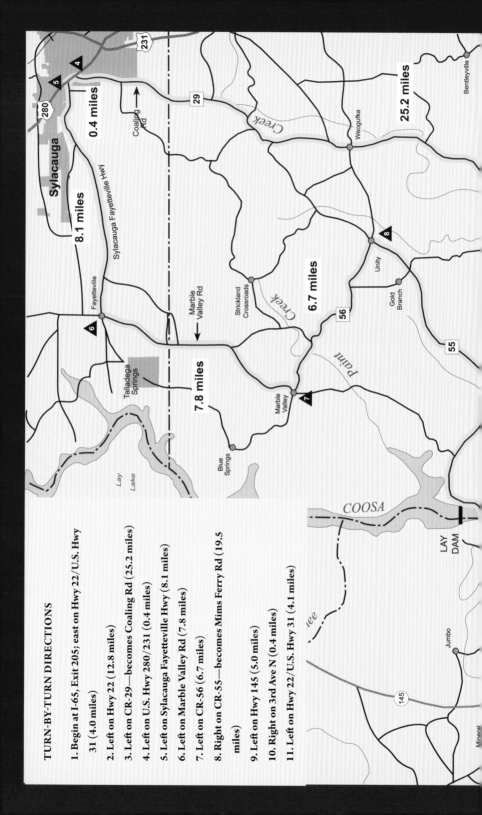

TURN-BY-TURN DIRECTIONS

1. Begin at I-65, Exit 205; east on Hwy 22/U.S. Hwy 31 (4.0 miles)

2. Left on Hwy 22 (12.8 miles)

3. Left on CR-29—becomes Coaling Rd (25.2 miles)

4. Left on U.S. Hwy 280/231 (0.4 miles)

5. Left on Sylacauga Fayetteville Hwy (8.1 miles)

6. Left on Marble Valley Rd (7.8 miles)

7. Left on CR-56 (6.7 miles)

8. Right on CR-55—becomes Mims Ferry Rd (19.5 miles)

9. Left on Hwy 145 (5.0 miles)

10. Right on 3rd Ave N (0.4 miles)

11. Left on Hwy 22/U.S. Hwy 31 (4.1 miles)

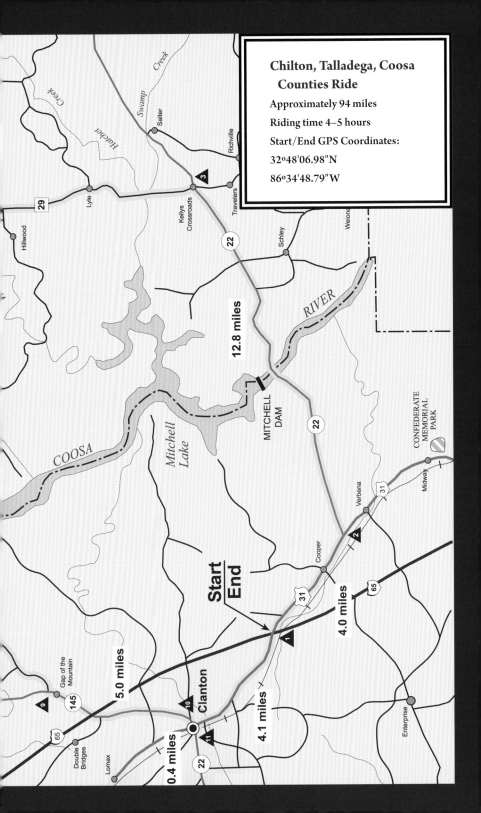

Chilton, Talladega, Coosa Counties Ride

Approximately 94 miles

Riding time 4–5 hours

Start/End GPS Coordinates:

32°48'06.98"N

86°34'48.79"W

four stores and little else, all dating back to the early twentieth century. If it's open, Caperton's Old South Store here is a unique experience.

From Weogufka, County Road 29 continues northward another eleven miles or so into Sylacauga (Turn 4), where the route briefly joins U.S. Highway 280/231 for 0.4 miles to Sylacauga Fayetteville Highway (Turn 5).

The next 8.1 miles to Fayetteville take you past Gantt's Quarry, where Sylacauga marble is taken from a deep pit. At a railroad crossing you'll see gigantic blocks of marble along the tracks to the left and right that were off-loaded more than forty years ago.

At Fayetteville the route heads south on Marble Valley Road (Turn 6) and through wide-open pastures and farmland for almost eight miles. You'll want to watch carefully for the left turn from Mar-

Crossing Weogufka Creek at Horsestomp Ford

ble Valley onto County Road 56 (Turn 7), as it is easy to miss.

The 6.7 miles on County Road 56 are characterized by a twisty, crooked road with pavement that varies in quality from okay to quite rough.

At Unity (Turn 8), the road turns southwest on County Road 55 toward the Coosa River and crosses it just below Lay Dam to reenter Chilton County. The twelve miles on this section pass through an area so remote that it's not uncommon at all to ride it without seeing another vehicle. Again—watch for deer here!

At the river, the road name changes to Mims Ferry Road and goes another 7.7 miles before reaching Highway 145 (Turn 9).

From this point the traffic density picks up considerably as the route crosses I-65 and returns to Clanton on Highway 145 to complete the loop on Highway 31 (Turns 10 and 11).

PART V

RIDES IN SOUTHWEST ALABAMA
Ride Loops 31–40

Boligee, Demopolis, Cuba Ride

Approximately 114 miles

Riding time 4–5 hours

Start/End Point GPS Coordinates:

32°47'48.03"N

88°01'51.79"W

THIS 114-MILE RIDE LOOP WEAVES in and out of the Tombigbee and lower Black Warrior river basins, through the unlikely-named towns of Cuba and Moscow, and past more than a half mile of quirky sculptures made from stylized rolls of hay and other common materials. Along the way the route also passes several stately antebellum-era plantation houses.

Beginning at Exit 32 on Interstate 20/59 at Lizzieville, the ride heads southeast through Boligee for 14.8 miles to Forkland on Highway 20.

At about the tenth mile of this leg, on the left you'll encounter an antebellum plantation house and schoolhouse on the same property, the Thornhill Plantation. Two more plantation homes, Rosemount Plantation and Strawberry Hill Plantation, lie a couple of miles farther down Highway 20. An antebellum-era tavern is situated at mile 14, and to the left about a block is the historic St. John's-in-the-Prairies Episcopal Church, established in 1834, both in the Forkland community.

When you've traveled about 1.7 miles after Turn 2 onto Highway 43, look to the right side of the road to see one of the most unusual displays in Alabama—or anywhere. For more than a half mile along

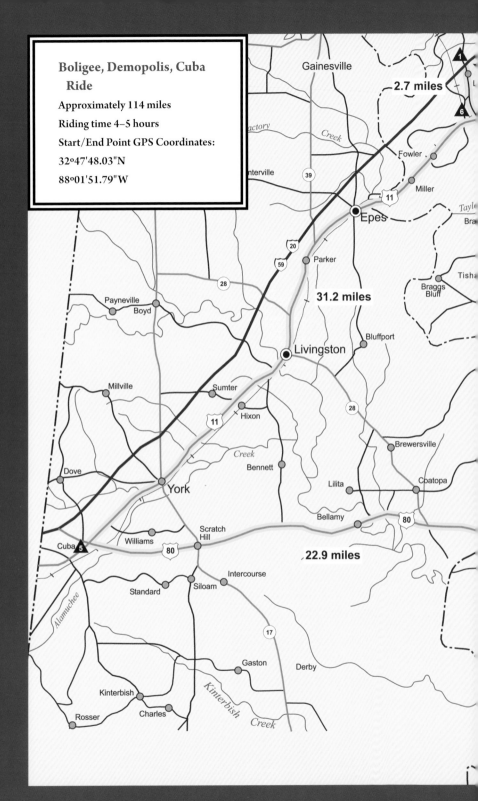

Boligee, Demopolis, Cuba Ride

Approximately 114 miles

Riding time 4–5 hours

Start/End Point GPS Coordinates:

32º47'48.03"N

88º01'51.79"W

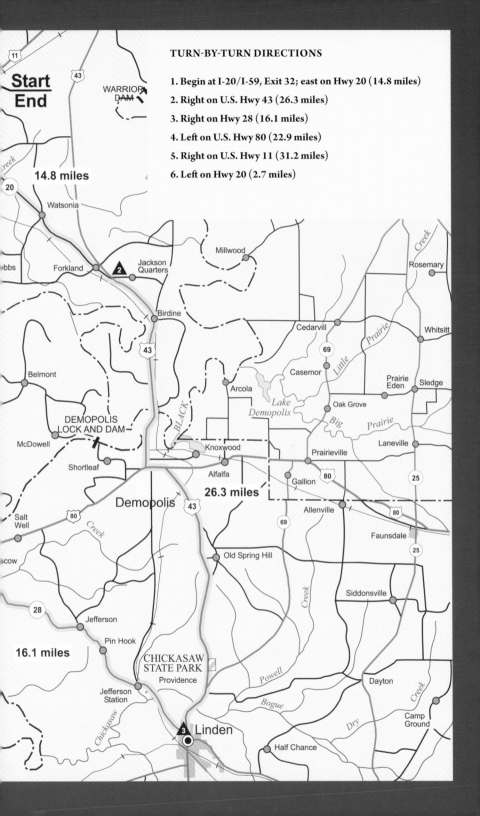

TURN-BY-TURN DIRECTIONS

1. Begin at I-20/I-59, Exit 32; east on Hwy 20 (14.8 miles)
2. Right on U.S. Hwy 43 (26.3 miles)
3. Right on Hwy 28 (16.1 miles)
4. Left on U.S. Hwy 80 (22.9 miles)
5. Right on U.S. Hwy 11 (31.2 miles)
6. Left on Hwy 20 (2.7 miles)

The driveway entrance to Jim Bird's sculpture field, along Highway 43

a field that fronts the road, you will see Jim Bird's whimsical and unique hay roll and scrap metal sculptures. Bird's driveway entrance has a menagerie of these characters made from whatever he no longer needed on the farm. A primitive wooden arch over the drive with "BIRD" spelled in four-foot-high bentwood letters confirms this is the place. The sculptures include characters such as Snoopy from the Peanuts comic strip, a real sailboat with hay rolls for ocean waves, and Sesame Street characters, among others. The most prominent is a forty-foot-high Tin Man from *The Wizard of Oz*. Bird once told me that the Tin Man was the only one he spent more than five dollars to make, and that was only because he had to buy the silver paint, which cost him forty dollars.

Continuing south, Highway 43 crosses the Black Warrior River just outside Demopolis. In the annual holiday tradition called Christmas on the River, lighted and decorated boats form a Christmas parade on the water. Bluff Hall, situated directly on the east bank of the Tombigbee River, tells a fascinating story of the Vine and Olive Colony (Napoleonic expatriates) that settled here.

Also in Demopolis, just 0.3 miles north of the Highway 43/U.S. Highway 80 intersection (pay special attention to signage here to stay on 43), is another antebellum mansion, Gaineswood, which was said to be the finest neoclassical house in the state in 1861 when it finally completed its twenty-year transformation from a rough-hewn log cabin. Tours of the house are available.

Continuing south on Highway 43, 6.6 miles after crossing U.S. Highway 80 at Demopolis, you'll come to another plantation mansion, but seeing this one requires a sharp left turn at Highway 1. Allen Grove, a Greek Revival plantation house completed in 1857, lies 0.9 miles down the road on the left.

The route continues south for another eight miles past Old Spring Hill to Linden, where it joins Highway 28 (Turn 3). At the historic community of Jefferson, two Greek Revival churches still stand and remain in use, one of them founded in 1820 by four Revolutionary War heroes buried in the church cemetery. Sixteen miles northwest of Linden, at Moscow, the route joins U.S. Highway 80 (Turn 4) for 22.9 miles into Cuba.

At Cuba (Turn 5), the route turns northeast for 31.2 miles on U.S. Highway 11. Along this stretch, you will catch glimpses of the grayish-white Selma chalk formation that underlies most of the Black Belt lands and lends its limy character to the soil. After about twenty-three miles, at Epes, just before the bridge crossing the Tombigbee

River, you'll find Fort Tombigbee, built by the French in 1735. Faint traces of the site still remain for the adventurous explorer.

About seven miles north of Epes is Main Street in Boligee, where north-south and east-west railroad lines intersect. An interesting old general store was here at one time, but now the town essentially encompasses city hall, the post office, a fire department, and a walking trail. On a hill to the right stand St. Mark's Episcopal Church and Friendship Baptist Church, both featuring bell towers as well as paired entrances that were used to separate male and female worshippers. Note the beautiful stained-glass windows of St. Mark's Episcopal Church, founded in 1852.

From Boligee, stay on Highway 11 until the route rejoins Highway 20 and backtracks to the starting point at the interstate.

Jim Bird's Snoopy sculpture

Left: The massive head of Bird's forty-foot-high Tin Man

Below: Bird's Tin Man sculpture, paying homage to *The Wizard of Oz*

Bladon Springs, St. Stephens Ride

Approximately 78 miles
Riding time 3–4 hours

Start/End Point GPS Coordinates:
31°44'05.92"N
88°11'58.86"W

THE STATE PARK AT BLADON SPRINGS has to be one of the smallest anywhere, but it does include campsites and picnic facilities as well as restrooms. This park is built around four mineral springs with concrete sunken pools run by manual pumps where guests once soaked in the supposedly curative mineral waters. In its heyday, it was a popular resort destination. Today it's usually not staffed all day, and the last time I visited I didn't see another person in more than an hour.

Actually, I much prefer the camping at Old St. Stephens Historical Park, whose turnoff you'll find at about the halfway point of this seventy-eight-mile ride. The park has better camping facilities at more reasonable rates and a camp store for necessities. There is also fishing, boating, and swimming in summer at Old St. Stephens, which was the little-known location of the Alabama territorial capital in the early nineteenth century.

Surprisingly, the roads in this part of the state are not entirely lacking curves due to the necessity to route in and around various rivers, creeks, and bayous.

This route begins and ends at Bladon Springs State Park. From the park, the first leg heads east on Bladon Road for 3.7 miles to U.S.

Church at Bladon Springs

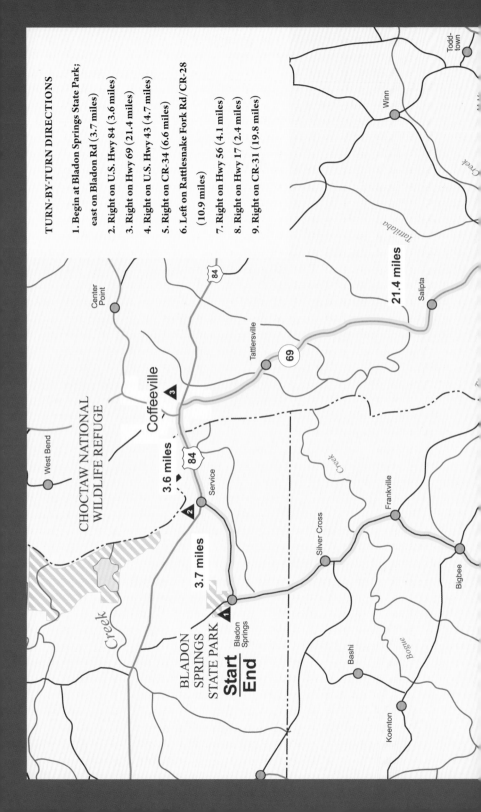

TURN-BY-TURN DIRECTIONS

1. Begin at Bladon Springs State Park; east on Bladon Rd (3.7 miles)
2. Right on U.S. Hwy 84 (3.6 miles)
3. Right on Hwy 69 (21.4 miles)
4. Right on U.S. Hwy 43 (4.7 miles)
5. Right on CR-34 (6.6 miles)
6. Left on Rattlesnake Fork Rd/CR-28 (10.9 miles)
7. Right on Hwy 56 (4.1 miles)
8. Right on Hwy 17 (2.4 miles)
9. Right on CR-31 (19.8 miles)

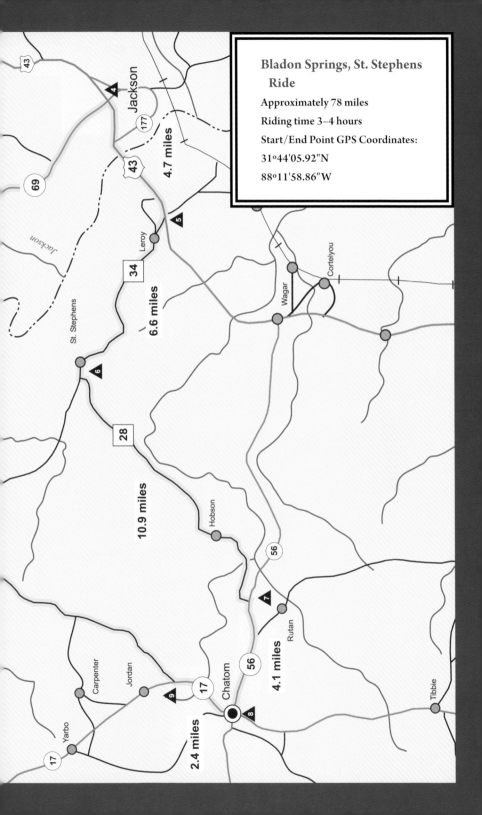

Bladon Springs, St. Stephens Ride

Approximately 78 miles

Riding time 3–4 hours

Start/End Point GPS Coordinates:

31º44'05.92"N

88º11'58.86"W

One of the pumps once used for springwater bathing at
Bladon Springs State Park

Highway 84 (Turn 2), where it joins that road for another 3.6 miles
to Turn 3 at Highway 69 about a mile after crossing the Tombigbee
River just south of Coffeeville.

The twenty-two-mile section between Coffeeville and Jackson
on Highway 69 weaves and winds through mostly low woodlands

Camping at Old St. Stephens Historical Park

with a surprising number of curves that seem tailor-made for the motorcycle. Here the road more or less parallels the river to its west a few miles as it heads southeast through the towns of Tattlersville and Salitpa.

At Jackson the route turns southwest on U.S. Highway 43 (Turn 4) and, after a couple of miles, crosses the Tombigbee again.

Just 2.7 miles after crossing the Tombigbee River, the route turns right onto County Road 34 at Leroy (Turn 5) and goes seven miles northwest toward the old city of St. Stephens.

Here (Turn 6), you'll turn left at Rattlesnake Fork Road/County Road 28. On the right about 0.7 miles before Turn 6 is the St. Stephens Museum, located in the old courthouse building for Washington County. Just a few hundred feet farther is Howell Road that forks to the right off County Road 34 where the St. Stephens United Methodist Church sits between the two roads. From there, signs show the way to the Old St. Stephens Historical Park about 2.5 miles off County Road 34.

Once a hub of commerce for south Alabama, St. Stephens sat astride the Federal Road and at one time boasted to have a population greater than that of Mobile. But by statehood in 1819, it was bypassed in favor of Cahawba as the first state capital, and today the town's buildings are gone and largely forgotten. There is an ongoing archaeological dig here.

Back on route, County Road 28 is a fun and twisting road through live oaks hanging with Spanish moss for almost eleven miles before it intersects with Highway 56 (Turn 7) outside Chatom.

After 4.1 miles into Chatom, the route joins Highway 17 for 2.4 miles at Turn 8, then goes right at Turn 9 onto County Road 31 through Bigbee and Frankville for almost twenty miles of fast-paced, sweeping, curvy road back to Bladon Springs.

Roland Cooper State Park, Davis Ferry Ride

Approximately 82 miles
Riding time 4–5 hours

Start/End Point GPS Coordinates:
32°02'43.29"N
87°14'46.46"W

THIS EIGHTY-TWO-MILE LOOP is the only ride in this book that must be done on a weekday. That's because Davis Ferry—which is probably the last of its type still operating in the southeastern United States—only runs Monday through Friday.

The entire loop runs through remote backwoods of Wilcox, Monroe, and Clarke counties, where there are few places to cross the Alabama River. So bypassing the ferry would mean an additional thirty miles to take the next bridge on U.S. Highway 84 at Claiborne.

I chose not to categorize this loop as a dual-sport motorcycle ride even though dirt roads make up two very brief sections on either side of the ferry landings. These are exceptionally well-maintained Perry County dirt roads that would be no problem for any family sedan, sports car, or street bike to navigate.

The loop begins and returns to Roland Cooper State Park on the Alabama River's Dannelly Reservoir northeast of Camden. The first two sections bring you into east Camden to connect with Highway 41 south—a very nice motorcycle road for this part of the state with numerous fast, sweeping turns over hilly terrain. You'll enjoy the 23.3 miles on Highway 41; and just before the Franklin community, the route turns right onto County Road 17 (Turn 4).

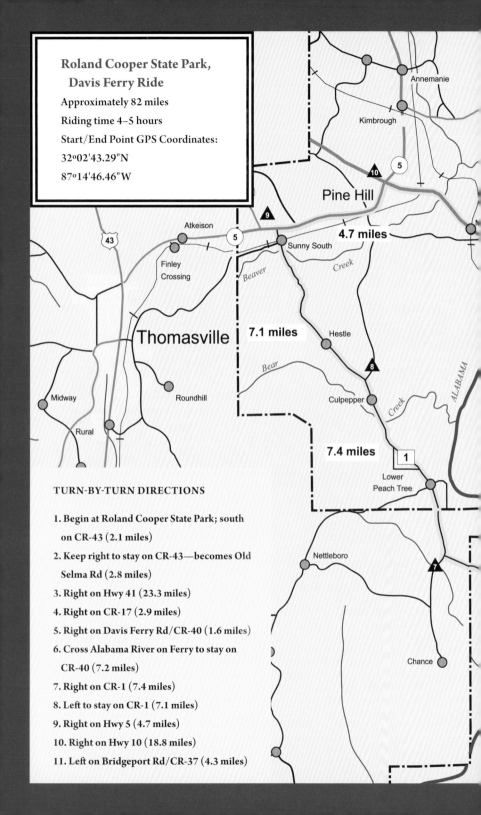

Roland Cooper State Park, Davis Ferry Ride

Approximately 82 miles

Riding time 4–5 hours

Start/End Point GPS Coordinates:

32°02'43.29"N

87°14'46.46"W

TURN-BY-TURN DIRECTIONS

1. Begin at Roland Cooper State Park; south on CR-43 (2.1 miles)
2. Keep right to stay on CR-43—becomes Old Selma Rd (2.8 miles)
3. Right on Hwy 41 (23.3 miles)
4. Right on CR-17 (2.9 miles)
5. Right on Davis Ferry Rd/CR-40 (1.6 miles)
6. Cross Alabama River on Ferry to stay on CR-40 (7.2 miles)
7. Right on CR-1 (7.4 miles)
8. Left to stay on CR-1 (7.1 miles)
9. Right on Hwy 5 (4.7 miles)
10. Right on Hwy 10 (18.8 miles)
11. Left on Bridgeport Rd/CR-37 (4.3 miles)

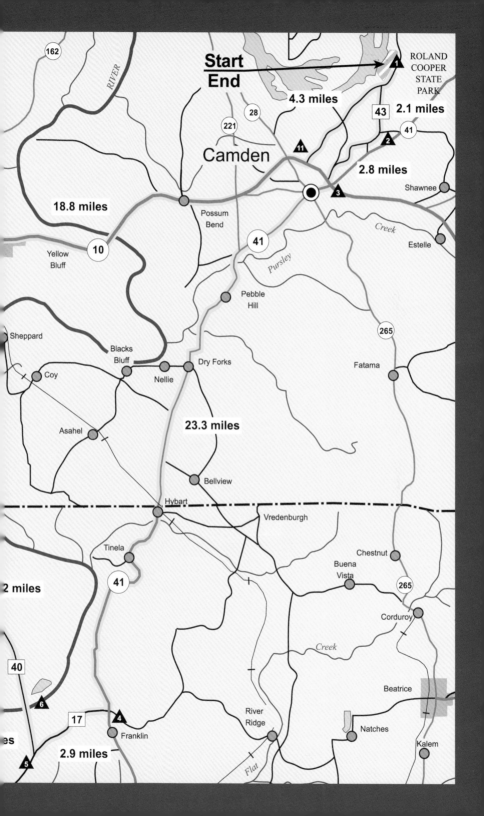

Davis Ferry, crossing the Alabama River

After 2.9 miles on County Road 17, Turn 5 will take you to Davis Ferry Road, a road that is 1.6 miles of almost manicured dirt down to the ferry landing.

County Road 40 in Monroe County, a fun dirt road

As mentioned above, the ferry does not operate on Saturdays or Sundays. It also does not operate from noon to 1 p.m. on weekdays, when the two ferry operators eat lunch. Once, we had the misfortune to arrive on the north side of the river at just about 12:05 p.m. We could see the ferryboat on the other side and the operators, but the ferry's motor didn't come to life until 1 p.m. sharp, when it motored across the river to pick us up.

Some readers may have never seen a ferry like this one. It is just long enough for two cars or pickup trucks at a time and has wooden ramps that one of the crew must crank up and down at each bank using a modified boat trailer wench. Steel towers on each bank are connected by a heavy steel cable high above the three hundred yards of water, and the ferryboat is connected at two points to this cable by other cables and pulleys attached near the bow and stern of the boat.

Power is supplied by a six-cylinder motor and transmission from

Crossing the Alabama River on Davis Ferry

Downtown in the community of Sunny South

a 1960s-era pickup truck connected to a paddle wheel on the upstream side of the boat. To cross, the operator simply puts the transmission in low gear or reverse and the paddle wheel begins churning the boat across. There is no charge for taking the less-than-five-minute ride on the ferry, which is operated by Perry County. On one trip the ferry captain told me that the boat came from Gees Bend near Camden in the early 1960s after Wilcox County shut down that crossing.

I would urge riders to be extra cautious when boarding or exiting the ferry because sometimes the wooden ramps can be somewhat slippery. The best way I've found to board is to approach the ramp with just enough momentum to coast up the ramp and onto the

Curving along Alabama Highway 41 in Monroe County

boat. You don't want to go too slow and have the rear wheel of your cycle begin spinning. Trust me on this.

Once you reach the north shore of the river, the first mile of the road is dirt (but in very good shape). At 7.2 miles north of the river, the ferry road (County Road 40) tees into County Road 1 (Turn 7) and continues for fourteen miles through Lower Peach Tree to Sunny South at Highway 5 (Turn 9).

After 4.7 miles on Highway 5, the route joins Highway 10 east at Turn 10 and crosses the Alabama River again en route back to Camden and the starting point (Turn 11).

Paul M. Grist State Park, Selma, Camden Ride

Approximately 125 miles

Riding time 4–5 hours

Start/End Point GPS Coordinates:

32°35'27.68"N

87°00'00.52"W

THIS 125-MILE RIDE COVERS terrain ranging from the sleepy and historic Alabama River city of Selma, with its numerous antebellum-era homes and Spanish moss–draped live oaks, to the open-sky river landscape around Camden, to the forested hills just south of the Talladega National Forest above Selma. And for those who so choose, a ferry ride across the Alabama River at Gees Bend is also an option.

Beginning at Paul M. Grist State Park—where camping, picnicking, and fishing are available—between Maplesville and Selma, the route heads south and then east (Turns 2 and 3) to join Highway 22 after 2.8 miles.

The next 15.7-mile leg of the route continues south on Highway 22, which becomes Highway 80 at Selma, crossing the Alabama River on the historic Edmund Pettus Bridge before intersecting with Highway 41 at Turn 4.

While in Selma, a right turn to stay on Highway 22 will lead to the Old Town neighborhood after a few blocks. Antebellum and Victorian homes, many of which have been restored, seem to be everywhere. Another interesting place to visit while here is the Live Oak Cemetery, which is on your left just 0.7 miles after leaving Highway 80. William Rufus King, founder of Selma, U.S. senator, and vice

TURN-BY-TURN DIRECTIONS

1. Begin at Paul M. Grist State Park; south on CR-37 (1.1 miles)
2. Left on CR-222 (1.7 miles)
3. Right on Hwy 22—becomes Hwy 80 (15.7 miles)
4. Right on Hwy 41 (34.3 miles)
5. Right on Hwy 10 (2.0 miles)
6. Right on Hwy 28 (16.6 miles)
7. Right on Hwy 5 (28.2 miles)
8. Right on CR-38 (4.0 miles)
9. Right on CR-45 (1.7 miles)
10. Left on CR-6 (5.4 miles)
11. Right on Hwy 14 (0.3 miles)
12. Left on CR-6 (5.3 miles)
13. Right on Hwy 219 (0.5 miles)
14. Left on Centenary St/ CR-16 (2.8 miles)
15. Left on CR-37 (6.5 miles)

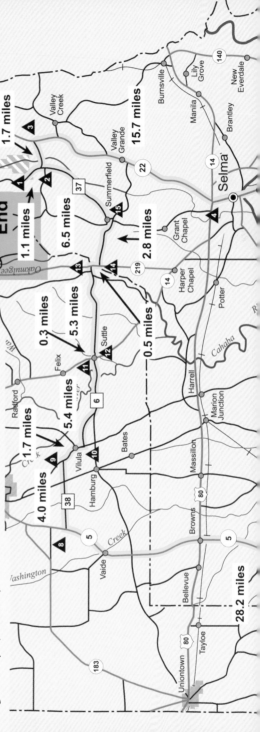

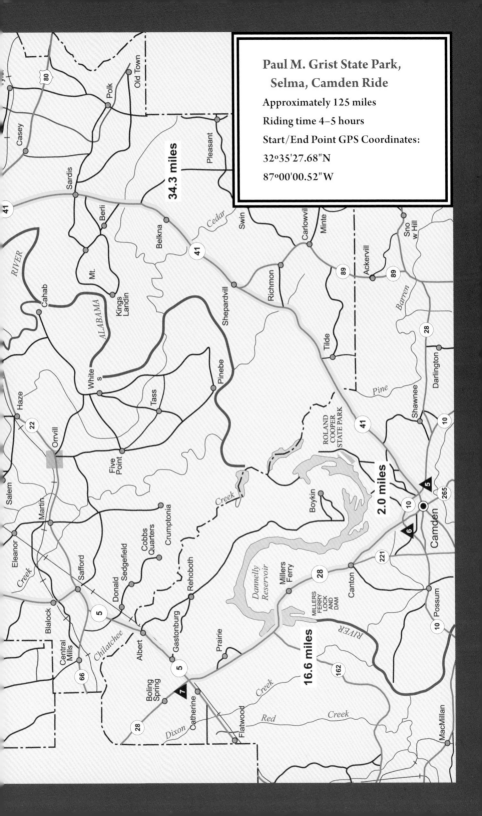

**Paul M. Grist State Park,
Selma, Camden Ride**

Approximately 125 miles

Riding time 4–5 hours

Start/End Point GPS Coordinates:

32º35'27.68"N

87º00'00.52"W

Pausing in the Old Town district of Selma

Riding under the beautiful Spanish moss at Live Oak Cemetery

Lake at Paul Grist State Park

president of the United States, is buried here. The cemetery is one of only a handful of Southern cemeteries listed on the National Registry of Historic Places. Its grounds are literally covered in sprawling oaks draped in Spanish moss. It's a nice, quiet place to stop and relax.

The 34.3-mile segment from Selma to Camden on Highway 41 quickly becomes a fine stretch for motorcycling, generally following ridgelines through farm country and woodland with many sweepers through a series of rolling hills.

At Camden you'll take a right (Turn 5) onto Highway 10 and then another quick right onto Highway 28 toward Millers Ferry and continue 16.6 miles northwest to Highway 5 at Catherine (Turn 7).

This is the section where the Gees Bend Ferry provides an optional route. After going 3.4 miles from Turn 5, look for Ellis Landing Road on the right and signs to the ferry landing.

The ferry, which was shut down for more than four decades, resumed operation with a new boat in 2006. It would be a good idea to check the ferry schedule before planning a trip. The ferry has a Web site with scheduling and fare information (www.geesbendferry.com). The departures from the Camden side of the river are scheduled for every hour and a half, but don't be surprised to have to wait a while for the next ferry crossing.

Once on the northern side of the river, continue north on Highway 29 until it connects with the mapped route at Highway 5.

Back on the mapped route at Catherine (Turn 7), the ride stays on Highway 5 for 28.2 miles almost to Marion. Then it begins a series of eastward sections back to the Paul M. Grist State Park starting point (Turns 8 to 15). Much of this final part follows winding country roads past small family farms alternating with heavily forested hills.

Calera, Montevallo, Centreville, Sprott, Maplesville Ride

Approximately 108 miles
Riding time 3–4 hours

Start/End Point GPS Coordinates:
33°06'12.16"N
86°44'19.23"W

THE 108 MILES OF THIS LOOP touch Shelby, Bibb, Perry, and Chilton counties and offer a sampling of landscapes that characterize the geographic center of the state. Roads on this ride pass through wide-open pastureland, through miles of farmland broken occasionally by creeks and hollows with heavily forested areas, and through part of the southern end of the Talladega National Forest.

Beginning at Exit 228 on Interstate 65, the ride follows Highway 25 west for 31.6 miles through Calera, Montevallo, and past the Brierfield Ironworks Historical State Park to Centreville. This first section is mostly open two-lane roads winding up and down gentle hills past large homes, farms, and pastures.

In Montevallo, the University of Montevallo campus is also home to the Alabama Traffic Safety Center's motorcycle safety program—highly recommended for either people learning to ride or experienced riders seeking to hone their riding skills.

At Brierfield, five miles farther down Highway 25, there is a historical park built around an early brick blast furnace that's been partially preserved. Brierfield Ironworks Historical State Park offers camping, picnicking, and some hiking trails.

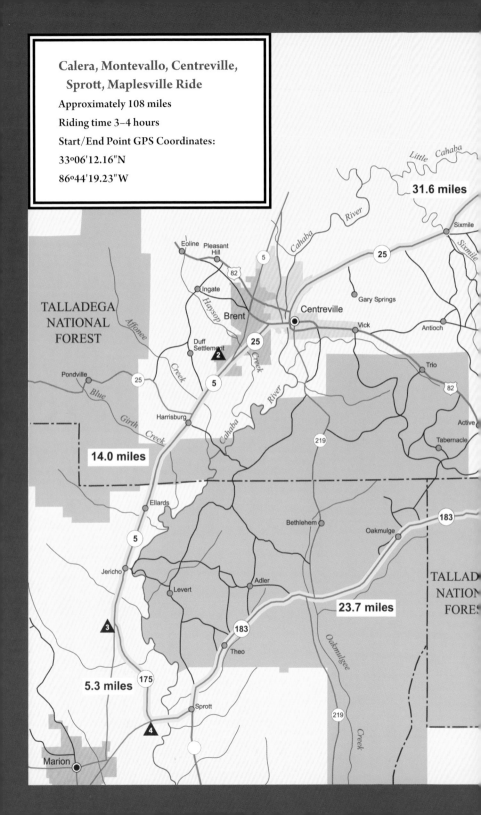

**Calera, Montevallo, Centreville,
Sprott, Maplesville Ride**

Approximately 108 miles

Riding time 3–4 hours

Start/End Point GPS Coordinates:

33°06'12.16"N

86°44'19.23"W

31.6 miles

14.0 miles

23.7 miles

5.3 miles

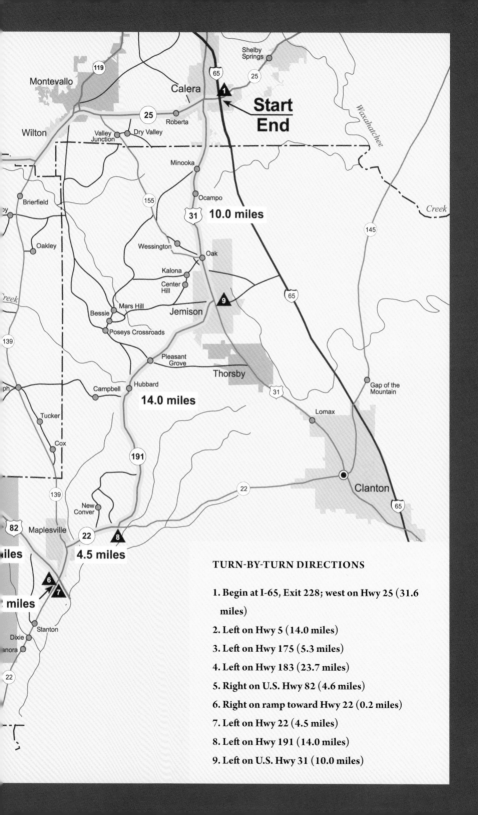

TURN-BY-TURN DIRECTIONS

1. Begin at I-65, Exit 228; west on Hwy 25 (31.6 miles)
2. Left on Hwy 5 (14.0 miles)
3. Left on Hwy 175 (5.3 miles)
4. Left on Hwy 183 (23.7 miles)
5. Right on U.S. Hwy 82 (4.6 miles)
6. Right on ramp toward Hwy 22 (0.2 miles)
7. Left on Hwy 22 (4.5 miles)
8. Left on Hwy 191 (14.0 miles)
9. Left on U.S. Hwy 31 (10.0 miles)

Covered bridge at Brierfield Ironworks Historical State Park

Turn 2 at Centreville begins a fourteen-mile southward section of this ride on Highway 5 that is mostly straight and smooth through a rural landscape.

A few miles north of Marion, the route turns left on Highway 175 and goes past the Perry Lakes Park entrance after about three miles, where an abandoned fire tower was moved from near Demopolis and rebuilt as a bird-watching tower that offers dramatic panoramas from a platform one hundred feet over the cypress swamp below. To reach the tower, walk about a quarter mile on an elevated boardwalk through the swamp. The park is adjacent to the state fish hatchery and the Cahaba River and boasts structures (a picnic pavilion, restrooms, and a swinging bridge) designed and built by the world-famous Rural Studio architectural program at Auburn University.

At Turn 4, the route turns northeast on Highway 183. After crossing the Cahaba River, the road forks at Sprott. Between Highway

183 and Highway 14 there are a cotton gin, store, and post office that formed the subject of a famous photograph by Walker Evans in the mid-1930s.

From just north of Sprott to U.S. Highway 82 near Maplesville, the ride passes through twenty miles of the Talladega National Forest.

After a 4.6-mile stretch on U.S. Highway 82 beginning at Turn 5, you'll turn onto Highway 22 (Turns 6 and 7) and follow that road through the old town of Maplesville.

At Turn 8 the ride heads north for fourteen miles through rolling hills and long, sweeping turns into Jemison (Turn 9), where it continues north on U.S. Highway 31 back to the start.

Clanton, Selma, Billingsley Ride

Approximately 106 miles
Riding time 4–5 hours

Start/End Point GPS Coordinates:
32°53'17.50"N
86°37'26.49"W

I HIGHLY RECOMMEND TAKING this 106-mile ride in early spring-time when the peach trees are in bloom. Cutting through the heart of Alabama's biggest peach-growing region, this route features sections where pink blooms seem to cover the hills for miles during the early spring.

This ride also runs through the Old Town district of Selma and travels past numerous antebellum-era homes and the landmark Live Oak Cemetery in that area.

You'll begin at Exit 212 on Interstate 65 (the one with the peach-painted water tower) and follow Highway 145 southwest into Clanton, where the route joins Highway 22 west (Turns 2 and 3).

Highway 22 passes by many old southern homes—some maintained or restored and others overgrown and returning to nature—as it winds through Maplesville and Plantersville en route to the historic and scenic city of Selma.

This route leaves Highway 22 at J. L. Chestnut Jr. Boulevard (Turn 4) to begin a tour of the Old Town sections of Selma. In the first block after turning on Mabry Street (Turn 5), you will see the stately Sturdivant Hall, a mansion built in 1852 that today looks much as it must have when the Civil War began. It hosts several events each year, including a ball that's part of the Battle of Selma Reenactment in April. Tours of Sturdivant Hall are available Tuesdays through Saturdays.

Driving farther down Mabry Street to Dallas Avenue/Highway 22, you'll see a number of other pre–Civil War homes, interspersed with newer buildings; and the same is true for the streets several blocks east and west of Mabry Street.

At Dallas Avenue the route goes right (Turn 6) for about four blocks before turning left into Live Oak Cemetery at King Street (Turn 7). Immediately on the right is the grave of the only vice president of the United States to be buried in Alabama: William Rufus King. King was the founder of Selma and a U.S. senator. Also buried here is Alabama's first black congressman, Benjamin Sterling Turner. The moss-draped live oak trees for which the cemetery was named were transplanted here from Mobile in 1879. For anyone interested in Alabama history, this cemetery is a worthwhile stop.

From Live Oak Cemetery, the route works its way back to High-

Chilton County peach orchard in bloom

TURN-BY-TURN DIRECTIONS

1. Begin at I-65, Exit 212; southwest on Hwy 145 (3.1 miles)
2. Right on 3rd St N (0.2 miles)
3. Right on 4th St N—becomes Hwy 22 (43.2 miles)
4. Right on J. L. Chestnut Jr. Boulevard (0.3 miles)
5. Left on Mabry St (0.5 miles)
6. Right on Dallas Ave/Hwy 22 (0.4 miles)
7. Left on King St—Live Oak Cemetery (0.1 miles)
8. Left on Selma Ave (0.7 miles)
9. Right on Hwy 80/Broad St (2.9 miles)
10. Left on Hwy 41 (3.0 miles)
11. Right on Water Ave/Hwy 48 (3.1 miles)
12. Right on Hwy 14 (6.7 miles)
13. Left on Hwy 1 (14.2 miles)
14. Right on U.S. Hwy 82 (0.2 miles)
15. Left on Hwy 37 (20.3 miles)
16. Right on CR-29 (3.5 miles)
17. Right on CR-77 (3.4 miles)
18. Left on Bell Ln Rd (0.4 miles)

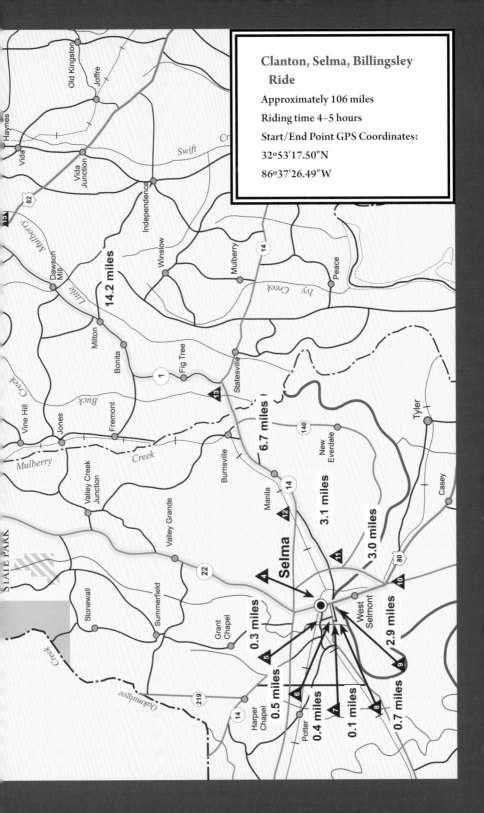

Clanton, Selma, Billingsley Ride

Approximately 106 miles

Riding time 4–5 hours

Start/End Point GPS Coordinates:

32°53'17.50"N

86°37'26.49"W

Sturdivant Hall, Selma

way 80 (Turns 8 and 9) and south across the Alabama River on the historic Edmund Pettus Bridge, made famous by the "Bloody Sunday" incident when the first Selma-to-Montgomery march was brutally halted by state troopers who attacked marchers with tear gas and nightsticks. The event helped focus national and international attention on the struggle for civil rights and led to passage of the 1965 Voting Rights Act.

After 2.9 miles on Highway 80, the route turns northeast on Highway 41 (Turn 10) and then right on Water Avenue after 3 miles (Turn 11) to connect with Highway 14 after another 3.1 miles (Turn 12).

Just after Burnsville, the route turns left on Highway 1 (Turn 13)

Beneath the historic Edmund Pettus Bridge in Selma

for 14.2 miles of surprisingly curvy roads to U.S. Highway 82, where it goes right for just 0.2 miles before turning left on Highway 37 (Turns 14 and 15).

The 20.3 miles on Highway 37 cut through numerous Chilton County peach orchards. At Billingsley, to stay on Highway 37 you must make a right turn over the railroad track. From Billingsley to Highway 22, you'll find the sections where blooming peach trees dramatically paint the landscape in shades of pink.

At County Road 29, the route turns east (Turn 16) and works its way back to the starting point after about seven miles (Turns 17 and 18).

Mobile Bay Ferry Ride

Approximately 115 miles
Riding time 5–6 hours

Start/End Point GPS Coordinates:
30°39'16.63"N
87°54'43.85"W

THIS 115-MILE RIDE CIRCUMNAVIGATES Mobile Bay and includes a ride on the Mobile Bay Ferry connecting Fort Morgan and Dauphin Island, one of only three ferries still operating in the state.

Beginning at Exit 35A on Interstate 10 at the northeast corner of the bay, the first leg of the ride heads south for 7.3 miles on U.S. Highway 98 to Alternate U.S. Highway 98 (Turn 2).

After 2.5 miles, the route turns right on Fels Avenue in Fairhope and again left (Turns 3 and 4) to stay on Alternate U.S. Hwy 98/Scenic Highway 98. In this 16.3-mile section, the ride follows the eastern shore of Mobile Bay before turning inland just north of Weeks Bay near Barnwell. Just over three miles after crossing the Fish River, the route turns south on Highway 49/Magnolia Springs Highway at Magnolia Springs (Turn 5).

At Bon Secour, a sleepy fishing village to the north of Oyster Bay, the route turns north on County Road 10 (Turn 6) for 1.4 miles, then right on Styron Road to stay on County Road 10 (Turn 7) for another 2.5 miles to Highway 59 (Turn 8).

After 4.9 miles on Highway 59, there is a westward turn onto Highway 180 (Turn 9) toward Fort Morgan and the ferry landing 20.7 miles to the west. This section of Highway 180 follows

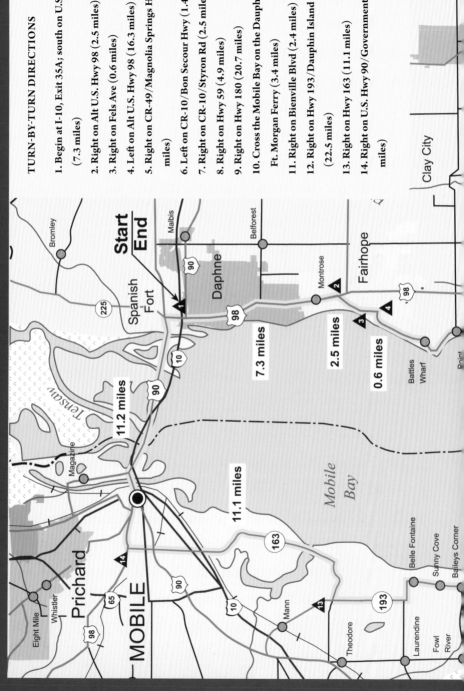

TURN-BY-TURN DIRECTIONS

1. Begin at I-10, Exit 35A; south on U.S. Hwy 98 (7.3 miles)

2. Right on Alt U.S. Hwy 98 (2.5 miles)

3. Right on Fels Ave (0.6 miles)

4. Left on Alt U.S. Hwy 98 (16.3 miles)

5. Right on CR-49/Magnolia Springs Hwy (8.3 miles)

6. Left on CR-10/Bon Secour Hwy (1.4 miles)

7. Right on CR-10/Styron Rd (2.5 miles)

8. Right on Hwy 59 (4.9 miles)

9. Right on Hwy 180 (20.7 miles)

10. Cross the Mobile Bay on the Dauphin Island–Ft. Morgan Ferry (3.4 miles)

11. Right on Bienville Blvd (2.4 miles)

12. Right on Hwy 193/Dauphin Island Pkwy (22.5 miles)

13. Right on Hwy 163 (11.1 miles)

14. Right on U.S. Hwy 90/Government St (11.2 miles)

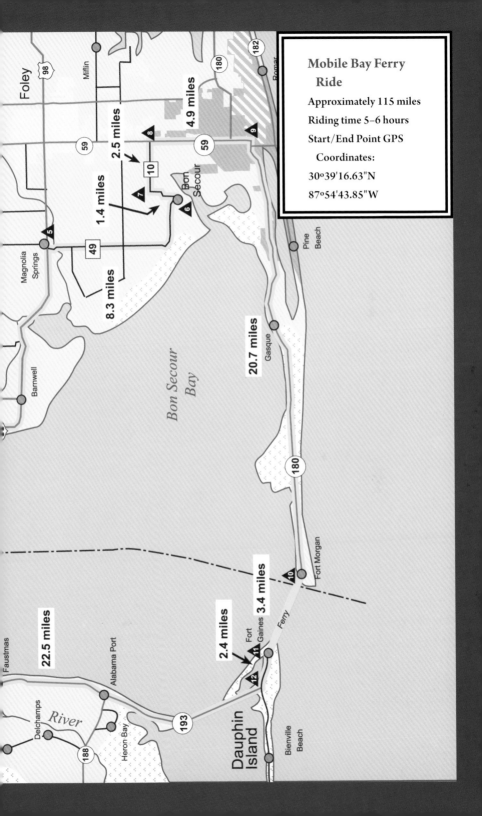

Mobile Bay Ferry Ride

Approximately 115 miles

Riding time 5–6 hours

Start/End Point GPS

Coordinates:

30°39'16.63"N

87°54'43.85"W

Foley

98

Miflin

182

180

2.5 miles

4.9 miles

8

10

59

59

9

1.4 miles

7

Bon Secour

6

49

5

8.3 miles

Magnolia Springs

Pine Beach

Barnwell

Bon Secour Bay

20.7 miles

Gasque

180

Fort Morgan

3.4 miles

10

22.5 miles

Faustmas

Alabama Port

2.4 miles

Fort Gaines

11

12

River

Delchamps

Heron Bay

193

188

Dauphin Island

Bienville Beach

Ferry

Looking across the Dauphin Island Bridge

the southern shore of Little Lagoon in Gulf Shores for the first six miles and continues along a peninsula that extends westward into the mouth of Mobile Bay where the historic fort is located. This section of the ride passes through the seven-thousand-acre Bon Secour National Wildlife Refuge, where a number of trails are popular with bird-watching enthusiasts who go there to see the more than 370 species of birds that migrate through the area.

The ferry runs on a regular schedule year-round, with departures

every forty-five minutes, but it's not uncommon to wait up to an hour before making the fifteen-minute trip across the bay to Dauphin Island.

As of this writing, the fare for a motorcycle with one rider was $8 and an additional $4.50 for a passenger. Additional information on the ferry schedules and fares is available at the Mobile Bay Ferry Web site: www.mobilebayferry.com/schedule.html.

Fort Morgan, named for Revolutionary War hero Daniel Morgan,

Above: Waiting
for the ferry from
Dauphin Island

Left: Crossing from
Fort Morgan to
Dauphin Island
on the Mobile Bay
Ferry

Our Lady of Bon Secour Church

Riding under a canopy of live oaks in Magnolia Springs

Beach off Fort Morgan Road in Baldwin County

Entrance to Bankhead Tunnel in Mobile

is a good place to take a break while waiting for the next ferry. Completed in 1834, the star-shaped fort was surrendered by Confederate forces during the Battle of Mobile Bay in the Civil War. Today the fort is open to visitors for tours.

Following the 3.4-mile ferry ride across the bay (Turn 10), the route begins its northward leg on Bienville Boulevard (Turn 11).

After 2.4 miles, you'll turn north on Highway 193/Dauphin Island Parkway (Turn 12) for 22.5 miles, first crossing the western edge of the bay on a span that climbs to a height of eighty feet, then following the western shore of Mobile Bay and crossing the Fowl River.

At the intersection with Highway 163, the route turns right (Turn 13) and stays on this road 11.1 miles into Mobile at Government Street/U.S. Highway 90 (Turn 14).

The final 11.2 miles pass through downtown Mobile beneath a shaded canopy of live oaks and then through the 0.7-mile-long Bankhead Tunnel at the north end of the bay. This final section on U.S. Highway 90 also passes by the USS *Alabama* Battleship Memorial Park on the extreme northern end of Mobile Bay en route to the starting point at Interstate 10.

Greenville, Fort Deposit, Burnt Corn Ride

Approximately 132 miles
Riding time 5–6 hours

Start/End Point GPS Coordinates:
31°51'02.62"N
86°38'26.97"W

THE FIRST TWELVE MILES of this 132-mile ride follow the thoroughly enjoyable winding Highway 185 from the starting point at Exit 130 on Interstate 65 at Greenville to Fort Deposit. Follow the signage to stay on 185 toward Fort Deposit.

This part of central Alabama has numerous old farmsteads and miles and miles of timberland, interspersed with aged small towns with weathered-plank stores, old cotton gins, and more relics from Alabama's past.

From Turn 2 at Fort Deposit, the route heads northwest for 9.3 miles on County Road 45, a narrow road through mostly pine forests broken up by the occasional farmhouse or barn.

At Highway 21 (Turn 3), the roadway becomes wider and faster with better pavement and passes through more miles of pines until Turn 4 at Freedom Farm Road/County Road 59. Just 0.4 miles after you turn onto this road, Wakefield Plantation will appear on the right, with its one-of-a-kind Steamboat Gothic design. The Furman area also boasts several other antebellum-era homes and churches.

Almost immediately the road narrows and begins to resemble a tunnel through the Spanish moss hanging from the trees for the next

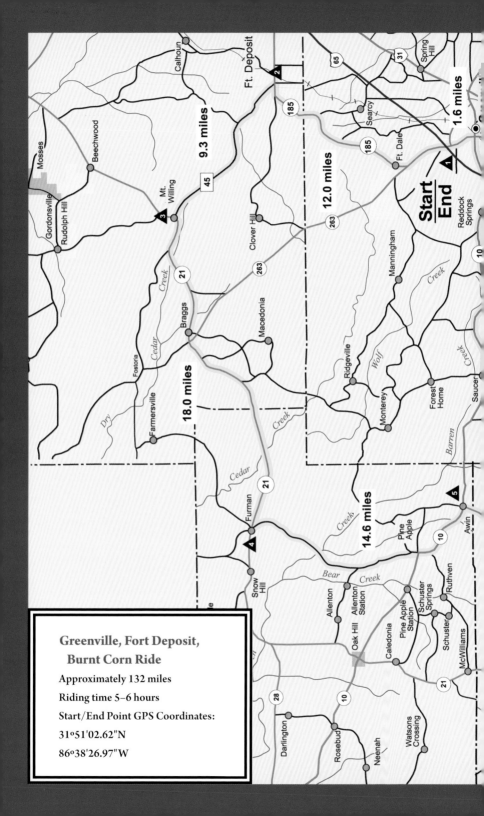

Calhoun

Ft. Deposit

2

65

31

Spring Hill

185

Searcy

1.6 miles

9.3 miles

Beechwood

185

Ft. Dale

Mosses

Gordonsville

Rudolph Hill

Mt. Willing

3

45

Clover Hill

12.0 miles

263

Start
End

Reddock Springs

10

Cedar Creek

21

Braggs

263

Macedonia

Manningham

Creek

Fostoria

Ridgeville

Wolf

Forest Home

Saucer Creek

Dry

Farmersville

18.0 miles

Cedar

Monterey

Creek

Barren

Cedar

21

Furman

14.6 miles

Creek

Pine Apple

5

Awin

10

4

Snow Hill

Bear

Creek

Allenton

Allenton Station

Oak Hill

Pine Apple Station

Caledonia

Schuster Springs

Schuster

Ruthven

McWilliams

21

28

10

Darlington

Rosebud

Neenah

Watsons Crossing

Greenville, Fort Deposit,
Burnt Corn Ride

Approximately 132 miles

Riding time 5–6 hours

Start/End Point GPS Coordinates:

31º51'02.62"N

86º38'26.97"W

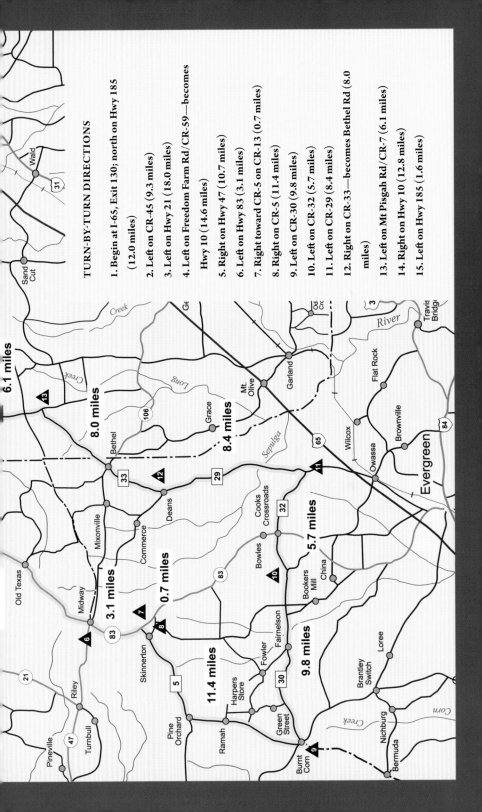

TURN-BY-TURN DIRECTIONS

1. Begin at I-65, Exit 130; north on Hwy 185 (12.0 miles)
2. Left on CR-45 (9.3 miles)
3. Left on Hwy 21 (18.0 miles)
4. Left on Freedom Farm Rd/CR-59—becomes Hwy 10 (14.6 miles)
5. Right on Hwy 47 (10.7 miles)
6. Left on Hwy 83 (3.1 miles)
7. Right toward CR-5 on CR-13 (0.7 miles)
8. Right on CR-5 (11.4 miles)
9. Left on CR-30 (9.8 miles)
10. Left on CR-32 (5.7 miles)
11. Left on CR-29 (8.4 miles)
12. Right on CR-33—becomes Bethel Rd (8.0 miles)
13. Left on Mt Pisgah Rd/CR-7 (6.1 miles)
14. Right on Hwy 10 (12.8 miles)
15. Left on Hwy 185 (1.6 miles)

Town hall in
Pine Apple

fourteen miles and through the town of Pine Apple (which has an interesting town hall/post office).

Just past Pine Apple, the route turns right (Turn 5) on Highway 47 for about ten miles, then left on Highway 83 at Midway (Turn 6).

After 3.1 miles on Highway 83 you'll see a dirt cut-through road on the right (Turn 7) that connects with County Road 5 (Turn 8). Riders not comfortable with the 0.7-mile dirt road can stay on Highway 83 another mile to the intersection with County Road 5.

The next turn (Turn 9) at County Road 30 comes at the 11.4-mile mark on Highway 5, but you'll want to continue a half mile past the turn to check out the old town of Burnt Corn. Its last store closed

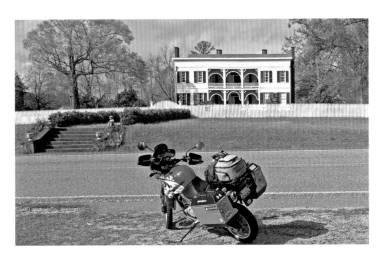

Wakefield Plantation in Furman

Going off-route to stop in the quaint town of Burnt Corn

A few of the time-worn buildings in Burnt Corn

around 2005, but four or five weathered buildings remain that are reminiscent of the old days in south Alabama.

After you return to County Road 30, the route continues east for 9.8 miles on that road, then on County Road 32 (Turn 10) for 5.7 miles, and then north on County Road 29 (Turn 11) for 8.4 miles. The landscape through this part of the ride is very rural, and stores are few and far between.

You'll ride the next 22.5 miles from Turn 11 to Turn 13 on County Road 29, then County Road 33, then Mount Pisgah Road all the way to Highway 10 at Turn 14. The roadway is mostly narrow as it winds through pine forests and past farms, and the pavement is a semi-rough tar-and-gravel composite.

For the next 12.8 miles on Highway 10, the roadway is smooth two-lane blacktop with wider shoulders, and it cuts through farmsteads and pine-forested hills. At Turn 15, the route rejoins Highway 185 north for 1.6 miles back to the starting point.

Spanish moss draping live oaks near Pine Apple

RIDE LOOP 39
Hope Hull, Lowndesboro, Fort Deposit Ride

Approximately 88 miles
Riding time 4–5 hours

Start/End Point GPS Coordinates:
32o15'59.55"N
86o21'17.32"W

THIS EIGHTY-EIGHT-MILE RIDE is just north of the 132-mile-long Ride Loop 38: Greenville, Fort Deposit, Burnt Corn Ride, and the two might actually be combined for a long day ride if time allows. These rides cover similar territory, although this one includes the truly unique antebellum town of Lowndesboro. Because they share one 9.3-mile section of Highway 45 between Fort Deposit and Highway 21, that section could be eliminated if the rides were combined. Still, the entire loop would total around two hundred miles.

Beginning at Interstate 65, Exit 164 (Hope Hull exit), the first leg of this ride heads south on U.S. Highway 31 for 6.5 miles to County Road 24 (Turn 2), where it turns west for 4.5 miles, crossing I-65 to a left turn on County Road 26 (Turn 3). These first eleven miles are mostly flat and pass between wide-open pasture and farmlands.

In the next leg, beginning at Turn 3 on County Road 26, the landscape becomes a mixture of both farm and woodland, and the sixteen miles between Turns 4 and 5 on County Road 37 are a continuation of similar scenery, but with more curves approaching Fort Deposit.

The section between Turns 6 and 7 on County Road 45 runs mostly through pine forests. It is this section that would be omitted if combining this ride with Ride Loop 38.

269

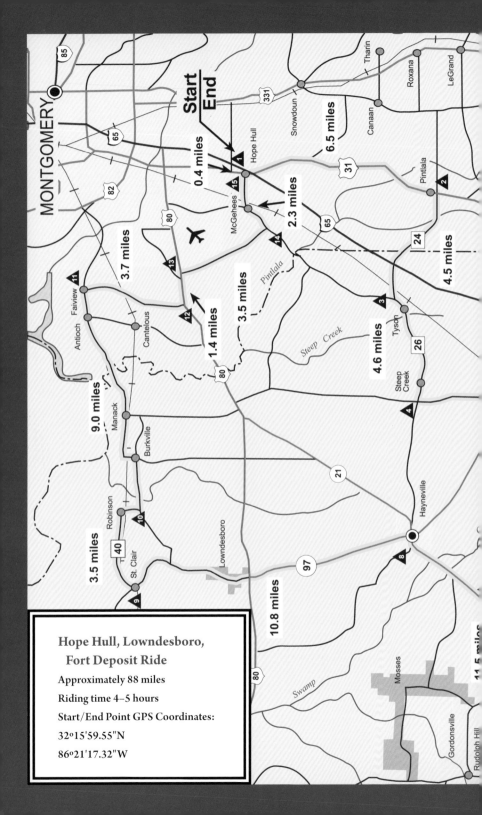

Hope Hull, Lowndesboro,
Fort Deposit Ride
Approximately 88 miles
Riding time 4–5 hours
Start/End Point GPS Coordinates:
32º15'59.55"N
86º21'17.32"W

TURN-BY-TURN DIRECTIONS

1. Begin at I-65, Exit 164; south on U.S. Hwy 31 (6.5 miles)

2. Right on CR-24/Cloverfield Rd—becomes CR-6/Tyson Rd (4.5 miles)

3. Left on CR-26 (4.6 miles)

4. Left on CR-37 (16.0 miles)

5. Right on Hwy 185 (0.9 miles)

6. Right on CR-45 (9.3 miles)

7. Right on Hwy 21 (11.5 miles)

8. Left on Hwy 97—becomes CR-29 (10.8 miles)

9. Right on CR-40 (3.5 miles)

10. Left on Brown Hill Rd—becomes Old Selma Rd (9.0 miles)

11. Right on Mitchell Young Rd (3.7 miles)

12. Left on U.S. Hwy 80 (1.4 miles)

13. Right on Felder Rd (3.5 miles)

14. Left on Wasden Rd (2.3 miles)

15. Right on Hwy 31 (0.4 miles)

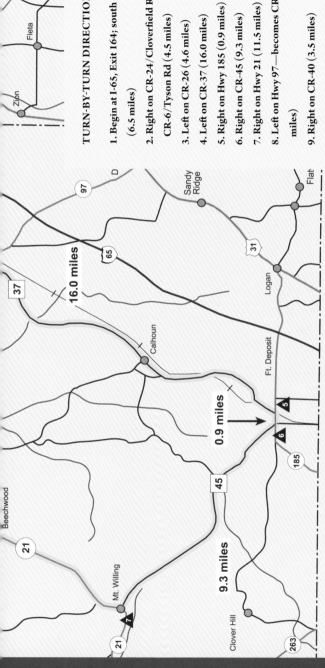

At Turn 7, which makes a right onto Highway 21, the route heads toward the Lowndes County seat at Hayneville 11.5 miles to the northeast. Here, at Turn 8 the route joins Highway 97 north through Lowndesboro just across Highway 80.

Riding through Lowndesboro is like taking a ride through the Old South before the Civil War. About 1.5 miles after crossing Highway 80, the winding road passes a half-dozen antebellum churches and stately mansions, several of which are on the National Registry of Historic Places. The original dome from Alabama's first state capitol in Cahawba tops the historic CME Church. It took a month and four teams of oxen to move the copper-plated dome forty-five miles from Cahawba, located on the Alabama River at its confluence with the Cahaba River.

Another nearby off-route site well worth visiting lies seven miles west of the intersection of Highway 97 and Highway 80 at Lowndes-

Lowndesboro's CME Church, topped with the original state-capitol dome

boro. The Lowndes County Interpretive Center on Highway 80 features an extremely well-produced interactive multimedia presentation and museum focusing on the Selma-to-Montgomery march for voting rights in 1965.

Leaving Lowndesboro, Highway 97 becomes County Road 29 and winds its way northward through some hills before intersecting with County Road 40 (Turn 9) alongside a railroad crossing.

After turning right on County Road 40, the ride follows the railroad eastward toward Montgomery on what becomes the Old Selma Road after Turn 10. At Mitchell Young Road the route turns south (Turn 11) and goes 3.7 miles to U. S. Highway 80 (Turn 12), where it turns east for 1.4 miles before going south on Felder Road (Turn 13).

From here the start point is only about 6 miles: 3.5 on Felder Road to Wasden Road (Turn 14), then another 2.3 miles back to Highway 31 (Turn 15).

Camping on the Alabama River

Mobile Bay, Bayou La Batre, Grand Bay Ride

Approximately 90 miles

Riding time 4–5 hours

Start/End Point GPS Coordinates:

30º34'51.62"N

88º10'13.92"W

THIS NINETY-MILE RIDE BEGINS at Theodore to the west of Mobile and goes south to pass both Bellingrath Gardens and Bayou La Batre before heading north to Grand Bay.

The starting point is Exit 15 (15A if you are headed west and 15B if you are headed east) on Interstate 10, about ten miles southwest of downtown Mobile. The first 2.2 miles go south on U. S. Highway 90 before turning left on Bellingrath Road to continue southward another 12.2 miles (Turn 2).

The left turn for Bellingrath Gardens occurs at about the eight-mile mark of this section. Just follow the signs for another 1.4 miles. Bellingrath Gardens is one of the area's major tourist attractions and offers a variety of things to see, including tours of both the museum/house and the expansive gardens, where something is in bloom any time of year. There is even a riverboat ride on the Fowl River.

Back on the route, at Turn 3 the ride joins Highway 188 for 3.7 miles west to Clark Road at Turn 4. This part of the route (Turns 4 to 8) ventures off the main artery of Highway 188 and travels first through the Coden community at Clark Road and then 3.9 miles along the south shore at Bayou La Batre, where shrimp boats are both built and put to sea.

Shrimp boats in Bayou La Batre

After turning on Clark Road, the roadway reaches the shoreline after about one-half mile and follows it past several cottages, including an older home at 0.6 miles called Royal Oaks, with a drive lined by massive live oaks. After 1.1 miles, the road returns briefly to Highway 188, crosses a bridge over Bayou Coden, then turns left again on Alba Abvenue to Shell Belt Road, which follow the shoreline again through Bayou La Batre for 3.9 miles before rejoining Highway 188 again.

This section through the blue-collar fishing village of Bayou La Batre features a number of shipyards where shrimping trawlers and other boats are made, as well as passes hundreds of working shrimp boats tied to the docks. Photo opportunities abound here!

Back on Highway 188 (Turn 8), the route heads northwest

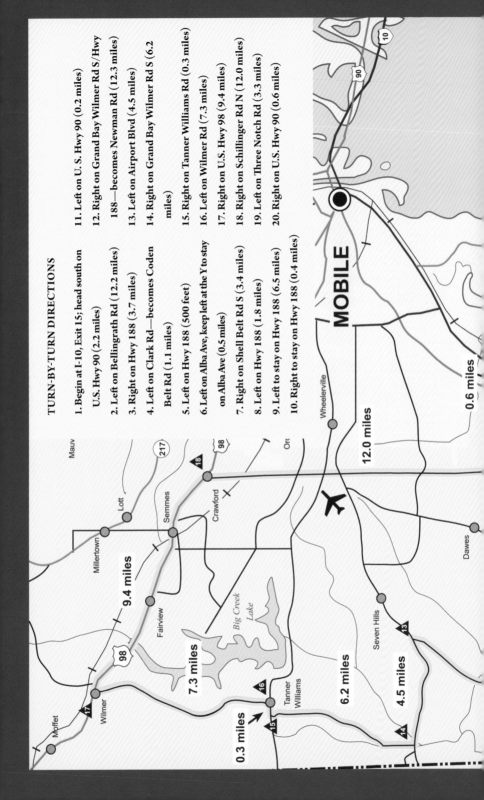

TURN-BY-TURN DIRECTIONS

1. Begin at I-10, Exit 15; head south on U.S. Hwy 90 (2.2 miles)
2. Left on Bellingrath Rd (12.2 miles)
3. Right on Hwy 188 (3.7 miles)
4. Left on Clark Rd—becomes Coden Belt Rd (1.1 miles)
5. Left on Hwy 188 (500 feet)
6. Left on Alba Ave, keep left at the Y to stay on Alba Ave (0.5 miles)
7. Right on Shell Belt Rd S (3.4 miles)
8. Left on Hwy 188 (1.8 miles)
9. Left to stay on Hwy 188 (6.5 miles)
10. Right to stay on Hwy 188 (0.4 miles)
11. Left on U. S. Hwy 90 (0.2 miles)
12. Right on Grand Bay Wilmer Rd S/Hwy 188—becomes Newman Rd (12.3 miles)
13. Left on Airport Blvd (4.5 miles)
14. Right on Grand Bay Wilmer Rd S (6.2 miles)
15. Right on Tanner Williams Rd (0.3 miles)
16. Left on Wilmer Rd (7.3 miles)
17. Right on U.S. Hwy 98 (9.4 miles)
18. Right on Schillinger Rd N (12.0 miles)
19. Left on Three Notch Rd (3.3 miles)
20. Right on U.S. Hwy 90 (0.6 miles)

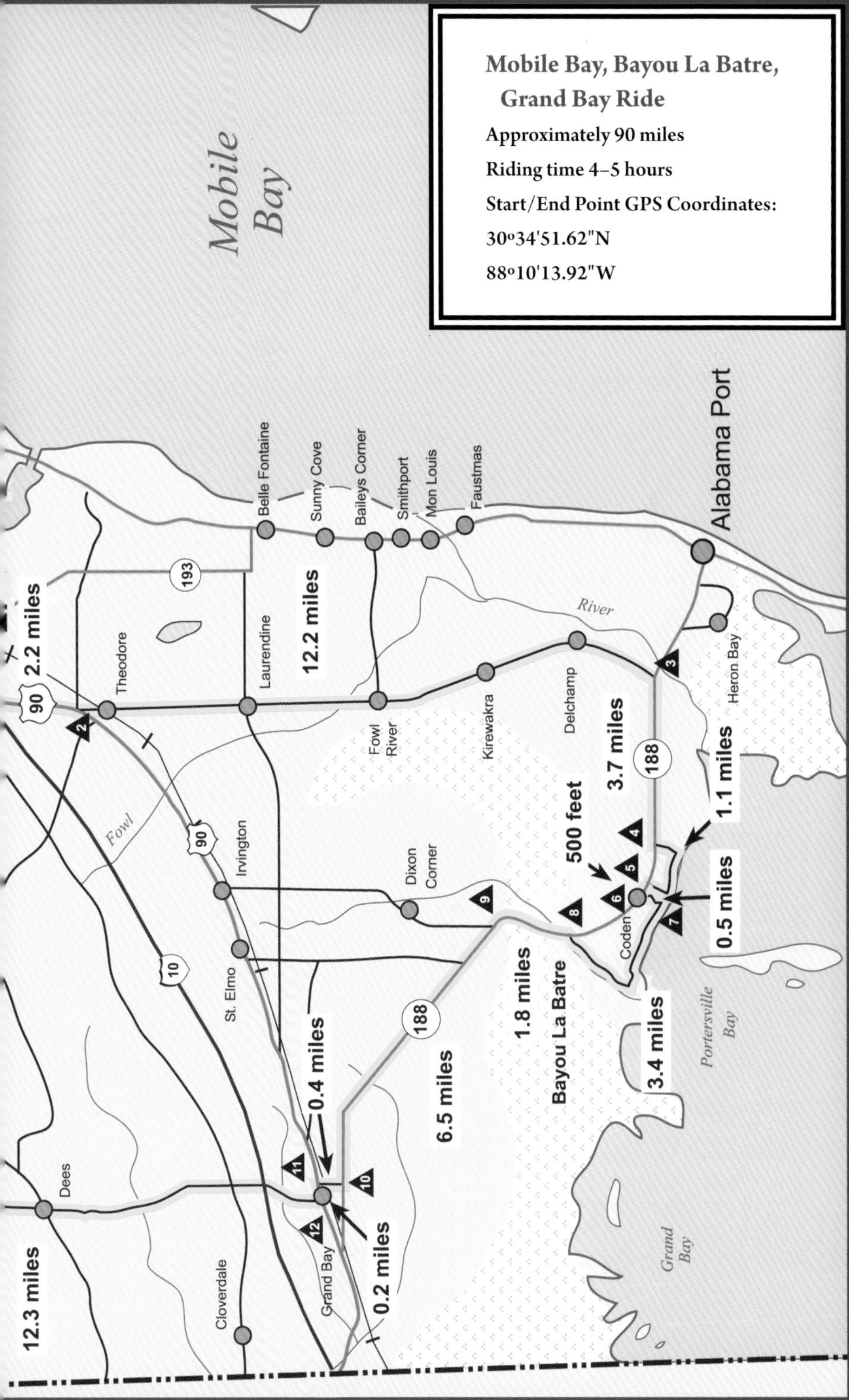

Mobile Bay

Mobile Bay, Bayou La Batre,
Grand Bay Ride

Approximately 90 miles

Riding time 4–5 hours

Start/End Point GPS Coordinates:

30º34'51.62"N

88º10'13.92"W

Alabama Port

Belle Fontaine

Sunny Cove

Baileys Corner

Smithport

Mon Louis

Faustmas

River

193

2.2 miles

90

Theodore

Laurendine

12.2 miles

Fowl River

Kirewakra

Delchamp

3.7 miles

188

1.1 miles

Heron Bay

3

Fowl

2

90

Irvington

Dixon Corner

500 feet

4

5

6

7

0.5 miles

St. Elmo

10

9

8

Coden

1.8 miles

Bayou La Batre

3.4 miles

Portersville Bay

188

6.5 miles

Dees

11

0.4 miles

12

10

0.2 miles

Grand Bay

Cloverdale

12.3 miles

Grand Bay

into Grand Bay, less than four miles from the Alabama-Mississippi state line.

Continuing north, the ride follows Grand Bay Wilmer Road 12.3 miles through a patchwork of farmland after a very brief 0.2-mile left on U. S. Highway 90 (Turns 11 and 12).

At Turn 13, the ride goes left on Airport Boulevard for 4.5 miles and comes within less than a mile of the Mississippi line before going north again on Grand Bay Wilmer Road (Turn 14).

From there the ride continues north through typical south Alabama farm country for 6.2 miles. It then takes a right on Tanner Wil-

Approaching the fishing village of Bayou La Batre

liams Road for 0.3 miles (Turn 15), and turns left onto Wilmer Road (Turn 16) for another 7.3 miles to the northernmost point of the loop at Wilmer.

Turn 17 at Wilmer begins the southward leg of the route on U.S. Highway 98. This 9.4-mile section contains the last curves on this ride. At Turn 18 on Schillinger Road, the road stays perfectly straight for 12 miles due south, then straight due east between Turns 19 and 20 on Three Notch Road for 3.3 miles back to U. S. Highway 90 and the 0.6-mile ride back to the starting point.

Pausing at Royal Oaks Plantation on Mobile Bay

PART VI

RIDES IN SOUTHEAST ALABAMA
Ride Loops 41–50

Chattahoochee State Park, State Line Ride

Approximately 79 miles
Riding time 3–4 hours

Start/End Point GPS Coordinates:
31°00'38.29"N
85°02'28.01"W

CHATTAHOOCHEE STATE PARK, SITUATED in the extreme southeast corner of the state where Alabama, Georgia, and Florida meet, is the start and finish point for this seventy-nine-mile loop.

The park, which is managed by Houston County, offers camping and fishing on a lake where the state record shellcracker (weighing in at four pounds, four ounces) was caught in 1962. I have found it sometimes difficult to locate any staff at this remote park, so I recommend calling ahead if you are planning to camp there: 334-699-3607.

The ride begins by heading west from the park entrance on County Road 8 and stays a few miles north of the Alabama-Florida state line through Turns 2 to 6 at Grangeburg. This entire section is made up of good two-lane country roads through pastures and cultivated farm fields.

From here to Cottonwood (Turn 7) and on to State Line (Turn 8), the road contains noticeably more curves and at times during the summer it passes through tunnel-like areas of Spanish moss–draped trees.

At State Line, the ride heads north for 5.9 miles before turning east on East Smithfield Road/County Road 33 (Turn 9).

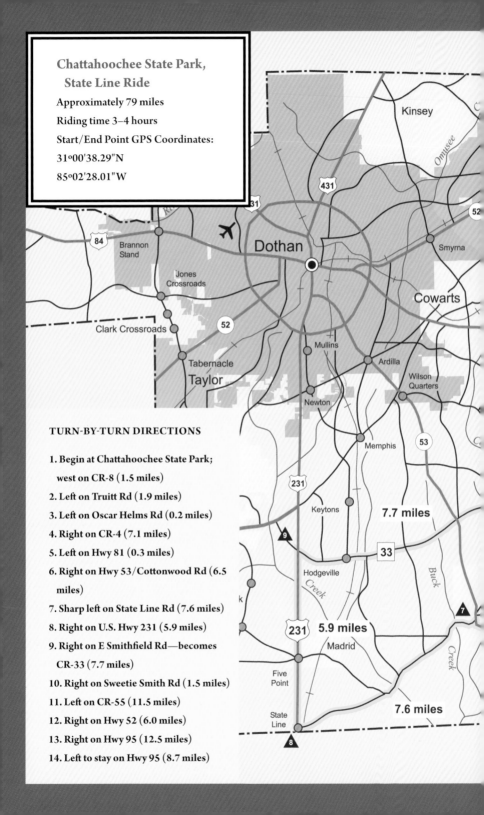

**Chattahoochee State Park,
State Line Ride**

Approximately 79 miles

Riding time 3–4 hours

Start/End Point GPS Coordinates:

31º00'38.29"N

85º02'28.01"W

Kinsey

Dothan

Brannon
Stand

Smyrna

Jones
Crossroads

Cowarts

Clark Crossroads

52

Tabernacle

Taylor

Mullins

Ardilla

Wilson
Quarters

Newton

TURN-BY-TURN DIRECTIONS

Memphis

53

1. Begin at Chattahoochee State Park;
   west on CR-8 (1.5 miles)
2. Left on Truitt Rd (1.9 miles)
3. Left on Oscar Helms Rd (0.2 miles)
4. Right on CR-4 (7.1 miles)
5. Left on Hwy 81 (0.3 miles)
6. Right on Hwy 53/Cottonwood Rd (6.5
   miles)
7. Sharp left on State Line Rd (7.6 miles)
8. Right on U.S. Hwy 231 (5.9 miles)
9. Right on E Smithfield Rd—becomes
   CR-33 (7.7 miles)
10. Right on Sweetie Smith Rd (1.5 miles)
11. Left on CR-55 (11.5 miles)
12. Right on Hwy 52 (6.0 miles)
13. Right on Hwy 95 (12.5 miles)
14. Left to stay on Hwy 95 (8.7 miles)

231

Keytons

7.7 miles

33

Hodgeville

Creek

5.9 miles

231

Madrid

Five
Point

State
Line

7.6 miles

Buck

Creek

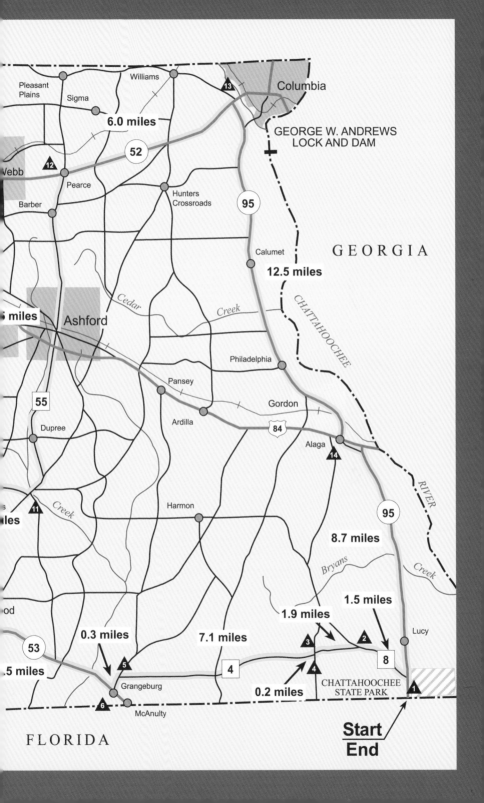

Parked outside the Chattahoochee State Park entrance

Turn 10 at Sweetie Smith Road continues to track east for 1.5 miles before the route joins County Road 55 for an 11.5-mile northward leg through the old town of Ashford and on to a right turn at Pearce (Turn 12) onto Highway 52. From County Road 33 into Pearce the roads are continuously passing through typical farm country for south Alabama with wide, sweeping fields and pastures.

When the route turns south for the final twenty-one miles on Highway 95, the road becomes noticeably narrower and the terrain more wooded. In this section (Turns 13 and 14), Highway 95 stays one to two miles west of the Chattahoochee River and, after about five miles, passes by the massive Farley Nuclear Plant, which generates about nineteen percent of the electric power supplied by Alabama Power Company.

Immediately after crossing U.S. Highway 84, the route takes a right at Turn 14 to stay on Highway 95 and the final 8.7 miles back to Chattahoochee State Park.

Eufaula, Abbeville, Clayton Ride

Approximately 140 miles
Riding time 5–6 hours

Start/End Point GPS Coordinates:
31°59'15.16"N
85°06'51.56"W

THIS 140-MILE LOOP FOLLOWS the Walter F. George Reservoir south through Eufaula and then west through Abbeville and north through rolling hill country.

This route begins at Lakepoint Resort State Park, where a wide range of lodging, dining, and camping options are available, about six miles north of Eufaula. The first part of the ride on U.S. Highway 431 passes numerous stately homes along tree-lined streets in the old river town of Eufaula. After 14.1 miles, the route turns left onto Highway 95 (Turn 2) to follow the western shoreline of the lake, and again takes a left onto Highway 97 at Turns 3 and 4. Throughout this section of the ride, the roads generally run adjacent to or near the lake on the left and open into wide cultivated fields broken up by woodlands on the right.

At Turn 5, just west of the Walter F. George Lock and Dam, the route turns west on Highway 10 for 11.7 miles into Abbeville, where it turns south on Highway 27 at Turn 6.

Turn 7 marks the southernmost point of the ride, where the route takes a sharp right onto Highway 69. After 7.7 miles on Highway 69, at Turn 8 you'll take a right onto Highway 105 for 3.3 miles.

Turn 9 onto Highway 35 continues north for 4.9 miles, and from

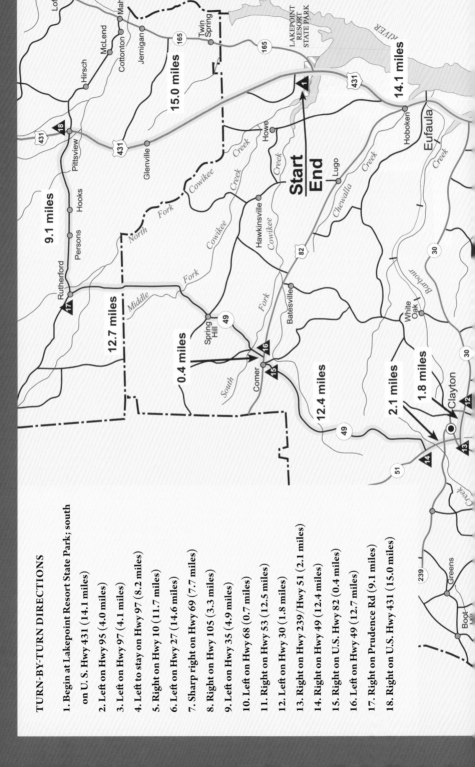

TURN-BY-TURN DIRECTIONS

1. Begin at Lakepoint Resort State Park; south on U. S. Hwy 431 (14.1 miles)

2. Left on Hwy 95 (4.0 miles)

3. Left on Hwy 97 (4.1 miles)

4. Left to stay on Hwy 97 (8.2 miles)

5. Right on Hwy 10 (11.7 miles)

6. Left on Hwy 27 (14.6 miles)

7. Sharp right on Hwy 69 (7.7 miles)

8. Right on Hwy 105 (3.3 miles)

9. Left on Hwy 35 (4.9 miles)

10. Left on Hwy 68 (0.7 miles)

11. Right on Hwy 53 (12.5 miles)

12. Left on Hwy 30 (1.8 miles)

13. Right on Hwy 239 / Hwy 51 (2.1 miles)

14. Right on Hwy 49 (12.4 miles)

15. Right on U.S. Hwy 82 (0.4 miles)

16. Left on Hwy 49 (12.7 miles)

17. Right on Prudence Rd (9.1 miles)

18. Right on U.S. Hwy 431 (15.0 miles)

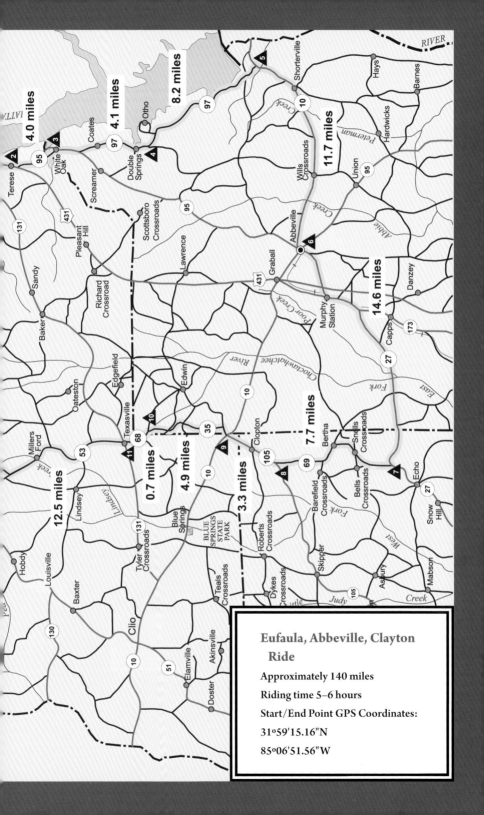

Eufaula, Abbeville, Clayton
Ride

Approximately 140 miles

Riding time 5–6 hours

Start/End Point GPS Coordinates:

31°59'15.16"N

85°06'51.56"W

this point northward the roads become increasingly curvy as the terrain has more hills and is more heavily forested through the town of Texasville (Turns 10 and 11).

The next major town is Clayton (Turns 12 and 13), where the northward direction of the route continues at Turn 14 on Highway 49 toward Comer. In this 12.4-mile section the roadway narrows and runs almost entirely through heavily forested, hilly country.

At Comer the route joins U.S. Highway 82 east for just 0.4 miles before continuing northward on Highway 49 (Turns 15 and 16). The 12.7-mile stretch between Turns 16 and 17 continues to run mainly through forests, but the road and right-of-way are somewhat wider here with a few more farms.

Turn 17 at Rutherford onto Prudence Road eventually connects with U.S. Highway 431 9.1 miles to the west at Turn 18. From there, the starting point at Lakepoint Resort State Park is approximately fifteen miles.

Southeast Alabama magnolias near Abbeville

Blue Springs, Smuteye, Ozark Ride

Approximately 122 miles
Riding time 5–6 hours

Start/End Point GPS Coordinates:
31°39'50.45"N
85°30'27.49"W

TOUCHING FIVE SOUTHEAST ALABAMA counties, this all-rural ride loop follows similar terrain throughout its length, alternating between pastures or cultivated fields and woodlands over rolling hills. The scenic route passes through parts of Dale, Barbour, Bullock, Pike, and Coffee counties over its 122 miles.

The ride begins at Blue Springs State Park just a few miles east of Clio—birthplace of former Alabama governor George Wallace—on Highway 10. The park is a great place for motorcycle camping and in summer offers swimming as well as fishing in the cool spring-fed lake. As of 2008, the park even added wireless Internet.

From Blue Springs, the route heads west on Highway 10 for 3.2 miles to Highway 131 (Turn 2), then turns left on County Road 33 after 1.9 miles (Turn 3), followed by an immediate left on Blue Springs Road after 0.1 miles (Turn 4). After 5.9 miles, Turn 5 takes a right on Planer Mill Road at Louisville for 0.2 miles.

At Louisville the route joins Highway 51 for a 2.2-mile stretch (Turn 6) before turning north on County Road 27 (Turn 7) for 9.7 miles, the last 0.9 miles of it after joining County Road 9 (Turn 8).

Here the route heads north on Highway 239 for 18.3 miles (Turn 9), all the way into the Bullock County seat at Union Springs. Along

TURN-BY-TURN DIRECTIONS

1. Begin at Blue Springs State Park; west on Hwy 10 (0.5 miles)
2. Right on Hwy 131 (1.9 miles)
3. Left on CR-33 (0.1 miles)
4. Left on Blue Springs Rd—becomes Carpenter Mill Rd (5.9 miles)
5. Right on Planer Mill Rd (0.2 miles)
6. Slight left on Hwy 51 (2.2 miles)
7. Left on CR-27 (8.8 miles)
8. Right at CR-9 to stay on CR-27 (0.9 miles)
9. Left on Hwy 239—becomes U.S. Hwy 29 (18.3 miles)
10. Left on U.S. Hwy 82 (0.5 miles)
11. Left on Hwy 223 (26.5 miles)
12. Left on U.S. Hwy 29—becomes Hwy 93 (10.4 miles)
13. Left on U.S. Hwy 231 (10.7 miles)
14. Left on Hwy 51 (4.0 miles)
15. Right on Hwy 123 (3.0 miles)
16. Left on CR-19 (4.8 miles)
17. Right on CR-113 (0.2 miles)
18. Slight right on CR-15 (2.1 miles)
19. Left on CR-60—becomes Hwy 105 (12.6 miles)
20. Left on Hwy 10 (5.8 miles)

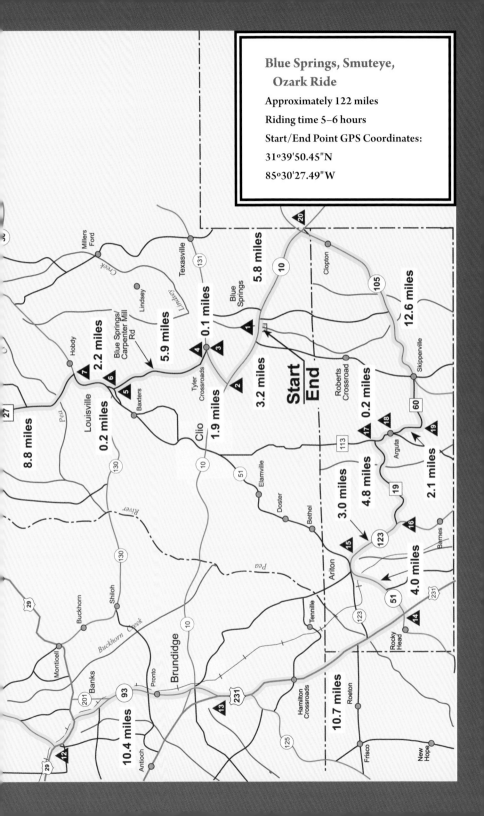

Blue Springs, Smuteye,
Ozark Ride

Approximately 122 miles

Riding time 5–6 hours

Start/End Point GPS Coordinates:

31º39'50.45"N

85º30'27.49"W

this stretch of Highway 239, however, after 5.6 miles, the route passes through the colorfully named community of Smuteye. Originally called "Welcome," the community became known as Smuteye because when men hung out around a local blacksmith's forge, their faces would become so covered in smut from the fire that only their eyes would be left visible. According to at least one account, moonshine often accompanied these gatherings as the locals warmed themselves around the forge. Over time the name stuck, and today the community is known to all as Smuteye.

At a fork in the road sits the old Smuteye Grocery building, long

Old grocery building in the community of Smuteye

ago closed down. Interestingly, the yellow door of the building is a hand-painted wanted poster for 1930s bank robber John Dillinger.

If you happen to be in the area in November, you might want to stop for the community's Hog Killin' Time, according to local Web site www.smuteye.com.

From Smuteye, the route heads north to Union Springs, where it turns back south on Highway 223 (Turns 10 and 11).

The historic city of Union Springs marks the approximate halfway point of the ride and one of the few places on the route convenient to fill up a gas tank or belly. Although it's slightly off-route, a

detour to the Bird Dog Field Trial Monument, a life-size bronze statue of a championship bird dog that sits atop a granite pedestal in the middle of a main downtown street, is well worth the trouble. To see this attraction, continue north on Prairie Street for two blocks at the intersection with U.S. Highway 82 (Turn 10). Once a prosperous cotton town, Union Springs also boasts numerous early-twentieth-century mansions and churches, some of which were being restored as of this writing.

From Union Springs the route follows Highway 223 south for 26.5 miles to its southern terminus at U.S. Highway 29 (Turn 12), where the route continues southward for another 10.4 miles, becoming Highway 93 after the first 2 miles.

At Turn 13 onto U.S. Highway 231 in Brundidge, you'll reach the only section of the route with any four-lane road, and this lasts only for the final 3 miles of this 10.7-mile section.

The next left (Turn 14) at Highway 51 begins an eastward series of state and county roads (Turns 15–19) to work back to Highway 10 (Turn 20), 5.8 miles east of the starting point at Blue Springs.

Camping at Blue Springs State Park

Hope Hull, Ansley, Lapine Ride

Approximately 97 miles

Riding time 4–5 hours

Start/End Point GPS Coordinates:

32º16'00.77"N

86º21'18.31"W

THIS ROUTE EXPLORES THE LANDSCAPE just south of Montgomery over ninety-seven miles of mostly back roads through a landscape that starts wide and flat through enormous pastures and gradually becomes hillier to the south.

Beginning at Exit 164 on Interstate 65, the first section heads north on U.S. Highway 31 for 0.7 miles to Hyundai Boulevard/ Teague Road (Turn 2), where it turns east for 2.7 miles, passing just south of the Hyundai automobile-manufacturing complex.

At Turn 3 the ride turns south on U.S. Highway 331 for 2.6 miles before turning left on Snowdoun Chambers Road (Turn 4). The countryside really opens up with pasture after pasture across hundreds of acres. You'll take pleasure in the "big sky" feeling of this terrain.

The southward sections of the ride begin at Woodley Road (Turn 5) and continue on Mount Zion Road (Turn 6), which later becomes Huffman Road and finally County Road 5. This 32.4-mile stretch runs almost all due south and is unusually curvy for this part of Alabama. The terrain gradually changes from farms and pastures to more woods and hills before County Road 5 intersects with U.S. Highway 29 at Turn 7 to continue southward.

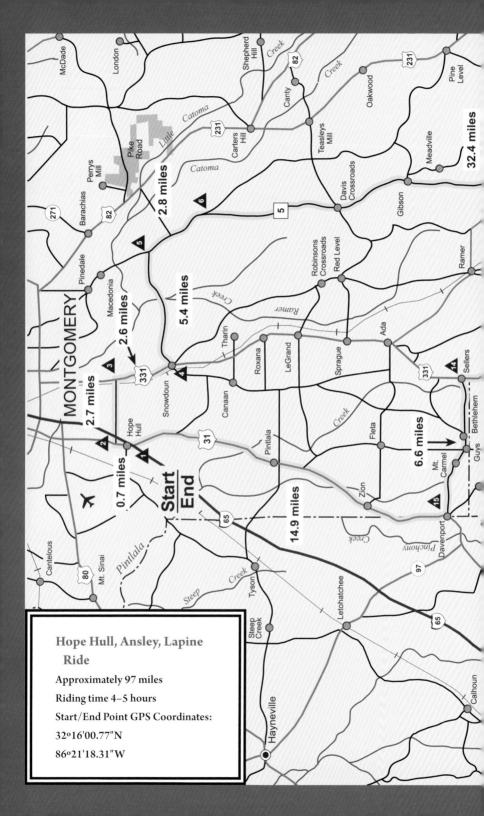

Hope Hull, Ansley, Lapine Ride

Approximately 97 miles

Riding time 4–5 hours

Start/End Point GPS Coordinates:

32°16'00.77"N

86°21'18.31"W

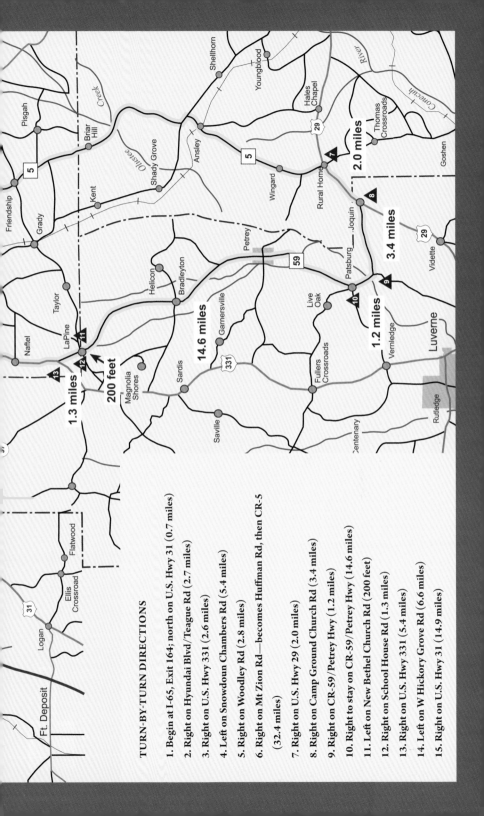

TURN-BY-TURN DIRECTIONS

1. Begin at I-65, Exit 164; north on U.S. Hwy 31 (0.7 miles)

2. Right on Hyundai Blvd/Teague Rd (2.7 miles)

3. Right on U.S. Hwy 331 (2.6 miles)

4. Left on Snowdoun Chambers Rd (5.4 miles)

5. Right on Woodley Rd (2.8 miles)

6. Right on Mt Zion Rd—becomes Huffman Rd, then CR-5 (32.4 miles)

7. Right on U.S. Hwy 29 (2.0 miles)

8. Right on Camp Ground Church Rd (3.4 miles)

9. Right on CR-59/Petrey Hwy (1.2 miles)

10. Right to stay on CR-59/Petrey Hwy (14.6 miles)

11. Left on New Bethel Church Rd (200 feet)

12. Right on School House Rd (1.3 miles)

13. Right on U.S. Hwy 331 (5.4 miles)

14. Left on W Hickory Grove Rd (6.6 miles)

15. Right on U.S. Hwy 31 (14.9 miles)

After just 2 miles on Highway 29, the ride turns west on Camp Ground Church Road for 3.4 miles (Turn 8) and then begins its northern return leg at County Road 59/Petrey Highway (Turn 9). The route follows this road—including a right turn at Turn 10 to stay on County Road 59 after 1.2 miles—northward for a total of almost 16 miles. Here the road has more broad, sweeping turns than the sections going south.

There's a small left-then-right dogleg at Turns 11 and 12 in the sleepy old town of Lapine, a good place to stop and stretch for a bit.

When you leave Lapine, it's just 1.3 miles back to the junction with U.S. Highway 331 (Turn 13), and the 5.4 miles on this road are noticeably hillier and more wooded than most of the ride.

At Turn 14, the route heads west on West Hickory Grove Road for 6.6 miles of mostly flat riding through a mixture of farmsteads and woodlands with gently sweeping turns.

Turn 15 begins the final section of about fifteen miles of enjoyable two-lane road on U.S. Highway 31 that becomes progressively wider and flatter as it returns to the starting point.

Opposite: Catching sight of a deer along the roadside near Lapine

Opelika, Tuskegee Ride

Approximately 100 miles
Riding time 4–5 hours

Start/End Point GPS Coordinates:
32°37'54.38"N
85°22'20.28"W

THIS ONE-HUNDRED-MILE LOOP would make a nice afternoon ride in the spring or fall of the year. Much of the way it passes through farmsteads and woodlands on moderately winding, well-maintained roadways.

Beginning at Exit 60 on Interstate 85 in Opelika, the first leg heads south from the interstate for 0.5 miles on Highway 51 before making a left onto Highway 169 (Turn 2) for 26.5 miles. After the first few miles through commercial and residential areas, this leg of the ride opens up into a rural landscape typical of southeast Alabama, alternating between fields and forest and punctuated by the occasional abandoned rustic farmhouse or barn.

As Highway 169 continues southward, the roadway is characterized by easy, sweeping curves on good asphalt.

At Turn 5 the route makes a right and goes 2.2 miles on a four-lane section of U.S. Highway 431 to its intersection with Highway 26 and another right at Turn 6. As of this writing, this 14.9-mile stretch featured a fresh, almost manicured asphalt surface that inspires confidence as you lean through the predictable sweeping turns.

Just after the intersection with Highway 51 at the old town of Hurtsboro, the route turns northward on Highway 10/Tuskegee

Coasting on a shady Macon County road

Highway (Turn 7), another well-kept and enjoyable two-lane road with terrain similar to that of highways 169 and 26, only with a bit more forested areas. It maintains its backwoods feeling until just a mile or two before Turns 8 and 9 in historic Tuskegee. This historic Macon County city is best known for the work of George Washington Carver at the Tuskegee Institute and for the Tuskegee Airmen, the first African American pilots in the U.S. armed forces.

Leaving Tuskegee, the route follows U.S. Highways 29/80 for 7.3 miles east through the Tuskegee National Forest before turning southeast on U.S. Highway 80 (Turn 10) for 13.2 miles to the Lee County community of Marvyn.

The final northward section of the ride turns left onto Highway 51 for 13.6 miles on another good road that starts off rural and becomes progressively more residential before returning to the starting point.

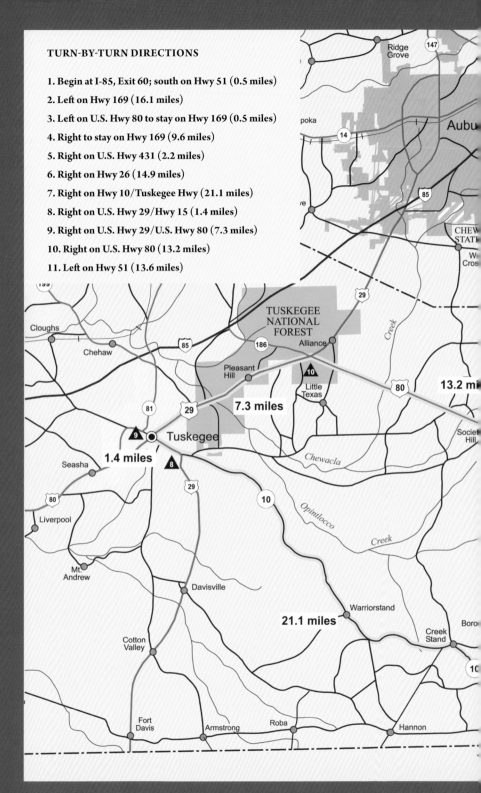

TURN-BY-TURN DIRECTIONS

1. Begin at I-85, Exit 60; south on Hwy 51 (0.5 miles)
2. Left on Hwy 169 (16.1 miles)
3. Left on U.S. Hwy 80 to stay on Hwy 169 (0.5 miles)
4. Right to stay on Hwy 169 (9.6 miles)
5. Right on U.S. Hwy 431 (2.2 miles)
6. Right on Hwy 26 (14.9 miles)
7. Right on Hwy 10/Tuskegee Hwy (21.1 miles)
8. Right on U.S. Hwy 29/Hwy 15 (1.4 miles)
9. Right on U.S. Hwy 29/U.S. Hwy 80 (7.3 miles)
10. Right on U.S. Hwy 80 (13.2 miles)
11. Left on Hwy 51 (13.6 miles)

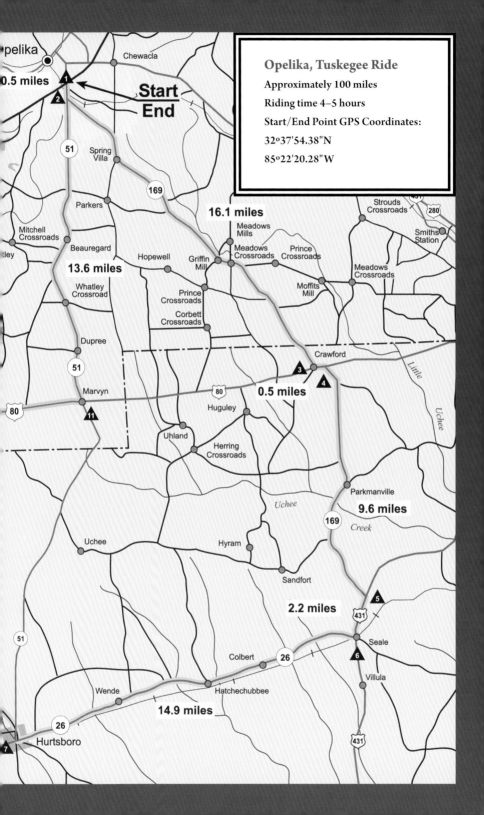

Florala, Geneva, Opp Ride

Approximately 94 miles
Riding time 3–4 hours

Start/End Point GPS Coordinates:
31º00'11.17"N
86º19'39.55"W

THIS EASY NINETY-FOUR-MILE LOOP begins and ends at Alabama's southernmost state park and passes through a town with one of the most unusual annual festivals in the country. Without stops, this mostly rural ride can easily be done in three hours.

Florala State Park, where the last campsite touches the Alabama-Florida state line, offers camping on the shores of the five-hundred-acre Lake Jackson, which actually straddles the state boundary line.

Starting at the park entrance on South Third Street in Florala, the first 0.1 miles of the ride goes northeast to join U.S. Highway 331 (Turn 2), which becomes Highway 54 after 1.3 miles at Turn 3.

For a road this far south on the mostly flat coastal plain, Highway 54's smoothly winding curves offer a pleasant contrast to the norm. Before terminating at Highway 52 after 15.9 miles (Turn 4), Highway 54 presents a nonstop series of enjoyable sweepers over gently rolling hills and even follows the southern boundary of the Geneva State Forest for a few miles.

Once you join Highway 52 just west of Samson, the next 16.9 miles prove noticeably straighter but still offer a scenic ride through terrain that varies between cultivated fields, pastures, and forest.

At Geneva (Turn 5), the route turns northward on Highway 27

for 16.7 miles, where you'll enjoy a section characterized by wide-open sky with sweeping curves through both rural and some more residential areas.

Turn 6 at Battens Crossroads is a left turn to the west on Highway 636, which over the next 20.9 miles becomes Highway 14 and finally Highway 134 before rejoining U.S. Highway 331 just outside Opp (Turn 7).

This Covington County city hosts what has to be one of the strangest annual festivals anywhere in the United States: the Opp Rattlesnake Rodeo. The event is held each spring and features a variety of snake-related events, including a snake show, snake races, and a chance to sample fried snake. There's even a beauty pageant—in which the lucky "winner" is draped with a live rattler.

In Opp, riders will encounter the only brief four-lane stretch of this ride on the U.S. Highway 331 bypass for about 3.7 miles. Then the road becomes two-lane and mostly straight for the remaining eighteen miles back to Florala and the starting point.

Canoeing on the Yellow River near Florala

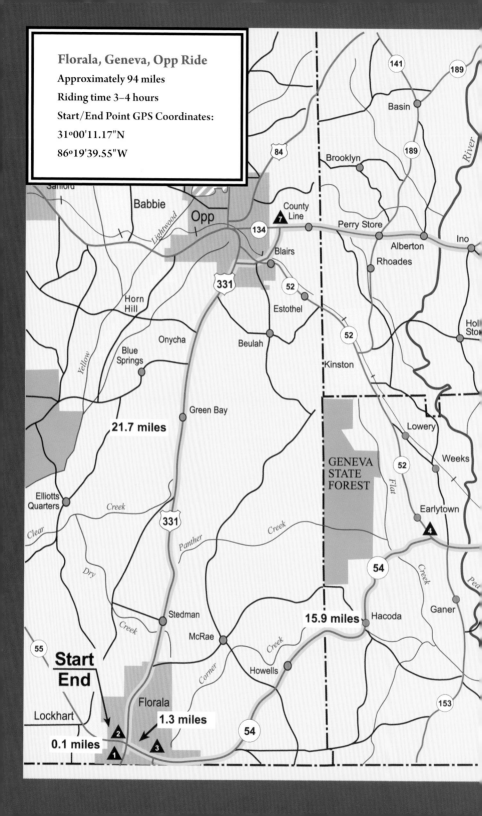

Florala, Geneva, Opp Ride

Approximately 94 miles

Riding time 3–4 hours

Start/End Point GPS Coordinates:

31º00'11.17"N

86º19'39.55"W

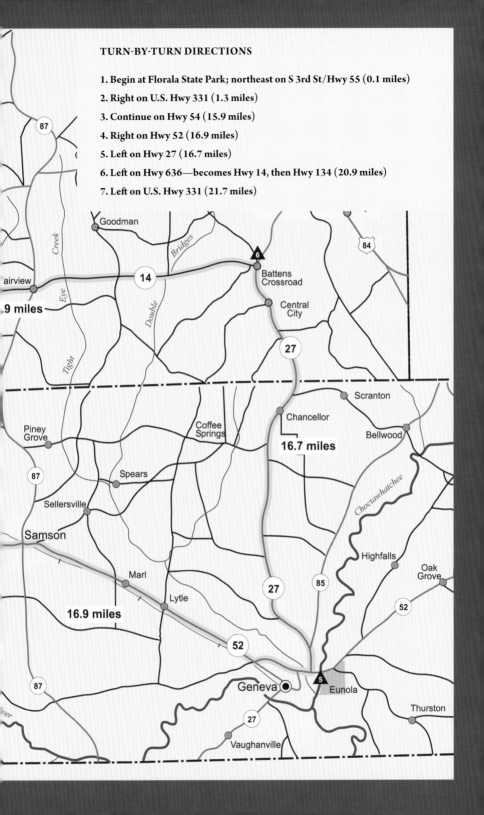

TURN-BY-TURN DIRECTIONS

1. Begin at Florala State Park; northeast on S 3rd St/Hwy 55 (0.1 miles)
2. Right on U.S. Hwy 331 (1.3 miles)
3. Continue on Hwy 54 (15.9 miles)
4. Right on Hwy 52 (16.9 miles)
5. Left on Hwy 27 (16.7 miles)
6. Left on Hwy 636—becomes Hwy 14, then Hwy 134 (20.9 miles)
7. Left on U.S. Hwy 331 (21.7 miles)

Evergreen, Andalusia, Brewton Ride

Approximately 120 miles
Riding time 4–5 hours

Start/End Point GPS Coordinates:
31°25'08.72"N
87°00'22.45"W

AFTER THE FIRST FIVE MILES or so through the town of Evergreen, this 120-mile ride loop stays almost entirely on rural back roads that are a pleasure to experience on a motorcycle.

Beginning at Exit 93 on Interstate 65 at Fairview, the first 4.2 miles on U.S. Highway 84 to Brooklyn Road are some of the busiest in traffic.

The 37.4 miles from Turn 2 at Brooklyn Road/County Road 42 to the outskirts of Andalusia at U. S. Highway 29 (Turn 3) pass through a mix of forests and farm fields with an occasional rustic farmhouse, barn, or store. This part of the ride has just enough sweeping curves to keep it interesting.

After turning south on U.S. Highway 29 outside Andalusia, the roadway follows similar terrain but has fewer curves and a more open feeling of expansive sky.

Much of the 11.9-mile section from Turn 4 to Turn 5 on Highway 137 runs through a pine forest with a wide-cut right-of-way and more fast, sweeping curves.

At Turn 5 the route turns west on County Road 4 just a couple of miles north of the Alabama-Florida line. Here the landscape is quite flat, but this road has an almost continuous series of smooth curves that make for a pleasurable ride.

As of this writing, a change in County Road 4 just before the Conecuh River crossing was not updated on any maps or GPS maps that I found. About three miles before County Road 4's terminus at U.S. Highway 29, a new road and bridge to the right crosses the river and the old road is now closed to traffic. I note this for riders who could be surprised to see the new road that may not yet be on their map or GPS, as this happened to me on my first ride through the area.

From the Turn 6 intersection with U.S. Highway 29 to the Turn 7 intersection with U.S. Highway 31 at Brewton, the distance is almost exactly ten miles, whereas my maps and GPS were showing it as about nine miles.

While passing through Brewton at Turn 7, look to the left to see a couple of historically inspired murals painted on the sides of downtown buildings.

Painted mural in downtown Brewton

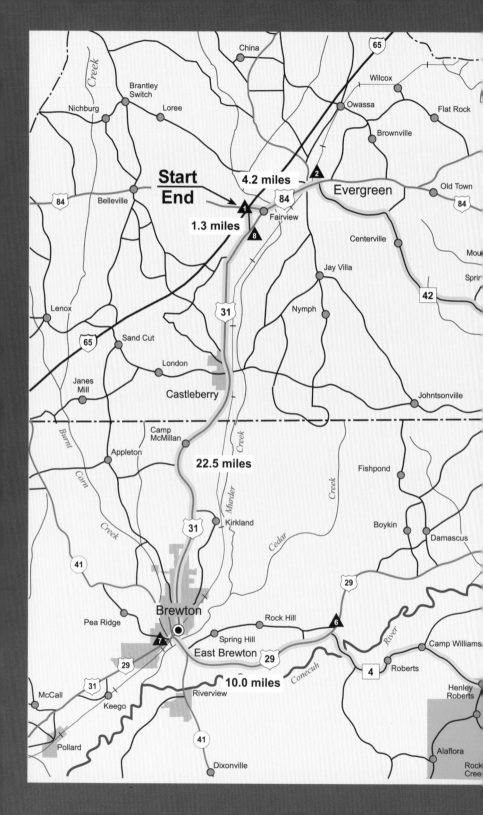

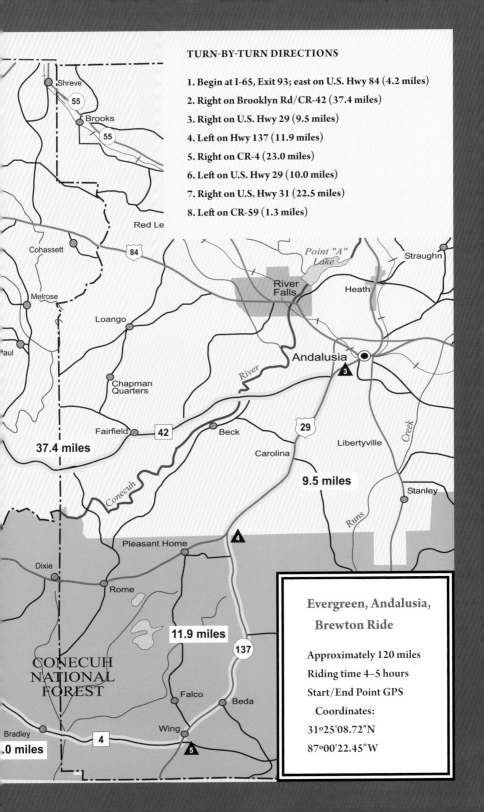

TURN-BY-TURN DIRECTIONS

1. Begin at I-65, Exit 93; east on U.S. Hwy 84 (4.2 miles)
2. Right on Brooklyn Rd/CR-42 (37.4 miles)
3. Right on U.S. Hwy 29 (9.5 miles)
4. Left on Hwy 137 (11.9 miles)
5. Right on CR-4 (23.0 miles)
6. Left on U.S. Hwy 29 (10.0 miles)
7. Right on U.S. Hwy 31 (22.5 miles)
8. Left on CR-59 (1.3 miles)

Shreve

55

Brooks

55

Red Le

Cohassett

84

Point "A" Lake

Straughn

Melrose

River Falls

Heath

Loango

aul

Andalusia

Chapman Quarters

3

River

Fairfield

42

Beck

29

Libertyville

Creek

37.4 miles

Carolina

9.5 miles

Stanley

Conecuh

Runs

Pleasant Home

4

Dixie

Rome

11.9 miles

CONECUH NATIONAL FOREST

137

Falco

Beda

Bradley

4

Wing

5

.0 miles

Evergreen, Andalusia, Brewton Ride

Approximately 120 miles
Riding time 4–5 hours
Start/End Point GPS
  Coordinates:
31º25'08.72"N
87º00'22.45"W

For the 22.5 miles from Brewton to Turn 8 near the starting point, U.S. Highway 31 passes through gradually more residential and commercial zones, though overall this section remains mostly rural in character.

From Turn 8 onto County Road 59, it's just 1.3 miles back to the starting point.

RIDE LOOP 48
Frank Jackson State Park, Stanley, Red Level Ride

Approximately 116 miles
Riding time 4–5 hours

Start/End Point GPS Coordinates:
31º17'35.90"N
86º16'28.08"W

ALL BUT ABOUT 3 MILES of the 116 miles of this loop stay on two-lane roads through rural south Alabama countryside.

The ride begins and returns to Frank Jackson State Park on Jackson Lake in Opp, where camping, fishing, picnicking, and hiking are available. In fact, if you decide to stay at this state park, this ride could be combined with Ride Loop 47: Evergreen, Andalusia, Brewton Ride, which travels in the same vicinity; or you could perhaps do the two routes on consecutive days with a night of camping in between.

The route begins at the state park entrance road and first follows Opine Street for 1.1 miles before turning south on U.S. Highway 331 (Turn 2) for 0.7 miles.

From there the route turns right on U.S. Highway 84 (Turn 3) and heads west for 6.6 miles—about 3 miles of which represent the only four-lane highway on the ride.

Turn 4 makes a left onto County Road 73/Cantaline Bridge Road for 1.3 miles, then a right on Coutny Road 45 at Turn 5 for 5.1 miles, continuing south. In this section the road winds left and right through a mixture of open pastures and wooded terrain.

The right turn onto County Road 32 at Turn 6 begins the west-

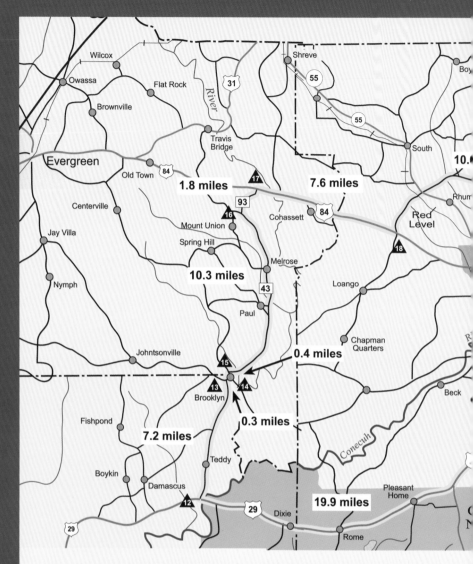

TURN-BY-TURN DIRECTIONS

1. Begin at Frank Jackson State Park, head east on Opine St (1.1 miles)
2. Right on U.S. Hwy 331/Hwy 9 (0.7 miles)
3. Right on U.S. Hwy 84 (6.6 miles)
4. Left on CR-73/Cantaline Bridge Rd (1.3 miles)
5. Right on CR-45 (5.1 miles)
6. Right on CR-32 (5.2 miles)
7. Left on Hwy 55 (1.3 miles)
8. Right on Hwy 55 Cutoff (3.5 miles)
9. Left on Andy Rd/CR-32 (1.2 miles)
10. Right on CR-31/1st Ave (0.9 miles)
11. Left on U.S. Hwy 29 (19.9 miles)
12. Right on Brooklyn Rd (7.2 miles)
13. Right on CR-6 (0.3 miles)
14. Left on CR-42 (0.4 miles)
15. Right on CR-43 (10.3 miles)
16. Right on CR-93 (1.8 miles)
17. Right on U.S. Hwy 84 (7.6 miles)

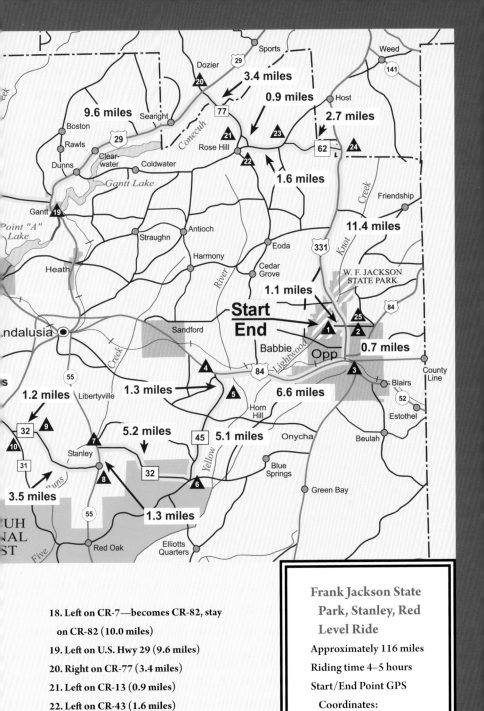

9.6 miles

3.4 miles

0.9 miles

2.7 miles

1.6 miles

11.4 miles

1.1 miles

Start End

0.7 miles

1.2 miles

1.3 miles

6.6 miles

5.2 miles

5.1 miles

3.5 miles

1.3 miles

18. Left on CR-7—becomes CR-82, stay
    on CR-82 (10.0 miles)
19. Left on U.S. Hwy 29 (9.6 miles)
20. Right on CR-77 (3.4 miles)
21. Left on CR-13 (0.9 miles)
22. Left on CR-43 (1.6 miles)
23. Right on CR-62 (2.7 miles)
24. Right on U.S. Hwy 331 (11.4 miles)
25. Right on Opine Street (1.1 miles)

**Frank Jackson State
Park, Stanley, Red
Level Ride**

Approximately 116 miles

Riding time 4–5 hours

Start/End Point GPS
    Coordinates:
31o17'35.90"N
86o16'28.08"W

ward section of the ride, with Turns 7 to 11 heading in that direction. The first zigzagging sections at Turns 7, 8, 9, and 10 pass similar scenery. Then at Turn 11, where the route joins U.S. Highway 29 for 19.9 miles, the road has a much more open feeling as it winds through gently rolling hills of farm fields and forest.

Turn 12 marks the beginning of the northward leg of the route at Brooklyn Road, which generally passes through a more forested landscape. At the town of Brooklyn after 7.2 miles, Turns 13, 14, and 15 make a right-left-right dogleg that continues north on County Road 43 for 10.3 miles to County Road 93 (Turn 16), a 1.8-mile cutoff road to U.S. Highway 84 (Turn 17). This entire section from Brooklyn to U.S. Highway 84 continues to wind through mostly forested areas, but the right-of-way and roadway are somewhat narrower than the section before.

Starry night camping in south Alabama

At Turn 17, the route begins an eastward leg for 7.6 miles on U.S. Highway 84 before making a left at County Road 7 (Turn 18) for 10 miles, which joins with County Road 82. Stay on County Road 82 when 7 branches off, which takes you through the Red Level community and finally forms a T into U.S. Highway 29 at Gantt (Turn 18).

The next 6.5 miles on U.S. Highway 29 follow the northwestern shore of Gantt Lake, passing numerous lake cottages and at least one private campground.

At Dozier (Turn 20), the route turns right on Highway 77 to continue eastward through Turns 21, 22, and 23 before turning south for 11.4 miles on U.S. Highway 331 at Turn 24.

After the final right onto Opine Street (Turn 25), it's just 1.1 miles back to the start.

RIDE LOOP 49

Baldwin County Ride

Approximately 97 miles
Riding time 3–4 hours

Start/End Point GPS Coordinates:
30°37'43.99"N
87°36'55.90"W

THIS NINETY-SEVEN-MILE RIDE loop stays entirely within Baldwin County east of Mobile Bay and west of the Alabama-Florida state line and passes by the site of the last major battle of the Civil War.

The beginning sections and final miles of this ride could hardly be more different, with the first miles passing through busy residential and commercial districts. In contrast, the route doesn't even pass a store for the last thirty-five miles.

Beginning at Exit 53 on Interstate 10, the route at first goes south and west for 17.7 miles on County Road 64 to Daphne (Turns 1 and 2).

U.S. Highway 98 (Turn 3) begins the northward leg of 4.6 miles that continues for another 24 miles on Highway 225 (Turns 4 and 5).

About 4.5 miles after joining Highway 225, on the left you will see the entrance to Historic Blakeley State Park, where more than twenty thousand Federal and Confederate forces fought the last major battle of the Civil War. The park offers camping, hiking trails, tours of the battlefield, and even tour boat rides on the Tensaw River. Each April the park hosts a reenactment of the battle, and each October it hosts a bluegrass music festival.

Continuing northward on Highway 225, one of the few roads in this area with both hills and curves, the route parallels the Tensaw River west of Bay Minette to May Tower. At Stockton (Turn 6), you'll turn left onto Highway 59 and, after 1.4 miles, make a right turn on Maytower Road (Turn 7).

This point begins the easterly portion of the ride. After 6.6 miles on Maytower Road/County Road 94, the route turns left on Rabun Road/County Road 47 (Turn 8) and follows it for 10.4 miles to U.S. Highway 31 at Perdido (Turn 9).

Interstate 65 in this section offers a last chance for you to fill up with gas for the final thirty-two miles back to Interstate 10 at the starting point. (I learned this the hard way.)

After going south for 1.3 miles on U.S. Highway 31, the route turns left onto Phillipsville Road/County Road 61 (Turn 10) and stays just west of the Alabama-Florida line to the road's intersection with County Road 112/Old Pensacola Road (Turn 11).

County Road 112 continues to follow the state line southeast for 12.3 miles through a pine forest to Gateswood (Turn 12), where the route returns to the starting point seven miles after you turn right on County Road 64.

Camping at Historic Blakeley State Park

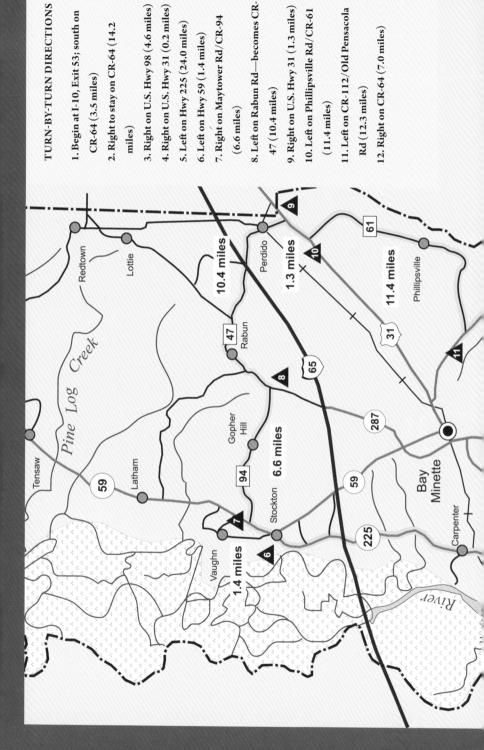

TURN-BY-TURN DIRECTIONS

1. Begin at I-10, Exit 53; south on CR-64 (3.5 miles)
2. Right to stay on CR-64 (14.2 miles)
3. Right on U.S. Hwy 98 (4.6 miles)
4. Right on U.S. Hwy 31 (0.2 miles)
5. Left on Hwy 225 (24.0 miles)
6. Left on Hwy 59 (1.4 miles)
7. Right on Maytower Rd/CR-94 (6.6 miles)
8. Left on Rabun Rd—becomes CR-47 (10.4 miles)
9. Right on U.S. Hwy 31 (1.3 miles)
10. Left on Phillipsville Rd/CR-61 (11.4 miles)
11. Left on CR-112/Old Pensacola Rd (12.3 miles)
12. Right on CR-64 (7.0 miles)

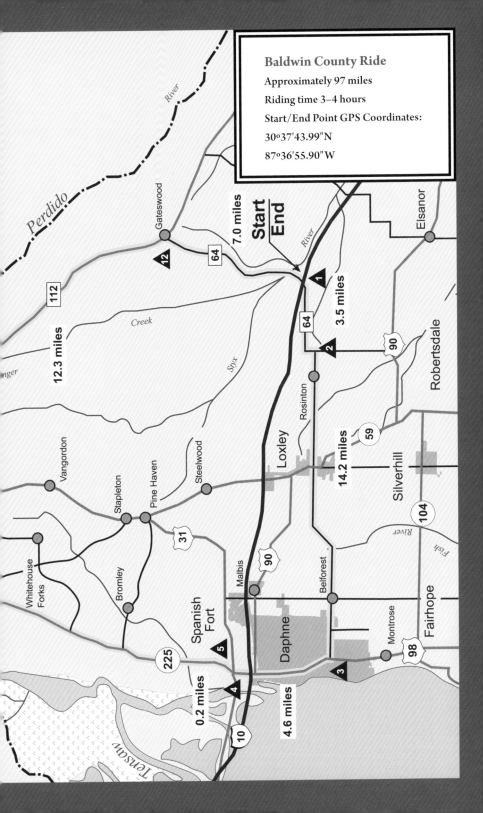

Baldwin County Ride

Approximately 97 miles

Riding time 3–4 hours

Start/End Point GPS Coordinates:

30°37'43.99"N

87°36'55.90"W

Fort Deposit, Luverne, Brantley Ride

Approximately 98 miles
Riding time 3–4 hours

Start/End Point GPS Coordinates:
31°59'06.43"N
86°31'46.88"W

WINDING THROUGH THE ROLLING low hills and valleys of south central Alabama on mostly two-lane country roads, this ninety-eight-mile loop is a great way to enjoy a low-stress springtime or autumn afternoon. In fact, the only four-lane stretch is the nine miles from Luverne to Brantley.

Passing through parts of Lowndes, Butler, and Crenshaw counties, the ride begins at Exit 142 on Interstate 65, just east of Fort Deposit, and heads east on Highway 185 for 2.3 miles to its terminus at U.S. Highway 31.

Continuing eastward, the route joins U.S. Highway 31 for less than 200 feet before turning right onto County Road 4 (Turn 2) for another 6.5 miles to a left turn at Bowden Road (Turn 3), which becomes Old Meriwether Trail after a few miles.

After 6.0 miles, Turn 4 takes a right onto County Road 28 for 1.2 miles; then Turn 5 is a right onto Highway 59 for 20.5 miles. This extended section is characterized by long, sweeping turns through typical central Alabama countryside with the occasional farm separating long stretches of wooded low hills.

At Turn 6 just east of Luverne, the route joins U.S. Highway 29 and turns right into town. For the next stretch, which includes the only four-lane section, the route is on U.S. Highway 29 for almost ten miles to Brantley. Pay special attention to road signs in order to stay on the route. Then it follows U.S. Highway 29 to Turn 9 at Highway 106, which heads westward for 15.8 miles, mostly through rolling low hills and pine forests.

Because stores and gas stations are few and far between after you leave U.S. Highway 29, it would be advisable to fill up if necessary before the turn at Brantley.

Turn 10 begins the northerly part of the route on Halso Mill Road/Highway 59 for 16.1 miles, a road with narrower right-of-way but running through similar terrain with a few more pastures and farm fields than Highway 106.

At U.S. Highway 31 (Turn 11), the route turns right and continues north, paralleling Interstate 65 for 12.4 miles before turning left onto County Road 79 at Turn 12. This 1.7-mile cut-through road connects with Highway 185 at Turn 13, just 0.9 miles from the starting point.

Riding Highway 185, where this ride loop begins and ends

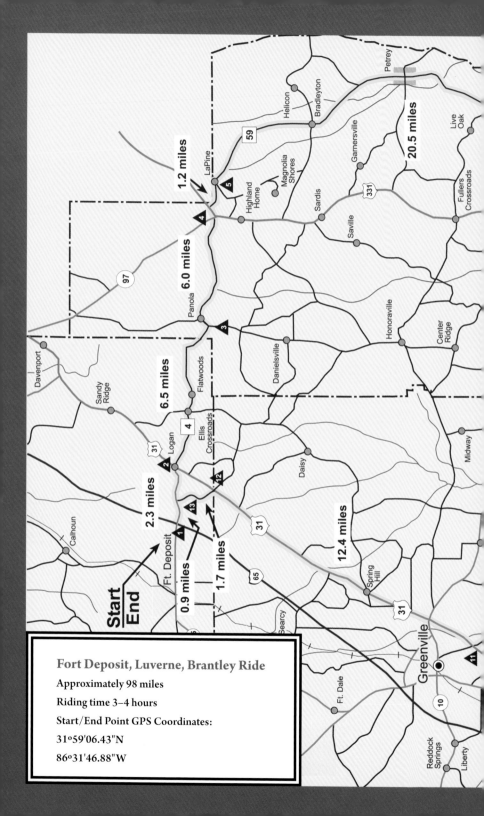

Fort Deposit, Luverne, Brantley Ride

Approximately 98 miles

Riding time 3–4 hours

Start/End Point GPS Coordinates:

31º59'06.43"N

86º31'46.88"W

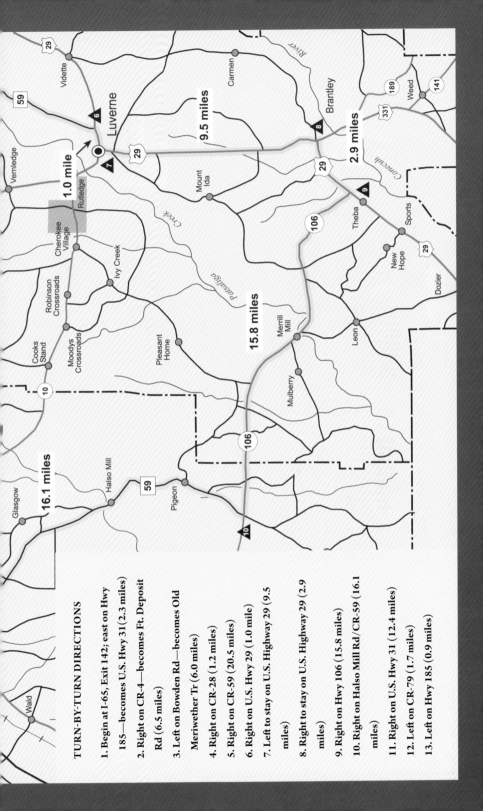

TURN-BY-TURN DIRECTIONS

1. Begin at I-65, Exit 142; east on Hwy 185—becomes U.S. Hwy 31 (2.3 miles)

2. Right on CR-4—becomes Ft. Deposit Rd (6.5 miles)

3. Left on Bowden Rd—becomes Old Meriwether Tr (6.0 miles)

4. Right on CR-28 (1.2 miles)

5. Right on CR-59 (20.5 miles)

6. Right on U.S. Hwy 29 (1.0 mile)

7. Left to stay on U.S. Highway 29 (9.5 miles)

8. Right to stay on U.S. Highway 29 (2.9 miles)

9. Right on Hwy 106 (15.8 miles)

10. Right on Halso Mill Rd/CR-59 (16.1 miles)

11. Right on U.S. Hwy 31 (12.4 miles)

12. Left on CR-79 (1.7 miles)

13. Left on Hwy 185 (0.9 miles)

The Barber Vintage Motorsports Museum. Photo courtesy D. McCalla, BVMM2010.

INDEX

Page numbers in bold refer to illustrations.

29 Dreams, 176

Abbeville, 287, **290**
accidents. *See* safety
Adams Gap, 181, **182**, 191
Addison, 146, **150**
Alabama Mountain Lakes region, 51
Alabama River, **23**, **34**, 157, 225, **228**, **230**, 232, 233, 248, 272, **273**
Alabama Traffic Safety Center, 14–15, 239. *See also* Motorcycle Safety Program
Alabaster, 202
Alberta City, 145
Alexander City, 167
Aliceville, 128
Allen Grove Plantation, 215
Altoona, 44
Andalusia, 310, 315
Anderson, 119
Ansley, 297
Arkadelphia, 90, 136–37
Arley, 106

Ashford, 286
Ashland, 188
Ashville, 40, 46

Baldwin County, **258**, 320
Bangor, 91
Bankhead National Forest, 99, **104**, 106, **107**
Bankhead Tunnel, **259**, 260
Barber Motorsports Park, **47**, 50
Barber Vintage Motorsports Museum, 50, 172, 176, **328**
Barbour County, 291
Barnwell, 251
Battens Crossroads, 307
Battleground, 76, 110
Bay Minette, 321
Bayou Coden, 275
Bayou La Batre, 274–**75**, **278**
Bear Creek, 61, 132
Bear Creek Reservoir, 132
Beaver Mountain, 47
Belgreen, 132

Bellingrath Gardens, 274

Bibb County, 239

Bibb Graves Bridge, 157

Billingsley, 240, 250

Bird Dog Field Trial Monument, 296

Bird, Jim, 214; sculptures, **214**, **216–17**

Birmingham, 40, 172

Black Belt, 128, 215

Black Warrior River, 140–41, 144, 211, 215

Bladon Springs State Park, 218, **219**, **222**, 224

Blount County, 40, 44–45, 83, 86, 90, 136; covered bridges, 83, 90. *See also* Easley Bridge; Horton Mill Bridge; Swann Bridge

Blount Springs, 83, 86, 95

Blountsville, 86

Blue Springs State Park, **17**, 291, **296**

Bluff Hall, 215

Boligee, 211, 216

Bon Secour, 251, **257**

Bon Secour National Wildlife Refuge, 254

Brantley, 324–25

Bremen, 106

Brewton, **311**, 314, 315

Brierfield, 239

Brierfield Ironworks Historical State Park, 239, **242**

Brilliant, 132

Brompton County, 46

Brooklyn, 318

Brookwood, 141

Brundidge, 296

Brushy Creek, 106

Brushy Lake, 102, **104**, 105

Buck's Pocket State Park, 54–**55**

Bucksnort, 37

Bug Tussle, 137

Bull Gap, 188, 195

Bullock County, 291

Burnsville, 250

Burnt Corn, 264, **265**, **266–67**, 269

Butler County, 324

Cahaba River, 197, 200, 202, 242, 272

Cahaba River National Wildlife Refuge, **200**

Cairo, 123

Calera, 200, 239

Camden, 225, 231–33, 237–38

Camp Hill, 166, 169

camping, motorcycle, 16–26; packing and packed size, 18–20, 34; gear, 21–25

Canyon Mouth Picnic Area, 56, 60–61

Caperton's Old South Store, **160**, 206

Carbon Hill, 105

Carns, 67

Cathedral Caverns State Park, 37

Catherine, 237–38

Centreville, 239, 242

Chandler Mountain, 41

Chandler Springs, 194

Chatom, 224

Chattahoochee River, 286

Chattahoochee State Park, 283, **286**

Cheaha Creek, 181

Cheaha State Park, 81, 177, **180**, 183, 184–**85**, **189**, 191

Chilton County, 203, 207, 239, **245**, 250

Christmas on the River, 215

Claiborne, 225

Clairmont Gap, 191

Clanton, 161, 203, 207, 244

Clarke County, 225

Clarkson, 146

Clarkson/Legg Covered Bridge, **147**

Clay County, 180–81, 188

Clayton, 290

Cleburne County, 183

Cleveland, 87, 91

Clio, 291

Cloudland, 61

Cloudmont, 62

CME Church, Lowndesboro, 272

Coal City, 47

Cochrane, 128

Coden, 274

Coffee County, 291

Coffeeville, 222

Colbert Ferry, **114**, 116

Coleman Lake, 82

Columbiana, 200

Comer, 290

Conecuh River, 311

Cook Springs, 47, 172, **173**, 176

Coosa County, **20**, 157, 160–61, 203

Coosa Mountain, 176, 197

Coosa River, 157, 161, 203, 207

Coosa Wildlife Management Area, 161

Cordova, 137

Cottonwood, 283

Covington County, 307

Crane Hill, 110

Crawford Cove, 41

Crenshaw County, 324

Crooked Creek, 106, 147

Cropwell, 172

Crow Mountain, 67

Cuba, 211, 215

Cullman, 89

Cullman County, 136, **147**

Cumberland Plateau, 70

Dadeville, 162, 169

Dale County, 291

Dannelly Reservoir, 225

Daphne, 320

Dauphin Island, 251, 255, **256**;
    Bridge, **254**

Davis Ferry, **4**, 225, **228, 230**

Dawson, 55

Deal's Gap, North Carolina, 173,
    197. *See also* Tail of the Dragon

Deatsville, 157

Deerlick Creek Park, 144

DeLorme *Alabama Atlas and
    Gazetteer,* 3

Demopolis, 215, 242

DeSoto State Park, 56, 62

Devils Den Waterfalls, 182

Dodge City, 106, 110

Dog Town, 60

Double Springs, **102**, 103, 105

Dozier, 319

dual-sport motorcycles, vii, x, 3,
    77–82, 90–95, 99–105, 177–83,
    191–96, 225

Dudleyville, 166; General Store,
    163

Dunavant, 176

Easley Bridge, **86–87**, 95

Eberhart Point, 60–61

Edmund Pettus Bridge, 233, 248,
    249

Eldridge, 103

Elk River, 119, 123

Elkmont, 123

Elmore County, 157

Enon: convenience store, 71, **76**

Epes, 215–16

Etowah County, 40, 44

Eufaula, 287

Eutaw, 128

Eva, 71

Evergreen, 310

Fairhope, 251

Fairview, 71, 310

Falkville, 71

Farley Nuclear Plant, 286

Fayette, 124

Fayetteville, 206

Fish River, 251

Five Points, 51, 145, 168

Florala, 306–7

Florala State Park, 306

Florence, 111, 118

Florette, 71

Forkland, 211

Fort Deposit, 261, 269, 324

Fort Morgan, 251, 255, **259**

Fort Payne, 56

Fort Tombigbee, 216

Fowl River, 260, 274

Frank Jackson State Park, 315

Franklin, 225

Frankville, 224

Freedom Hills Overlook, 116

Friendship Baptist Church, 216

Furman, 261, **265**

Gainesville, 128–**29**

Gaineswood, 215

Gallant, 41

Gantt, 319

Gantt Lake, 319

Gantt's Quarry, 206

Garden City, 86, 90

Gateswood, 321

gear, 5; boots, 8–10; gloves, 8–10; helmets, 6–8; jacket and pants, 10–11; rain, 11–14

Gedney's, 156

Gees Bend, 231, 233, 237

Gees Bend Ferry, 237–38

Geneva State Forest, 306

Global Positioning System (GPS), 3–4

Google Earth, 3

Google Maps, 3

Gordo, 124

Goshen Hollow, 67

GPS. *See* Global Positioning System

.Gpx file. *See* GPS

Graces High Falls, 61

Grand Bay, 274, 278

Grangeburg, 283

Grant, 37

Grantley, 81

Green Pond, 202

Greene County, 128

Greenville, 261, 269

Gulf Shores, 254

Hackleburg, 133

Haleyville, 99, 132

Hamilton, 115, 118

Hammondville, 66

Hanceville, 89

Hartselle, 146

Hawk, 156

Hayden, 83, 89, 95

Hayneville, 272

Heflin, 81–82, 156

Historic Blakeley State Park, 320

Historical Society, St. Clair County, 47

Hodges, 133

Hope Hull, 269, 297

Horn Mountain, 188, 191, 194–**95**

Horse Pens 40, 41

Horseshoe Bend National Military Park, 162–**63**, 166, 168

Horton Mill Bridge, 87, **94**, 95. *See also* Blount County

House Road Bridge, **94**

Houston, 107

Houston County, 283

Hurtsboro, 302

Hyundai Motor Manufacturing Alabama, 297

instruction, riding, 14–15

Interstate 10, 251, 260, 274, 320–21

Interstate 20, 46–47, 81, 153, 172

Interstate 20/59, 128, 141, 211

Interstate 22/Corridor X, 99, 115, 132, 140

Interstate 59, 40, 66

Interstate 65, 71, 83, 89, 90, 106, 136, 146, 157, 197, 203, 239, 244, 261, 269, 297, 310, 321, 324–25

Interstate 85, 168, 302

Isbell, 132

Jackson, 167, 222–23

Jackson County, **37**, **70**

Jackson Lake, 306, 315

Jacobs Mountain, 36

James H. Miller Jr. Electric Generating Plant, **140**

Jasper, 99

Jefferson, 215

Jefferson County, 40, 45, 136, 141

Jemison, 243

Jena, 128

Jesse Owens Museum, 110

Jim Walter No. 4 Mine, 141

Joe Wheeler State Park, 119

John Looney Pioneer House Museum, 46

Johnnie's Creek, 60–61

Jones Chapel, 110

Jordan Lake, 157

Kellys Crossroads, 160, 203

Kentuck Off-Road Vehicle (ORV) Area, 182

Kentuck ORV Area. *See* Kentuck Off-Road Vehicle (ORV) Area

Kinlock Falls, 103

Kowaliga Bridge, 162

Lacon, 76, 146

LaFayette, 169

Lake Chinnabee, 181

Lake Guntersville State Park, **50**, 51, **54**

Lake Jackson, 306

Lake Lurleen State Park, 124–25

Lake Martin, 162

Lake Martin Dam, **167**

Lakepoint Resort State Park, 287, 290

Lamar Marshall's Warrior Mountains Trading Company and Indian Museum, 103

Lanett, 168

Langston, 51

Lapine, **301**

laws, state of Alabama, 6–7

Lay Dam, 161, 203, 207

Lay Lake, 157

Lee County, 303

Leeds, **47**, 50, 172, 176, 197

Leroy, 223

Letcher, 37

Lewis Smith Lake, 106. *See also* Smith Lake Park

Lexington, 119, 123

Linden, 215

Lineville, 180, 185, 188

Little Lagoon, 254

Little River Canyon, 56–**57**, **60**, **62–65**

Little River Falls, 56, 60

Little Tallapoosa River, 153

Live Oak Cemetery, 233, **236**, 244–45, 248

Lizzieville, 211

Locust Fork, 88, 91, 94–95, 140. *See also* Swann Bridge; Warrior River

Logan Martin Dam, 172–73, 197

Logan Martin Lake, 172

Lookout Mountain, 56, 61–62, 66

Louisville, 291

Lower Peach Tree, 232

Lowndes County, 272, 324

Lowndes County Interpretive Center, 273

Lowndesboro, 269, 272–73

Luverne, 324

Lynns Park Community, 137

Macon County, **303**

Magnolia Springs, 251, **258**

Maplesville, 233, 243, 244

Marion, 238, 242

Marvyn, 303

Maytower, 321

Maytown, 140

Mellow Valley, 168

Menlo, Georgia, 61

Mentone, 56, 62

Midway, 264

Millers Ferry, 237

Millerville, 188

Mitchell Dam, 203

Mitchell Lake, 157

Mobile, 224, 245, **259,** 260, 274

Mobile Bay, 251, **254, 256,** 259–60, 274, **279,** 320

Mobile Bay Ferry, 251, 255, **256**

Monroe County, 225, **229, 231**

Monte Sano State Park, 36

Montevallo, 197, 200, 239; University of, **12,** 14–15, 239

Moody Gap, 67

Moscow, 211, 215

Motorcycle Safety Program, 14–15, 239. *See also* Alabama Traffic Safety Center

Moulton, 99, 103

Mount Cheaha, 153, **182,** 184, **188–89,** 190, 191, 196

Mulberry Fork, 90, 144. *See also* Warrior River

Murphy Creek, 83, 95

Mushroom Rock, 61, **62**

Nances Creek, 81

Natchez Trace Parkway, 111, **114–16**

Nauvoo, 105

Nectar, 95

Neely Henry Lake, 46

New Site, 162

Northport, 141, 144

Oak Mountain State Park, 197

Oakville Indian Mounds Park, 110

Odenville, 46

Old Spring Hill, 215

Old St. Stephens Historical Park, 218, **223,** 224

Old Town, 233, **236,** 244

Omaha, 153

Oneonta, 40, 44–45, 89

Opelika, 302

Opp, 306–7, 315

Opp Rattlesnake Rodeo, 307

Our Lady of Bon Secour Church, **257**

Oyster Bay, 251

Ozark, 291

Paint Rock River, 36

Paul M. Grist State Park, 233, 238

Pearce, 286

Pell City, 172

Penton, 168

Perdido, 321

Perry County, 225, 231, 239

Perry Lakes Park, 242

Phil Campbell, 132

Pickens County, 128

Piedmont, 81

Pike County, 291

Pine Apple, **264, 268**

Pine Glen, 82
Pine Level, 157
Pine Mountain, 44
Pine Torch Church, 105
Pinson, 44
Plantersville, 244

Rabbittown, 103
Ragland, 47
Rainsville, 55
Ranburne, 153
Rash, 67, 70
Rebecca Mountain, 188
Red Bay, 115
Red Hill, 162
Red Level, 319
Remlap, 44
Rickwood Caverns State Park, 83,
   89
Roanoke, 153, 156
Rock Creek, 106, 110
Rock Spring, 118
Rock Zoo, **66–67**
Rogersville, 119, 123
Roland Cooper State Park, 225
Rosa, 87, 95
Rosemount Plantation, 211
Royal Oaks Plantation, 275, **279**
Rutherford, 290
Ryan Creek, 110

safety, 5–15. *See also* Alabama Traf-
   fic Safety Center; gear; Motor-
   cycle Safety Program
Salitpa, 223
Samson, 306
Sand Mountain, 51, 54–55, 66, 70
Scottsboro, 54, 66
Section, 54–55
Selma, 233, **236**–37, 244–45,
   248–49
Sessions, 166
Sewanee, Tennessee, 70
Shanghai, 123
Shelby County, 239
Shoal Creek, 82
Simpson Creek, 110
Sinclair's Restaurant, 162
Sipsey River, 124
Sipsey River Gorge, 99
Sipsey Wilderness Area, 99
Skyline, 37
Skyline Wildlife Management Area,
   36
Smith Lake Park, 110
Smuteye, **294–95**
South Sauty Creek, 54
Speake, 110
Springville, 40, 45, 46
Sprott, 242–43
St. Clair County, 40, 46–47

St. John's-in-the-Prairies Episcopal
Church, 211
St. Mark's Episcopal Church, 216
St. Stephens, 218, 223–24. *See also*
Old St. Stephens Historical
Park; St. Stephens Museum;
St. Stephens United Methodist
Church
St. Stephens Museum, 223–24
St. Stephens United Methodist
Church, 224
Stanley, 315
Stemley Bridge, 172
Sterett, 176
Stevenson, 70
Stockton, 321
Straight Mountain, 41, 89
Strawberry Hill Plantation, 211
Sturdivant Hall, 244–45, **248**
Sumter County, 128–29
Sunny South, **230**, 232
Swann Bridge, **88–89**. *See also*
Blount County
Sylacauga, 194, 206

Tail of the Dragon, 173, 197. *See
also* Deal's Gap, North Carolina
Tail of the Lizard, 173
Talladega, 190, 194
Talladega County, 203
Talladega Creek, 188

Talladega Mountains, 153, **156**,
184, 191. *See also* Mount
Cheaha
Talladega National Forest, 77, 82,
177, **183**, 191, **196**, 233, 239,
243
Tannehill State Park, 197, 202
Tattlersville, 223
Tennessee River, 51, 66, 70, 71,
111, 114, **115, 116,** 118
Tennessee-Tombigbee Waterway,
129
Tennessee Valley Authority (TVA),
132
Tensaw River, 320–21
Texasville, 290
Theodore, 274
Thornhill Plantation, 211
tire: goo, 30–31; inner tubes,
29–30; repair, 27–31; tubeless
tires, 28–29
Tishomingo State Park, 115
Tom Hendrix's rock wall, **117,** 118
Tombigbee River, **129,** 211, 215,
222–23
tool kit, 31–33
Top Hat BBQ, 86. *See also* Blount
Springs
Trimble, 110
Tupelo Pike, 66–67
Tuscaloosa, 141, 144

Tuscaloosa County, 141
Tuskegee, 303
Tuskegee Institute, 303
Tuskegee National Forest, 303
TVA. *See* Tennessee Valley Authority
Twin Oaks, 128

Union Bridge, **64**
Union Springs, 291, 295–96
Unity, 207
USS *Alabama* Battleship Memorial
    Park, 266

Vandiver, 176, 197
Vincent, 173, 197

Wadley, 168
Wakefield Plantation, 261, **265**
Waldo Covered Bridge, 188
Walker County, 136, 141, **145**
Walker Gap, **40,** 41, 44
Walls of Jericho, 36
Walnut Hill, 166
Walter F. George Lock and Dam,
    287
Walter F. George Reservoir, 287
Warrior, 83, 136
Warrior River, 88, 90, 94. *See also*
    Locust Fork; Mulberry Fork
Warsaw, 129
Washington County, 224

Wedowee, 156
Weeks Bay, 251
Weogufka, 157, 160–61, 203, 206
Weogufka State Forest, 161
West Blocton, 201–2
Wetumpka, 157, 160
Whitehouse, 132
Wilburn. *See* Bug Tussle
Wilcox County, 225, 231
Wilmer, 279
Wilsonville, 200
Wind Creek State Park, 162, **166,**
    168
Windham Springs, 141
Winterboro, 194
Woodville, 37
Wren, 103, 107
Wyatt Gap, 176

Yellow River, **307**